Picnic at Mount Disappointment

Melissa Bruce holds an MA in Writing (UTS), a Diploma in Directing (NIDA) and a BEd (Vic. College). She has worked as a writer, teacher, stage manager, performance consultant and theatre director. Melissa has produced original stage, radio and educational plays and published short stories, poetry and articles. The Australian Society of Authors awarded her a mentorship to develop this debut novel.

Melissa Bruce

Picnic at Mount Disappointment

Acknowledgements

I wish to thank the Australian Society of Authors through its Mentorship Program and the Copyright Agency for its support of the ASA Mentorship Program through its Cultural Fund.

Excerpts from *My Brilliant Career* by Miles Franklin have been reproduced with kind permission of the Perpetual Trustee Company Ltd, as trustee of the Estate of Miles Franklin.

Many gifted and generous people have helped with the development of this book in various ways. I wish to thank mentor Gabrielle Carey, literary agent Gaby Naher, editors Thomasin Litchfield and Sophie Dougall, and many fine staff and peers at the University of Technology, including Debra Adelaide, Rosie Scott, Jean Bedford, Anthony Macris, Tegan Bennett Daylight, Isabelle Li, Alison Bell and Maureen O'Shaughnessy.

I'm also immensely grateful for precious encouragement, support and patience from A. Manning and The Campfire Ruffians, Z. Barta, S. Doctor, N. Ruscoe, N. Lambert, R. Proctor, S-G Anderson, P.T. Bruce, J. Bruce, the Connans and extended family & friends. Thank you all. This book would not exist without you.

For SGA and in memory of PTB

Picnic at Mount Disappointment is a work of fiction inspired by real events.

Picnic at Mount Disappointment
ISBN 978 1 76041 303 3
Copyright © text Melissa Bruce 2017 (www.melissabruce.com)
Cover image: Brooke Shaden (www.brookeshaden.com)

First published 2017 by
GINNINDERRA PRESS
PO Box 3461 Port Adelaide 5015 Australia
www.ginninderrapress.com.au

Contents

Part One	7
Part Two	82
Part Three	169
Part Four	229

I am a part of all that I have met
From *Ulysses*, Alfred Lord Tennyson

Part One

1

We're travelling north
along the Hume Highway
behind two Wilson trucks
stacked with everything we own.
Dad will drive up tonight
after he's stitched up a few more people.
My younger brother and I
sit in the dickie seat
of our stepmother's sky-blue Volvo.
Usually we torment the oncoming drivers
with crazy faces
but today our faces
are naturally strange
because the joke is on us.

Pipstar whispers,
'I feel like we forgot something.'
'Yeah,' I say, then call out,
'Did anyone pack our mother?'
Our new stepfamily ignore the question
so we start pulling faces secretly at them
and laugh out loud
but the joke is still on us.

It's the Year of the Child –
the first time the world has fully acknowledged
the rights of children –
but we haven't seen
any evidence of this.
We had no say in the move.

The couple in the car behind us wave.
It reminds me of Mum and Dad
in the audience
waving up at me
on the stage of my first ballet concert.
That was years ago
when everything was normal.

Pip gives them the peace sign
then after they pass us
he turns his hand back to front.

If life starts off well
then goes off the rails,
you expect it to get back on them.
Maybe it's best if life starts off the rails
so you grow up with low expectations.

We're heading north
to live on a farm
because of that dumb love letter;
the one I found under Dad's stuffed crocodile,
the croc he shot on his honeymoon
with my horrified mother.
I was going to take it to school for the
dangerous animal science class
but then I found something
much more scary
underneath it.

I know Mum's handwriting very well,
even though you can hardly read it,
but this letter was easy to read
because it wasn't written by Mum.

'My dream would be to live on a horse stud
with seventeen horses…'

Oh, she wrote other unsavoury things to Dad
about oil baths and candles and stuff
but the horsing around bit
stuck in my mind,
the way hair catches on a barbed-wire fence
when you try to sneak through.

We pass Pentridge Prison and Sarah,
our youngest stepsister
(one year older than Pip), says,
'What do you have to do to get in there?'
'Something wrong,' says Jackie, or Midstep as I secretly call her.
She's one year younger than me and two years older than Pip.
She's got a big bawdy life-be-in-it laugh
and an enviable supply of energy.
Must take after her father.
Christine – Bigstep, our new stepmother –
answers in her whispery soft voice,
'You're only locked up if you've done something terribly wrong.'

Today I feel like a prisoner.
What did I do?

We pass Fawkner Cemetery
where Dad's mother's kept
and where Dad's father is going to be kept
and Dad too I guess and
probably all of us in the end.

We pass McDonald's and Kentucky Fried (without stopping)
and drive on through Craigieburn
until there are less and less houses
and then pass the white-fenced estate of Robert Holmes à Court.

'Lucy,' whispers Pipstar,
short for Phillip the Pipster
(he's not very tall),
'how far away is this farm?'
I curl my top lip.

'Exactly one hour and a half
too far.'
Driving through Kalkallo, Pipstar looks vacant.
I whisper to him, 'Don't worry.
I'll look after you until she comes back.'
He says he doesn't need looking after,
'…and anyway, Dad says she's not coming back.'
That is possible.
That could be true but it's unlikely.
She's not dead.
On this matter I reassure him
but it's little consolation;
if she were dead then it wouldn't have been
a decision
to go away.

He looks like he's going to cry.
I try pulling silly faces
until he grins
but the rest of the trip we stare blankly
at the disappearing city –
the disappearing world as we've come to know it –
and all of this disappearingness
doesn't feel good.

2

I think our world
began turning upside down
the day that man came to the door.
I'm certain it was him
who started the snowball disaster.

'Your husband's having an affair with my wife,'
said the man at the door to my mother.

'Excuse me?' she said,
frozen
and holding her belly all pregnant with Pipstar.
'Your husband's having an affair with my wife,' he said.

That's when I first saw Mum cry.
She sat on the stairs
with her head in her hands and said twice,
'Not again.'

Things went downhill from there
in the department of Dad's extracurricular affairs
but our family was temporarily Velcroed together.

We splashed around in our
kidney-shaped pool
oblivious to the cracks
in the family foundations.

I walked to the private girls grammar school
in my neat blue uniform and navy hat
past the mansions with
manicured gardens (and manicured mothers),
past Mr Tolmer's Rolls-Royce,
hoping his company Toltoys
would hurry up with Bionic Barbie.

For special treats
Mum took me shopping for clothes,
into town on the number 8 tram
or to little boutiques off Toorak Road
and when we came home
I'd do fashion parades after dinner.

Mum made honey roast chicken for us,
and osso buco for Dad.
And interior-designed our whole house and
made everything perfect.
For dinner guests as well.

Gazpacho soup and duck à l'orange
where Pipstar and I
would spy from the stairs,
watch the women arrive in colourful muumuus,
their perfume infusing the house,
their lipstick marks on the glasses of Dubonnet and soda,
or half-sipped martinis with toothpicked olives.
A miracle,
the romance of it all,
after Mum's all-day-crazy-cook-tidy rush…
everything smooth and
humming along to 'Guantanamera'.

We saw her sneak out between courses
and leaf through the *Bulletin* magazine.
Maybe nobody noticed she initiated topics
but never elaborated on them.
The men's voices dominated the table.

She played the role of the doctor's wife
to perfection.
Kept the house in stylish order
though kids can make such a mess
and the ironing pile
grew higher and higher.
She must've missed her
independent days of *TV Week* success.

One day, when I was home sick from school,
she was ironing out the wrinkles in Dad's safari suit
and singing 'I Am Woman' along with Helen Reddy
and when the song ended,
she stopped ironing and singing and said,
'I gave up a television career for this?
Make sure you have a goal in life, Lucinda.'

On some days
there was yelling
and one day
I know the smashed teapot
was not an accident.

I heard her say on the phone to a friend,
'Well, Richard's father offered me money
not to marry Richard.
Maybe I should've taken up his offer.'

When Pipstar was almost four
we waved Mum and Dad's taxi
off to the airport
for their round-the-world trip.
First stop – the Pacific Islands.

Our French nanny
kept the house shipshape
and – like the library she worked in part-time –
extra quiet.

At first she was a very
foreign body
in our house,
which is what we told her
until we decided we liked her.

For six weeks
every Friday night
she gave us a present
sent from our parents.
Beautiful gifts
but I could tell (no foreign stamps)
they were wrapped before they left.

Story goes…
At the stopover in Paradise,
at the resort owners' dinner,
with pineapple cocktails and a purple sunset,
Dad suggested one of his crazy games.
'Let's say what we most want to do…and then do it!'
So he ran up and down the beach
naked.
The game went around the table until
the flares were lit
and the stars came out
and the sea was lapping the sand
with phosphorescence.
The manager of the tropical resort,
a tall dark handsome Frenchman,
looked straight at Mum and said to Dad,
'What I would mose like to dooo
is make lov weeth your wife.'
Everybody laughed.
Except Dad.

They continued around the world
and arrived home to Pipstar and me
and a pile of ironing
and a pile of letters from
the tall dark handsome Frenchman.

Mum slept in the spare room bunk
'because of the possums'.
'Just go and get it out of your system,'
said Dad to Mum, handing her an air ticket.
So she did –
she went.
But she hasn't come back.
He's still not out of her system.

3

'Wandong'
sounds like a Chinese rice paddy
not a one-shop pit stop, ninety minutes north of Melbourne.
It's host to the
'second largest truck 'n' country music festival
in the southern hemisphere'
and nothing else.
I can't stand country music.

Long dry grass
filled with crickets
screaming
as the shadows of clouds
pass haphazardly over paddocks
that roll down to the Hume Highway
where the train tracks run all the way to Sydney
(something I nearly did last night).

I'm a fish out of water
pretending to breathe without effort.

High on the hill of our front lawn
you can smell the fresh manure.

The sky is vast.

In the distance you can see
Mount Disappointment.
Promising.

The nearest neighbours
are crazy.
We found one of their seven kids
in our pantry.
Not eating.

Their pacers run in circles
around their dusty track,
whipped along by the father
in his harness,
round and round
day after day
in circles
going mad.

But it's the new stepfamily
I'm trying to come to terms with.

Dad's only here for weekends,
commuting from Melbourne
(he's a waterworks doctor – a plumber for humans),
so most of the time
it's just the Steps and Us.

My stepsisters, Midstep and Littlestep,
got two ginger kittens from their grandparents
who last night
shat all over our shared white bathroom.
(The kittens not the grandparents.)
I don't like cats.
We're a doggy family.
That's what it's like –
we're the dogs and they're the cats
and there's a whole lot of shit between us.

And although we're not poor
and my stepmother and stepsisters
are not all that ugly,
just call me Lucindarella.
It's unlikely there'll be a ball around here but
do you think I can hope for a prince?

Being relatively rich is looked down upon
in this district –

'Who are these toffs in the yellow diesel Mercedes
who come into town for their pink-iced buns
and live in the vast brown house on the hill
that they bought from the mayor of Melbourne?'

Ours is a 'hobby farm' – so the doctors call it.
Dad plays on the tractor sometimes.
Harrowing.

Mum calls
long distance
from Paradise.
'Why can't I come and live with you, Mum?'
'You can when you're eighteen, darling.'
That's what the judge said, apparently,
in the court case that Dad must've won
because cases are won with money, I think,
and these days Mum's got none.

Another four years is a very long time
and a very big gap between Pipstar and me
so except for the fact that
we're in the same boat
we don't have too much in common.

Behind me is our house.
A long curved turd of brown bricks,
filled with poo-brown shag carpet, furniture and curtains.
When my grandfather walks his dog around the Toorak block
he's thrilled when his Jack Russell
produces a 'dog lolly'.
That's what I call where we live now:
Doglolly House.
The sun sets in its twenty-four rattling glass doors
where I pause to contemplate my new existence.
Here we are (yee haa),
the Brady Walton Prairie Bunch on Doglolly Hill.

4

Pipstar and I
were in the same boat last year
shooting rapids on the Howqua River
the day that Dad said,
'How would you like a nice lady to come and stay with us?
She has two daughters who could be really good friends.
She'd be like a housekeeper.'
We were staring at him.
'Or the nanny in *The Sound of Music*.'
Pipstar and I looked at each other.
It was weird without Mum
and the house needed keeping
but why would we want to have strangers
living with us?

The first day we met
the future Steps
we drove miles to take them out for a bush picnic.
I had to watch for bull ants. I'm allergic.
We tried to be nice
but didn't have much in common with
the 'housekeeper's' kids and
the hills were alive with the sound of trouble.
Was she more like the Baroness
than the Von Trapps' nanny?

Driving home, I sat next to Dad –
in Mum's seat.
The 'nice' lady's perfume
was all over the seat belt.
Dad said we needed someone
to care for us
and look after our house.
I said maybe *he* needed someone
to care for us
and look after our house.

Either way,
why would you wear so much perfume to a picnic?

One rainy day, Dad called me into our formal lounge
and sat me on the smoky-blue sofa
under the Alice-blue chandelier.
Quietly and slowly he told me,
'Your brother's too young to understand but...
your mother and I are going to get a divorce.'
It sounded like something rare you could buy in a pet shop.
I looked up into the blue glass drips of the chandelier
and they seemed to slowly blur and shatter.

'We'll have to sell the house,' he said.
'But why?' I asked.
'Because your mother wants half.'
'So give her half the house!' I said and
slammed the whole door.

I ran upstairs and
picked up their wedding photo –
all tulle and lace and smiles and bows and petals.
I took it out of the frame and on the back I wrote
in thick black ink,
TILL DEATH US DO PART,
then I tore the photo in half.

Not knowing who to be more upset with,
I stored the two pieces
in separate drawers
and divided some unframed part of myself in half as well.

After that,
the 'housekeeper'
and her two 'nice' daughters
moved into our granny flat.

I had a nightmare one night
and went up to Mum and Dad's room
and heard noises.

I didn't get
why the housekeeper
had to housekeep his bedroom
at three o'clock in the morning.

The wedding was horrid.
We all had to wear
multicoloured gingham dresses
lovingly handmade by Bigstep's mum,
and listen to a minister
crap on with stuff like
'…till death us do part.'

5

It's Saturday. Dad's home for the weekend.
He's cleaning his duck-shooting gun
with his trannie radio wailing out Wagner.
He opens the safety lock,
removes the two cartridges
and gives my brother
a lesson in gun safety.
Ironic really –
only recently
he accidentally shot a hole
through our bedroom window.

I doubt that Pipstar is into guns
but he's into Dad
and if you want time with Dad
you've got to be into what he's into.
Luckily he's into a lot.
I call him a 'life enthusiast',
which is charming
so long as you're feeling enthusiastic.
But Dad's got a short attention span.

I can hold it with a pretty basic joke
(doesn't take much to give him a laugh)
but if you want more than a minute of his
undivided time
you'd better have some Houdini tricks up your sleeve,
or be funny like Benny Hill, his comic hero.

In the background, Midstep is hooning around
on the new sit-on lawnmower.
Doglolly House
rests on an isolated island of
green grass
which I can see will forever be mowed by
Midstep and me.
Bigstep is apparently
allergic to mowing and
Dad has a twingey back
from standing too long over
anaesthetised people.
Littlestep is scared of it
and Pipstar is, according to Dad,
'too small to safely drive the machine'.
Poor Pip, he doesn't like horses;
the only thing he wants to ride is the mower.

Lucky school
doesn't start this week.
I've got period pain
and would rather be in hospital gowns
than a new uniform.
Not that we've got our new uniforms yet.
I hope they're a nice colour.
That's why I'm up at the house.
Bigstep is down at the saddle yard
grooming her new horse, Pirate,
who's sixteen hands tall and
steel-coloured with a white patch over his eye.

She put nail polish on yesterday
but it's already chipped.

At first I was pretty stand-offish,
not wanting to celebrate Bigstep's dream –
the one that got us here in the first place.
Then we got new ponies.
Mine is called White Sails.
He's the only one who's white. He glows in the dark.
I'd never been into horses,
it's ballet I like,
but Bigstep said you can learn to do ballet on a horse.
It's called dressage.
Have to see it to believe it.
And I have to say,
there's something wild about having a pet
who's three times your size,
so I might learn to ride
but not today
while my insides are falling out.

By dinner time, everyone's exhausted.
'It's the fresh air,' says Dad.

Bigstep might have been dux of her school,
as Dad likes to remind us often,
but she sure as hell can't cook and
certainly not honey roast chook
like Mum.

In the soup tureen
she's put
white rice
mixed with tinned stuff like
pale yellow baby corn, grey slimy champignons,
miniature green gherkins
and whole baby beets.
Minimal cutting, minimal preparation.

Pipstar says,
'What's that?'
'Fried rice salad,' says Bigstep,
brushing a little wisp of fair hair off her face.
'It isn't fried,' he replies, accurately.

'How about a little gratitude,' says Dad,
'for a lovely meal and a toast to Life on the Farm!'
He raises his glass
alone,
trying to turn us into a
Happy Family.

'What's that?' says Dad,
quickly pointing to the radio
(his perpetual companion and ally
that helps ward off conflict and silence).
We all shrug.
'A radio?' says Midstep.
'Beethoven's Piano Sonata Number 31 in A Flat Major.'
He says it like we forgot our ABC.

'Bait horven,' says Pip,
copying Dad's Austrian pronunciation of the master's name.
Poor Dad; where he came from
everyone knows about classical music.
He tries to bring aspects of his culture to us
but we're more interested in
Australian Crawl than the Viennese waltz.
And there's no point in learning German –
Who would we talk to?
I had ODed on schnitzel by the time I was eight,
the same age he was when his family escaped the Nazis.

Midstep changes the radio station.
'Hey!' says Dad.
'So what's THIS, Richard?' she says, increasing the volume
on the song 'Freak Out'.

'Hey,' says Dad screwing up his face, 'turn it back!'
but he has to do it himself because
she pretends she can't find the station.
She's totally into popular culture,
or 'pop culcha', as Dad describes it.
Music, clothes, gadgets.
It's gonna be hard to keep that up
living here in this wasteland with a one-shop town.

I watch Littlestep
quietly ignoring all of us –
with one hand holding her best friend,
Enid Blyton,
and the other hand holding her other best friend,
a spoon with vanilla ice cream.
Whenever she's not holding a spoon,
she's twirling her third best friend
which is one of her long mousey plaits.
Today it's the ice cream.
She eats it by shutting her eyes and blissfully
lipping over the cold stuff like an old lady without teeth.
She makes vanilla ice cream look like
the best thing you've ever eaten
which annoys me because it isn't.

So here we all are
surrounded by Dad's
freaky abstract paintings
on the poo-brown walls
with the twenty-four glass doors
rattling in the north wind
and Wagner cooking up a storm.
Looking around the table
it's clear
that none of us
have anything much in common.

Dad lights up his stinky cigar
and we all make a fuss
and send him outside
which seems to give us
permission
to get on with our separate lives
on this property together.

6

Our bedroom wing
is separated by a
breezy breezeway.

I have to share a room with Midstep
and Pip is in with Littlestep.
Between the bedrooms
is our white bathroom
where the kittens used to shit
until they were eligible for the outside world.

After fourteen years of
not sharing a room
it's a major shock
to the sock drawer.

I know why they call them
STEPsisters
because there's a big step
between them and you that you
can't (or maybe don't want to) cross.

I never had a sister
and I always wanted one
but what I've learnt is
you can't just have them delivered ready-made.
A good start would be to
arrive on the planet
through the same birth canal.

It's still early.
I got up at sunrise
and went searching for a place of my own –
somewhere I can escape
and think
and write my journal.

Near where Pipstar plays handball,
I found a way
to climb up on the roof.
There's a low dividing wall that hides the clothes line.
It's easy to reach if you stand on the barbecue.
Then, from the gutter you
carefully, quietly,
walk up the tiles to the chimney in the centre.
I won't let anyone ever know
it's my hideout.

I've been sitting here on the platform
that surrounds the chimney all morning.
It's the first time I think I've been able to breathe.
You can see two of our six dams
and the hay shed, the saddle shed and the dressage arena
and the alternative entrance gates
where they bring in the livestock.
You can see part of the Great Dividing Range
and how it links up with
Mount Disappointment.

A few trees are left in each paddock
for shade
usually near the water troughs.
That's what our farm is named after.
Yarrimbah means 'clumps of trees' in an Aboriginal language.
But those Aboriginal people didn't name our farm.
Dad did.
And even though Dad owns the farm
he doesn't really
because they didn't sell it.

Sometimes I think I hear their ghosts,
when the wind fills the air vent in a certain direction.

It's pretty quiet up here
on top of the world
save for the ghosts and the real conversations
that rise up from the lounge room fireplace through the chimney.
This could prove to be very
useful.

I open my bag,
take out my black fountain pen and
red faux-suede-covered journal.
It's pretty new.
I flick through some things I've written so far…

Dear Journie,
   What the hell are we doing here????

I try to think of something to write today
but I run out of inspiration.

On the platform beside me
is the huge silver air vent –
the one that catches the whisperings of
the Aboriginal ghosts.
It turns its hollow face left and right,
creaking in the breeze
like those clowns at the show you put ping-pong balls into,
only the air vent's mouth is its whole face
and it certainly isn't smiling.
We watch the world together,
Empty Ness and me.

7

Bigstep fills the sky-blue Volvo with petrol.
There's something vague in her manner,
even though she was dux of her school.

Something slightly soft and colour-washed,
from a romantic painting
(whereas Mum is like a Kodak colour photograph).
She moves slowly, gently,
as though slightly stoned or from another planet.
She stares across the railroad tracks
through her touch-of-mascara eyes…
lost in a dream.
Lost
in *her* dream.
I guess her wish
to have seventeen horses
didn't include us.

I wonder how would it be
to have someone else's uncomfortable teen
in your own home?
I don't know,
so she tells me.
Often.

First she drives Pipstar and Littlestep
to the primary school in Wandong.
It's so small all the kids share the same classroom.
My brother looks worried.
I want to hug him but he'd get embarrassed
so I give him the look – like we're both in the same boat.
This would help if we both felt the boat was floating.
I give him the thumbs up.
His thumbs do not reciprocate.

The teacher guides them both into the classroom.
Pip looks back at me like he's not meant to be here,
which he isn't.

Bigstep drops Midstep and me at the corrugated-iron shelter
to wait for the school bus.

The car skids off the gravel like she's
eager to return to her four-legged friends
(six now in her collection).
Soon she'll have more horses
than the piles of crime novels she borrows
from the mobile library.

An empty cattle truck rattles past,
interrupting our silent conversation.

The old bus takes half an hour
on a bumpy road beside the freeway
to get to the co-ed high school in Broadford.
Some of the stops have only a pink galah
waiting,
or a crow with its face in some roadkill.
Others have one or two kids
throwing stones at yellow signs
or stomping out secret cigarettes.

I sit beside Midstep.
She's wearing jeans, sneakers and an
orange T-shirt which sticks out like a sore thumb.
She refuses to wear our blue Grammar uniform
and is dreading the new local green one.
But you know what they say about first impressions.
So my socks are pulled up and
my hair is pulled tight in a ponytail with a blue velvet ribbon.
'You look like the Ayatollah Khomeini,' she says,
referring to my Jewish nose,
which she knows I would like to get rid of.
(Grandfather cut off half our name
but couldn't cut out our genes.)
I know it's funny, in principle,
but I'm not laughing.
We're not helping each other psych up for the day but
anxiety has its own way of managing things.

Broadford harbours a special blend of scents
resting between the tannery and the sewage plant.
It wafts through the one-of-each-shop kind of town
and then up Sunday (shit) Creek,
where gold was found in the late 1880s
but apparently not since.

The school is wedged between the dark pine forest
and the Hell's Angels' base.
I don't know where in Hell it is exactly
but some kids at the back of the bus
were freaking me out with some spooky stories.
This is nothing like the red-brick fortress of halls and
gymnasiums and chapels and lawns of
my old girls grammar school.

'What a dump,' says Midstep, looking at the wooden portables
and the mangy football oval with lonesome goalposts.
As I said, she's got a thing for popular culture
but this is about as unpopular as it gets.

'What the hell are we doing here?' she says.
I almost nod in agreement but decide just to shrug.
We can't be friends (or sisters).
It would mean that I accept our new life
and I don't.
I won't.
I'm willing it all away in the hope that it won't exist.
So I get off the bus in my own little bubble.

It bursts because
everyone is screaming
and running like it's World War III.
Kamikaze magpies swoop at the heads of children.
I never saw birds do this in South Yarra.
So we pile our bags on top of our heads
and run into Day One.

'Posh bitch,' they say.
'Stuck-up Toorak princess!'
Their green dresses hardly cover their bums.
'Who's the toff from the big smoke, eh?'
'What's ya name, Brace Face?'
'Lucinda.'
'You're in the wrong school, Metal Mouth,'
says the boy with tattooed knuckles.
'Ken oath,' says his mate, wringing his hands.
'Gotta smoke? I'm broke.'
Hey, Loose, you know what you need?'
says the head of some girl-gang
with dyed black hair, gelled up into an electric shock.
The gang – in unison – spell it out:
'What you need is a good fuck!'

There are no hymns or prayers or readings
at morning assembly in the chapel.
We stand outside (!) in the 'quad',
surrounded by portable classrooms
listening to announcements
interrupted by admonishments to noisy students.

It's weird having boys at school.

I look around
trying to imagine
how I can reverse time
change events
steer things in a different direction
so I don't end up here.

At the end of last year
our drama teacher said we were going to do *Pygmalion*.
In private, she said I should try for the role of Eliza.

Well, I can tell
there won't be any
Fair Ladies
in the school play here
unless they tell the
whole story
backwards.

Besides,
I don't feel as confident
as I did.

I go home in tears.
'Chin up,' says Dad on the telephone
from Melbourne, struggling for words.
Neither Dad nor Mum
can bear it when we're sad.
It makes them too unhappy.
Maybe they think it's their fault.
Best to try and fix it quick.
'Oh, first days are never easy, darling. You'll settle in.
Life's not always a picnic.
You heard what our prime minister said:
"Life wasn't meant to be easy."'

I wait for Mum to call from
Paradise
but when at last I hear the phone
it cuts out after only two rings.

8

We are fodder for fun for a month or so
when the novelty wears off
for some.

'You know what you need?'

Apart from feeling like an alien who lost her planet
there are other issues to deal with.
Testosterone in the classrooms.
Male students and teachers.
I'm used to an all-girls' school.
How can you possibly concentrate
when you're trying to look like a catch?

I do what I can to fit in at school.
Eventually,
I untie my hair,
hem up my dress,
begin to swear
and take up cigarette smoking.
It eliminates some of the joking.

But two things I'm finding hard to change
are my Toorak voice and the fact that I'm
the only one in the whole school with braces on my teeth.
I cover my face, especially when I'm eating,
and practise speaking more like a local –
azzo oim prevenning enny floys frm gittin in me meouf.

I'm only fourteen but I should plan
to not be a virgin
as soon as I possibly can.

9

The highlight of each week
is when Bigstep takes us into Kilmore.

Just beyond our drive
is the 'big dipper'
which always gets a scream out of us
as the car hits the bottom of the valley and lifts off.

We drive past the old bull with the ring in its nose
in the paddock surrounded by broken-down cars and tractors.

KILMORE
Spooky name.
Who would have called it that?
Maybe Squizzy Taylor,
the gangster guy
who had his hideout nearby.

POPULATION 3,958
WINNER OF THE TIDIEST TOWN 1972
Which is quite a long time ago really,
when it comes to rubbish.

We visit our post office box
which sometimes has a letter from Mum.
She writes one juicy letter per week,
on paper crinkled from the tropical heat,
and postcards (one of four images)
and 'Guess what!?' air letters with
who nearly stood on a deadly stonefish
and how the hurricane came so close.
Just the sight of her crazy handwriting
feeds my spirit
hugs my soul
but it's confusing because
they come out of order
and some take weeks
and some don't arrive at all.

Along with the post, there are four shops in Kilmore I like.
The newsagent: stationery gives me a hopeful feeling.
The haberdashery: like something out of the 50s.
(It is something out of the 50s.)
The saddlery: leather smells divine.
Shining silver spurs and bits and buckles.
Hand-stitched bridles and blue velvet riding attire.

And the famous Kilmore pie shop
with its wire door
that bangs shut with every hungry customer.
It smells yeasty-sweet
like everything's going to be fine.
The pies are fall-apart-fresh
and the pink-iced buns are
to die for.
They're all gone before we get home.

Of course there's the Red Lion pub
which is good for Chinese dinners
if you like Chinese dinners
and the racecourse
if you like horse races.

That's it.
That's Kilmore.
The highlight of our week.

10

It's a bit cooler now on the roof after school
and much easier to walk on the tiles with my shoes off.
I wish I could come up more often but I have to wait
until I'm certain I won't be seen.

Dear Journie,
*   Who are these people I'm sharing my home, my laundry, my moods, my hormones with??? Another big doozie with Bigstep and the Little Steps about everything and nothing. It's not that they're all that bad, it's just we have NOTHING in common. Dad's adopted a family for us but it isn't for us. We don't want them. Bigstep has to act like she's my mother. She couldn't be more different. After school, to get acceptance points, I walk the paddocks and practise smoking with Marlboro cigarettes that I buy from the girl with the shock-treatment hairdo.*
*   It's fourteen ks to the nearest town that has more than one shop. I'm too young to get a car licence.*

Phone calls to Melbourne are charged as 'long distance'. There's a quota per week. When I call my friends, they've got parties, excursions & school tasks that have nothing to do with me. They hardly ever call me but I answer all the calls I can, expecting the occasional beeps from Paradise. They echo & crackle & sometimes cut out completely. Mum always sounds like she's going to cry. I try to sound like I don't cry at all. Ever.

Poem: Conundrum
Mum left Dad
for another man
because Dad had other women.
I would have left too.
I was proud.
She was brave.
Followed her heart.
Broke the rules of the day.
A pioneering feminist!

But she left us with
the man who had betrayed her.

In the distance I see
Dad's tiny toy car,
the Yellow Peril,
the Scary Canary,
the noisy diesel Mercedes
which sticks out like a cow in a paddock full of sheep
and signals to all the farmers
that my Daddy's rich (and my Mummy's good-looking).
It's winding its way up the hill.
I can almost see him conducting his beloved Wagner
with his cigar and
the window open a crack
to let out the smoke
and any difficult feelings
about why his wife left him
for playing around and how he
hasn't really found anyone
who can truly replace her.

The Peril crunches up the gravel drive
panting and hot,
from the long trip home
with Dad on cruise control
to his great big house
and his beautiful wife
and I wonder
if he wonders,
'How did I get here?'

11

Midway into the term when we've 'settled in'
but none of us are settled,
Dad senses the need for a cheer-up.
'Family Day,' he says on the phone,
always trying to turn us into something we're not.
Instead of him coming home Friday night,
we're to drive down to meet him in town on Saturday morning.

The day begins
with me complaining about
how there's no Coco Pops left
for Pipstar and me
for breakfast.
She's hopeless at stocking the cupboards.
Lately Coco Pops,
even eaten dry,
are the highlight of my day
and later,
I won't be able to eat anything.

'Can't you see I've had more
important things on my plate?' says Bigstep,
applying lipstick without looking in a mirror.
'Well, I've got nothing on mine,' I say.

The long drive either way with the Steps
doesn't inspire me
but I'm not allowed to stay here alone.

I decide
instead of arguing
to be silent.
To let them feel my
fury
underneath.
For the whole drive,
I bombard them with missiles of the words
I don't speak
while Pipstar gets hypnotised to sleep
by watching the power lines.

It's not all their fault
that I'm unhappy
but you can only blame
what's in front of you.

At first in town
I have to have my braces tightened.
A special Saturday appointment
for which I'm supposed to be grateful
for not having to miss school next week.

It takes a millennium
for the tectonic plates of the earth to move
but they can get your teeth shifting
in a day or so.
The pain is like
a slo-mo oral earthquake
and for at least twenty-four hours,
liquid
is all you can eat.

Dad meets us and takes us to
Pellegrino's.

They eat spaghetti
followed by three colours of gelato ice cream.
You can tell how much he wants us all to get on,
to make the arrangement cosy,
free from guilt, discomfort and pain –
all neat like the Brady Bunch.
Where's Alice?
Perhaps if we had an Alice, things would all be okay?

Apparently,
there's no time for me
to visit a friend from my old school.

They're disappearing.

I sip my lemon granita,
try to get the ice to
numb the ache in my teeth
and the ache in my self.
I'm surrounded by my new family
but I feel like the Ugly Duckling.
Different but also invisible.

After the 'family' lunch
Dad takes my brother
for some 'Quality Time with my son'.
They see 'a boy's movie'.
We girls head off to see
My Brilliant Career.

I fall in love with the actress Judy Davis
and her proud, independent, ambitious character: Sybylla.
Her intensity, her purposeful face, so powerfully original.
The rebelliousness of her choices.
Her long dresses, aprons and lace petticoats with boots.
The hair tussled, escaping its Victorian roots and regulations.
Her conflict, her passion.
Her pain, her joy, her desire.

Imagine the whole world meeting you in a close-up.
Imagine the whole world sharing the depths of your feelings.
Imagine the whole world caring about your soul.

Sybylla,
against the odds
longs to escape her arduous farm life and
social expectations.
She wants to become a published writer,
someone with a voice.
She even refuses an offer of marriage
in order to reach her dream
which in 1900 is seen to be insane
for a woman.
My Brilliant Career is the name of her true-story novel
and through sheer determination
her dream is achieved.

The film
plants
a powerful seed
in my thinking.

I don't speak again
on the long drive home
but for very different reasons.
Midstep fiddles with her new Walkman.
Pipstar counts crows and I-spies with Littlestep,
while I brainstorm this whole new solution
to my out-of-control existence.
Bigstep turns on the radio news
about the first woman prime minister of England.
I bet no one believed in her dream before she fulfilled it.

That's what I want,
a brilliant career,
an escape route.
A way to be respected, heard, seen and understood.

A way to matter.
A way to get met.
Connected.
Close-upped.
Free.

I decide to become
a brilliant actress
so I won't be
up Doglolly stream
without a paddle
for the rest of my life.
So I won't be
nothing
and nobody
forever.

The idea gives me a burst of fuel.
A destination.
I'm suddenly in the driver's seat,
gripping the wheel
speeding
decidedly
into my future.

'What's wrong with Lucy?' says Littlestep,
trying to snap me out of my silence.
Midstep shrugs. 'Maybe she thinks she's special.'

12

Now that I've got my
purpose on the planet,
things have changed
somewhat.
I'm not so bothered by all the challenges
because everything is
useful –

for research
for character building
for building characters
for my memoir.

Back on the roof I quote Shakespeare
from a heavy gold-leafed tome that I found on Dad's bookshelf.
It was tricky climbing up with it but worthwhile.
My new bible.
    'To thine own self be true,
    And it must follow, as the night the day,
    Thou canst not then be false to any man'
or woman, I usually say.

I open my journal
and catch up on logging what's been happening.

Through the chimney
I hear my brother's clarinet, the same sequence
over and over.
I want to yell out,
SHUUUUUT UUUUUP
but my hideout here is a sacred secret.

This morning I saw a story in the local paper
about some horses who are going to be hired by a local farm
for a new film based on Banjo Paterson's poem
'The Man from Snowy River'.
I've decided to audition,
which is why I agreed to join Bigstep
for riding lessons.
I think my new-found enthusiasm
excited her.
Never mind the reasons.

Last weekend I learnt to ride the tractor.
Dad taught me.
He said, 'Maybe you can help out on the farm.'
It's a big machine

but it's basic.
I picked it up quickly.
He was impressed
and there we were
driving across the cow-padded paddock
with bark hanging off the trees in the breeze –
grass and earth and air and sky –
the hobby-farmer father and his daughter
working the land.
We even spotted a couple of roos.

Tomorrow he said he's going to teach me 'harrowing'.

Yeah, it isn't so bad up here after all.
What I like is the mornings.
Mist levitates above the dams.
The air is so fresh you can breathe it right down to your feet.
Magpies chat in the trees like a ladies' tea party.
The insects wake up in the long grass
and their hum feels like they are keeping the whole earth turning.

13

At last a ray of cultural light
at the school concert.
A tall blonde popular girl
sings a solo
with no accompaniment at all
until
everybody cries,
even me.
So pure.
Such a voice.
This girl is
Going Places.
I want to go with her.

When Monday comes
I'm heading out to my lone pine for lunch.
(It's tricky to eat with braces on your teeth
especially when no one else in the whole school wears them.)
I see the tall blonde singer and her friend
talking along the corridor.
I hear the singer say she forgot her canteen money.
So when they get close
I offer some coins
in passing.
She receives them all
in a frozen glare
then says,
'I don't need your fucken' charity,'
and throws them
spinning
under the lockers,
spinning, spinning,
all along the vinyl-tiled floor to the doors.
They laugh and leave
and when I can't see them any more
I head out to my tree.

I watch the country kids playing handball
and kicking soccer balls
and swapping bits of lunch and cigarettes.
The same groups tend to hang in the same locations.
I hear yelling and laughter and fights.
I see the token lonely fat kid near the shed.
It isn't too different really from
the kids in my old school grounds,
just a rougher backdrop.
The grass on the field is wild
and the concrete's got cracks
and behind us
instead of a city
there's a tall dark pine forest.
The uniform rules are pretty slack.

A lot of them wear their runners
but then there's a lot of running around.
I guess fresh air makes you want the wind in your hair.

After lunch
in the typing class,
ppp qqq ppp…
Singing Charity Rejector
wins the speed test.
All applause soon fades to hear my
p q p q p.
Electric Shock starts the class laughing.
I didn't learn typing at Grammar.

It's Mr Barley,
the school's favourite teacher,
who finally introduces me to the
Singing Charity Rejector.
'This is Jessica Harford,
who has legs all the way to the ground.'
He winks at her.
'Show Lucy the books that arrived in the library, Jess.'
I think she does it to please him.

'I love your voice,' I say. 'You could be famous.'
She rolls her eyes and laughs.
'What did he say your name was? "Loose"?'
'Lucy,' I say. 'Please don't call me Loose.'
'Yeah, strange name for the school virgin.'
How does she know
for certain?

14

It's Friday afternoon,
thank the Rural Gods.
The days and weeks at school are long.

Bigstep's taking Pipstar to the Wandong train stop
which is just a platform with nobody there.
Dad will drive him back from Melbourne in the morning.
He's carrying his clarinet case
and his overnight bag.
He looks small.

I decide to come for the short drive
to keep him company
and with some hope that she might stop
at the general store
and fill up with petrol
so I can somehow try to buy my own cigarettes.

'What time's your lesson?'
'Five-thirty,' he says, pulling a face.
'Is the teacher horrible?'
'Yes,' he says,
'mainly because you guys won't let me practise.'
'That's not true,' I say, though sometimes it is.

After I wave him off on the train,
Bigstep stops at the store
but the family who run it
are getting to know us
and I don't look sixteen.
I've got five smokes left
to last until Monday. Eek.

I decide to have one of them
out on my first ride alone.
To celebrate
the feeling of escape.
I stop in the paddock
where you can't see the house or the shed
and I dismount White Sails.
I let him eat grass around me,
swishing his tail
while I sit and enjoy the cigarette.

Sometimes he looks at me
with his lashy eyes.
I'm certain he knows what I'm thinking.

15

Before school,
Midstep finishes all the Coco Pops
so there's none left for breakfast again.
Bigstep doesn't stick up for me.
Why would she? I'm not one of her *real* children.
'I thought you were employed to look after us,' I say.
It's a bit rude but frankly, Dad gives her heaps of money.
She looks at me, hurt.
'I'm not employed,' she says. 'In case you didn't notice,
I married your father,
and you better begin to accept and respect it.'

I'm almost glad to get to school,
where Bigstep does a big embarrassing Uey
that doesn't make it quite around
and Midstep meets up with her dorky
magazine-swapping 'friend'
and I just hang around near the fence
waiting to hear the bell for the first lesson.

At lunchtime
I'm on the way out to my tree,
feeling hungry.
I pass the woodwork room where I see Jess
on her own
in goggles and gloves and earmuffs
working a loud wood shaving machine.
I've never seen a girl do anything like this before.

She lets the machine whine down to a halt.
'Are you lost?'
'No, just looking.'

She dusts the area where she was working.
'What are you making?'
'A table.'
'Jesus!'
'Yes, apparently Jesus also made tables but as you already know, I'm just Jess.'
'We didn't have woodwork at Grammar.'
'What the hell *did* you learn there? How to speak like the queen?'
I shrug. 'I guess – yes.'
She examines the leg of the unfinished table and begins to pack up.
'Are we going to get some lunch then?' she says.
'Is that a royal we?'
'Yes,' she says, faking a British accent,
'Shall we pick up a spot of lunch?'
'Um, thanks,' I say, trying to sound less queeny.
'Actually, I forgot it.'
'Just uctuuuually just buy some then.'
'I ran out of pocket money.'
'I thought you guys were rolling in dosh?'
'We don't get much cash. We go travelling instead.'
'Right,' she says, trying to work that one out.
She's packing away all the gear.
'So did your mum forget to make your lunch?'
'No. My mum forgot to come home from her travels.'
'Oh… So you have to make your own then?'
'Well, my Ugly Stepmother is not so great with a sandwich. I told her plenty of times I don't eat butter.'
She places the last leg on top of her unfinished table.
The air is floating with sawdust.
Without looking at me she says,
'I can lend you some dosh.'
'Thanks,' I say. 'I don't need ya fucken' charity.'
She laughs and mimics the queen,
'We do not need your farking cherity, ol' chap.'
It's funny the way she says it.
Cracks us up.

She takes me out to her bench,
to meet all her friends.
It's only just after Easter but
it feels like fucking Christmas.

16

I'm on the Red Rattler
heading down to Melbourne to have my
braces tightened again.
The only good thing about it is
I got the day off school.
Dad will pick me up
but unlike Pipstar after his clarinet lesson
I won't be able to eat anything but gelati.
At least it's Quality Time in the car
while Dad drives us back to the farm.

I listen to my new Walkman for a while
and just stare out the window, listening to 'Down to the Waterline'.
I'm totally into Dire Straits. Bigstep introduced me.

It's hard to imagine but outside the window
maybe those little people sitting on little tractors
and hanging out little washing in little back yards
all have big messy inner worlds and outer lives just like me.

Someone's left a newspaper
in my carriage and I read about
the terrible oil spill in Mexico.
And what Jimmy Carter's got to say
about Mother Teresa winning the Nobel Peace Prize,
which is like an Academy Award for people who do good things.

I take out my journal.

Dear Journie,
    Award Speech: Wow… I'm honoured to be amongst such extraordinary company… I never imagined I'd end up here on this stage. It's incredible! I haven't prepared a speech, so I'd just like to thank a few people… Firstly, the Academy… (Work on this later…)
    Made a new friend: Jessica Harford. She finally realised I was NOT an up-myself snob. I was only trying to look as cool as you can when you feel like a fish out of water. Note to self: My version of 'cool', looks like 'f*** off!'
    It was so great to share my ambitions with Jess. And to tell her more about how we came to be here. She laughed when I told her about Lucindarella – said the story sounded more like Rapunzel because we weren't poor & because I've got long hair & was taken to live in a castle on the hill.
    I've realised that as an actress, all the bad things in life can be useful.

Poem: Conundrum II
Dad's new woman and Mum's new man
are very important to them.
We are fitting in
to support their importance
(by order of the court).
But our parents keep (separately) telling us
that we are the most important things in their lives.

Is it something we did?
Is it us?
Is it me?

17

Before leaving town, Dad stops at Georges.
He says I can buy myself something special to wear.
It's exciting.
But with his unspecified budget
and brief attention span in a department store
I am overwhelmed and can't decide.

While I am not deciding,
he pulls out some expensive silk scarves
like the magician he was at my childhood parties.
'What do you think?' he says, 'The blue one or the red one?'
'Thanks, Dad,' I say. 'Scarves aren't really my thing.
Especially as I heard what happened to Isadora Duncan.'
'No,' he laughs, 'for Christine!'
I shrug. 'I don't know,' I say,
feeling uncomfortable that he's shopping for her
while he's shopping with me.
Red. Blue. Doesn't make any difference.
She doesn't wear scarves either.
I leave the store holding one bag
with only her red scarf in it.

When we arrive at the farm,
Dad makes a big fuss giving Bigstep her present.
It's not even her birthday.
I liked it when he gave presents to Mum.
When he gives them to Bigstep it feels weird.

She says something about
how messy I left my room.
Like as if I had time to clean it?
I went from the bus to the train.
But he supports her.
Nearly every time he comes home,
he takes her side
'because she's my wife'
and then when she's not looking
he winks at me
like I'm really the favourite.

Dear Journie,
    Is it more important to stand by your wife than your daughter?
    Especially when your wife is not your daughter's mum?

Right after dinner
at last
Mum calls from Paradise.
The line is good
and it must be a still day
because you can hear a little boat putting on the water.
'I'm looking out at the glassy sea,' she says,
from the small resort office. 'You should see the sunset!
It's pink and orange and purple. I really wish you could see it.'
Her voice catches on a ray of tropical sunshine,
'Love you, darling.'

I want to tell her that I met a new friend.
That I can ride a horse up Gallop Hill.
That the Steps are not as bad as I thought
(even though we have nothing in common)
and guess what? Guess what!
I know what I'm going to do…
I'm going to be an actress!
But the phone cuts out –
Beep beep beep beep beep.

18

Next morning Dad and I go
harrowing together.
He drives the ute.
I get to drive the tractor.
He trusts me to drive it
which makes me feel important.
I open the gates so efficiently,
like a farm girl,
for him to drive through.
On top of Ghost Gum Hill
he's already through –
I'm walking back to the tractor,
but it's vibrating so much
that it loosens its not-so-tight handbrake –

starts inching away from the gate
heading down to…
'Get on!'
yells Dad from the window of the ute.
I try but it picks up momentum.
'Get on. Get on! Get on the tractor!'
I try but its wheels are huge
and moving
and there's a harrow of spiked metal
dragging along behind it.
'Get on the bloody tractor!' he yells, driving along beside it.
It's rare to hear him swear.
'I can't!' I yell back, beginning to run. 'Too dangerous!'
It picks up speed
and takes off on its way,
careering down the steep hill
towards our biggest dam
at the bottom of the paddock.
He drives beside it,
I run behind it,
stopping at last to see the show of its
slow-motion sinking,
bubbles and all
like a hippopotamus drinking.
It turns its face up
at the last minute
half-bogged
half-sunk
lifeless.

An ambitious fly buzzes around Dad's face
preparing itself for the best moment to
zoom into his shocked open mouth.

I've got one eye on him
and the other eye on the tractor.
I don't think I've ever stood as still as this.

He gestures for me to get in the ute.
Drives me back.
No speaking.
I fumble with all of the gates.

The day goes slowly.
I hide out in my room
listening to 3XY.
At about one o'clock
Dad knocks and enters, before I've said enter.
'Come and check it for fire hazards,' he says.
He's obsessed with the farm catching fire.
'It's in the water,' I say.
But I don't think he wants me to speak.
We get to the bottom paddock,
all heaviness and disappointment between us.
We stand and stare at its twisted face,
the headlights like eyes
pleading towards the heavens.
No fires here.
'Poor thing,' he says, 'looks a bit sad.'
'Yeah…' I say, looking at the sorry creature.
And then he starts to laugh
and I am laughing and
we are laughing
together.
Nobody's hurt.
It's only a piece of machinery!
We are laughing so much
that we have to sit down
in the grass to stop from falling.
There are tears in our eyes –
not a cloud in the deepest bluest of skies
just a flock of high-flying birds going by and then simply
insects buzzing,
and the growing of the grass…

We wipe our eyes
and sniff.
'Well,' he says, 'haven't had a good laugh in ages.'
He wipes his eyes and sighs.
'I think we lost a good tractor,' he sniffs,
'but I'd just about say it was worth it.'

19

It's the long weekend.
Dad's gone duck shooting with Pip.
Bigstep's gone to visit her parents
and the Little Steps are with their father.
Jess invites me to stay
at her dairy farm in Wallan.

Her dad gets up at four a.m.,
gets me halfway under a cow.
Everything's splattery, stinky, mooing and wet.
No wonder cow's milk gives me diarrhoea.
I vow never to get milk out of a cow again.
Let alone drink it.

At night 'Ma and Pa'
sit in their tiny fibro house
with homemade floral curtains
in front of a large wooden telly.
We eat a huge roast chicken, like a turkey,
with crispy skin and stuffing.
Can't fit it all on my flowery plate.
When the peas go over the edge, Jessica says,
'So much for my posh friend,' and they laugh,
including me
but I nearly start crying as well
because I miss Mum.

Later the windows frost over as
the gas fire warms
the cockles of our hearts and
after dessert
they drink milky tea and we munch on homemade bikkies.
Her dad smokes a sweet pipe
and winks like the world is an okay place.
I didn't realise you could be so content with hardly any money.

We watch *Young Talent Time*.
'Jess,' I say, 'you could be on this show.'
'Don't be crazy,' she says.
'I'm not. You could.'
'I know,' she says, 'but why would I want to do that?'
'Don't you love singing?' I ask.
'I do. I sing all the time.'
She does, she sings all the time.
Today by the huge record player
she sang harmonies with
Linda Ronstadt, Joan Baez and Emmy-Lou Harris.
'Don't you want to be discovered?' I ask.
'By who? For what?'

During the next advertisement I ask,
'Is that a wedding dress?' pointing to the plastic-covered gown
hanging over the door to the bedrooms.
Nobody answers.
Mr Harford puts down his cup too fast
and Mrs Harford stares at the telly.
I look to Jess. She's shaking her head
frowning and miming, shhhh.
It seems to be
the only thing
in their house
that doesn't fit.

Next morning
after bacon and eggs
we're in the top paddock
smoking behind the trees.

We're watching over the neighbouring property.
'Bancini's,' she says. 'Italian.'
Pigs, chickens, ducks and rusty machinery surround the
square red-brick house.
She tells me the father gets his five kids to manage the farm.
'Slave labour,' she says, then loudly whispers, 'Mafia.'
The conflict apparently began when their ducks
got through the fence in the joint dam.
Another time, they saw the eldest son
being hit with a '4be2', whatever that is.
Mr Harford tried to intervene but
Mr Bancini threatened him with his shotgun.
'If you ever step on my property again…'
A ruling was made after that.
'We'll have nothing more to do with any of them.'

Strange how a prohibition makes you feel curious.

'So what's with the dress?' I ask, recalling the awkward moment.
She says it's her sister Stacey's.
'She called off the engagement just a week before the wedding,
which was meant to be last month.
Mum specially made the dress.
They don't know what to do with it. Or her.'
'Why'd she call it off?'
'She said she was having doubts and if she wasn't sure now
what if she never was.'
'Wise.'
'Mum's devastated. She thinks you only get one real chance,
that she's gonna be an old maid forever.'
'Well,' I say, 'better to be safe than sorry.'
Jess says, 'I dunno. I think she just got a case of the nerves.
Nice guy. Spunk. Teaches at the boys school.'

I tell her I'm not into weddings.
She says I'm 'tragically unromantic'.
'It's not the wedding. I like tulle. It's the vows.
They don't last.'
'You're just cynical,' she says, 'because of your parents.'
(Can't argue with that.)
She says, 'If you had parents more like mine…'

She snaps me out of my fantasy about parents more like hers by
singing her favourite Ronstadt song, 'Desperado'.

We compare notes on favourite singers.
I tell her I like Dylan, Van Morrison, Neil Young,
Leonard Cohen and Janis Joplin.
'How come you only like the ones that can't sing?'
'What do you mean?'
'None of them can sing.'
'Yes they can.'
'No they can't.'
'Well, how come they're so famous?'
'Good question!'

I put out my cigarette in the dead leaves
and spit on it so we don't start a fire.
Maybe she's got a point,
but this is the thing that proves to me
that anyone can be famous.

Dear Journie,
  I wish I could stay every weekend with Jess or simply just move in.

20

This week we both auditioned
for the school musical.
I can't sing but I gave it a go.
You don't have to be able to 'sing' to sing
and besides, there must be some speaking parts.

It's written by our music teacher
Neddy Zeichmann who is always
very publicly
impressed with Jess's voice –
always inviting her to sing the examples.
He looks like a young version of Einstein,
except he has messier hair.
We call him Mr Zed.
I can't wait to get the casting results.
They will see…
We will both be Somebodies
together.

I'm humming along practising
while we're all out riding together.
Not Dad – with his bad back from bending over his patients,
or Pipstar who hates horses that are
too big to join his plastic army.
Just me and the Steps.

Bigstep is on her giant horse, Pirate.
I'm on White Sails,
Midstep's on Prince
and Littlestep is on old faithful Anderson.
We're all flying up Gallop Hill
and halfway up
in mid-air
Bigstep looks across at me
and smiles –
I can't help smiling too.
If it weren't for her
we wouldn't have our wild hair streaming
in the breeze of her crazy dream.
After lunch I sneak up to the roof
for a cigarette
and to practise the love scenes
I'll have to play
in front of audiences one day.

I don't get tired from fresh air any more.
It's normal.
When we spend a day in town, that's when I feel wrecked.
Yeah, I'm getting used to the wide open spaces
with enormous skies filled with tumbling clouds and
rising and setting suns and stars you can almost hang onto.

On Sunday I take White Sails out
to the edge of our farm, alone.
I dismount to let him munch some grass
and he swishes some flies with his tail.
I'm beginning to fall in love
with the personalities of horses.
Before I thought they were all the same
but horses are totally individual
whenever you get to know them.

After I finish my cigarette
I check it's just White Sails and me
and then I follow this inspiration to
take off all my clothes.
It's a crazy sensation
to be outside
in a wide open paddock,
naked.
This is definitely not something that
you can do
in the city.

21

It was cold and dewy and dark
when we set out early this morning
but the sun's slowly gaining strength,
infusing little bits of itself
in the spring wattle and roadside daisies.

There's a whole bunch of us heading to Flowerdale
on an overnight horse trek.
According to the map it's about forty ks one way.

We've packed saddlebags and backpacks with
food and drinks and a toothbrush and
something to sleep in tonight.
The preparation has been extensive,
emotionally at least.
It's only one night but we discussed it for weeks.
I bet Ned Kelly headed out for months
without any preparation.

At least we look the part
in our riding hats, joddys, R.M. Williams boots and Driza-Bones.
Not Dad.
He's in a different costume
with his tails and his grandfather's top hat
over his Austrian lederhosen.
Thank the Rural Gods we're taking the back roads and tracks.

After the chaos of the morning start,
we've settled into a rhythm
and we're moving along
at a good pace on Dry Creek Road
heading into Mount Disappointment State Forest.
It's a little bit spooky but thrilling.
I'm awestruck by the dignity of trees
and the way they filter rays of tangible light.
The forest has a cathedral-like grandeur
that puts the city to shame
and the sound of horses walking
is the ultimate sound of
Journey and Destination.

I imagine the early explorers, Hume and Hovell,
trekking past these same tree trunks.

How slowly and surely
they mapped our already discovered country.
How vast a land for the Aboriginal people
who only travelled by foot.

We have ten horses altogether.
Bigstep's on Pirate and the Little Steps are on their ponies.
There's Uncle Henrik and one of his sons, Mathew, Midstep's age.
Also with us is Uncle Raul and two of his kids:
Andrea (my age) and Bobby, a year older than Pip.
Everyone loves Bobby because
even though he's a little bit 'sandwich short of a picnic',
it makes him loveable and innocent forever –
like he wouldn't know bullshit if he stepped in it.
Which he did.

We hardly ever see our cousins. I wish they lived closer.
They're crazy-fun and they ride.

Dad has bought a Percheron horse.
It looks like a Clydesdale, only bigger.
In fact, it's the biggest horse there is.
Dad named him Spade because
aside from his fluffy white fetlocks and pink freckled lips
he's 'black as the ace of spades'.
Dad is not riding.
He says he used to ride with my grandfather
around the volcanic rocks of Mount Buffalo
and the woods of Emerald and before that the Austrian fields
but his back's too much of a risk these days
to brace itself for a fall.
So he's bought an old milk cart and renovated it,
with Holden wheels and comfy old car seats.
With his gigantic horse pulling the cart
he's up front, leading the way
like some Chariot of the Gods.

Pipstar is sitting beside him helping with every little thing
in between asking a thousand questions
about shooting ducks and orchestras.

In the back of the cart there is precious cargo,
food, supplies, water, coats,
but Dad also, in a moment of patriotic madness,
invited two international guests.

The man is a famous pianist
with a Russian name I can't pronounce, like Krankivich.
My grandfather's the president of Musica Viva
and often hosts visiting players and Dad got inspired
to introduce this one to the Aussie bush.
Krankivich lives in 'dreary London'
and can hardly identify a species of gum tree let alone a koala.
He doesn't seem too inspired.
He's awfully handsome but looks like a fish out of water.
For once I don't feel like I am this fish.

The other guest is a celebrated photographer
from New Zealand.
Dad met Petra on a boat leaving from dreary England,
when he was, in her words, 'a handsome young ship's doctor,
all in white uniform with Paul Newman eyes'.
I get the feeling he might've married her there and then
if she hadn't been on her honeymoon with an equally handsome dentist.
She's ultra enthusiastic. Photographs EVERYTHING.
Even us.
'Stop! Stop! That's perfect! The light. The light! Stop!'
Her excitement is nice
but we have to get to Arthur's Creek before night-time.

Also on the cart is Katie; Dad's German short-haired pointer.
She's always quivering, petrified.
'Sit, sit!' says Pipstar every five minutes,
as Krankivich tries unsuccessfully to stop her sitting on his feet.

Pip swaps seats with Petra to try and manage Katie
and now Petra and Dad can't stop laughing
about I don't know what
and her crazy gutsy earthbound laugh
casts itself out through the Great Dividing Range.

I'm riding beside Andrea. Her horse is much taller than mine.
We're first behind Dad's chariot.
And behind us is Littlestep, riding beside Bobby,
then Midstep beside Matthew
and Bigstep is last,
the remnants of her lipstick beaming with joy
as she rides between Uncle Henrik and Uncle Raul.

My uncles don't look like Dad at all.
They were adopted by Dad's parents during the Holocaust.
But today it's like we're all totally related.
Even with the Steps,
it feels like one big
happy family.
Funny how
this Great Dividing Range
has brought us all together.
Even with Petra, who's clicking away,
capturing us in Time.
It's only Kranki who's out of place,
tapping his fingers on his knees like he really should be
back at the concert hall, practising his concerto.

Sometimes everyone's chatting and laughing
and sometimes everyone's looking around at the trees and the birds
and the enchanted rays of downward light
and all you can hear are hooves on the road
and the wheels of the cart
and the click of the camera.

By mid-morning we come to a dam at Main Mountain Road.
We tie up the horses and let them munch grass
and fill up buckets of water for them to drink.

Dad boils real billy tea on the little gas cooker
and we eat Uncle Henrik's home-made Vanillekipferl biscuits.

We head off again.
The further we get away from home the more it feels like a
real adventure.
After the recent rain
the bush is excited with new growth
and everything's thriving
but you wouldn't want to be here in a dry spell;
if there was a fire, you'd never get out alive.

We're heading up a steep hill when Spade suddenly stops still
and cannot or will not budge.
We're only halfway there so it's a bit of a concern.
We all have to dismount and take turns to lead the horses
and push the cart, for half an hour to the top.

Petra thinks it's hilarious.
She's pushes with all her might
then rushes back to record the scene.
Bigstep has one eye on all the horses and one eye on Petra.
Dad can't push, he's protecting his back
but he's big on the instructions.
Krankivich is walking behind us all,
just looking after his fingers.
Occasionally he looks backwards,
as though he might hitch a ride.
Not a car in sight.

Heading downwards now, though strangely,
it's easier riding upwards.
(Well, maybe not for the horse.)
The sky is denim blue
with some cotton wool clouds floating around.

There's a gentle breeze
and the sound of happiness in the trees in the shape of birds.
There's a prize for spotting the first koala
but nobody's won it.

After seeing a lot of nothing but trees and singing daggy songs like
'Climb Ev'ry Mountain', 'Edelweiss' and 'Waltzing Matilda',
we come to a clearing where Dad decides we'll stop for lunch.
Our bums are feeling bony
and the hairs have rubbed off the inside of our legs.
We unsaddle and tie the horses on long leads
and look after their water.
My uncles unpack the picnic box they prepared.
It's a little shaken up from travelling on the cart but
still an al fresco extravaganza.
There's rye bread, salami, pastrami, Liptauer and gorgonzola cheese,
pickled gherkins, duck paté, sauerkraut and potato salad.
Also some sliced apfelstrudel.
We eat like we've been lost in the bush for weeks.

I look at Dad sipping billy tea,
puffing on his big cigar, telling jokes and stories.
The master of ceremonies,
in his element,
perfectly at home in the Aussie bush,
his beloved adopted continent,
and I suddenly glimpse
how our move to the country
makes absolute sense.

Tonight we'll be staying at the property of an author.
His widowed wife is letting us and the horses sleep the night.
The author wrote about a heifer who learned the value of freedom
but nobody wanted to publish a book about a cow,
so he self-published, won a literary award and became successful.
Dad says his last book took twenty-two years to write!
(Remind me not to become an author.)
'So you see,' says Dad to the mob, 'the lesson is, "Never give up."

Who said that?' he asks as a quiz.
Bobby says, 'You did, Uncle Richie,' and everyone laughs.
Dad says, 'No, my little kipferl, it was Winston Churchill,'
and Bobby looks around for the very man himself.

Late afternoon and the trek is on track
but the horses start to shy a bit
at the shadows and rubbish bins and cars.
Katie barks at a bull in a paddock,
a passing horse float, a dog on a chain, a twig.
It's as though we're having to readjust to civilisation.
Suddenly Pirate rears up with a neighing screech
and Spade gets a fright and bolts ahead,
faster than we've ever seen.
Petra screams with delight, Krankivich yells, and Dad calls out,
'WOAHHHHHH BOY WOAHHHHHH…'

I canter ahead to rescue them
while my cousins collect the stuff that fell off the cart.
First I find Pip who's fallen off
but says he's fine, he's all right.
Spade has eventually pulled over
near an extra juicy patch of grass
at the entrance to somebody's apple orchard. He's no fool.
Dad gives me a 'that was a close one' look.

Kranki refuses to get back on the cart
which doesn't matter because
even though we're on level roads now
we can't get Spade to budge.
Frustrating because we're not far from our destination.
We have to ask the orchard owner
if they mind hosting him and the cart overnight.
Dad calls Moira to pick them up
leaving us to meet them at Flowerdale.

By dark, my inner legs are rubbed raw,
my bum's made of gravel and we're all utterly exhausted.

The horses are walking with long reins and drooped necks.
It's impossible to imagine returning to Wandong tomorrow.

We arrive at the gates of Spring Flower Valley after nine o'clock,
unsaddle and tend to the horses while
Kranki gets Mrs Devison to call a taxi to take him
back to Melbourne. Lucky he's got lots of money.
Seeing him get in the taxi, I sort of feel sorry for him.
All day he looked like he totally didn't belong here at all,
which gives me the unexpected revelation that
I totally did.

We eat a big roast lamb that Moira has prepared.
It's a bit overcooked because we're late
but it's fine because we were almost ready to eat a live horse.
For dessert she's made a beautiful pie from locally picked apples
with fresh home-made ice cream.

Bigstep makes a toast to Dad for the whole terrific idea
and I say sorry for all the doubts I had.
'You didn't trust me, did you?' he says.
'Not really,' I say.
'Well, good,' he says. 'You know what I've always taught you…'
Pipstar and I join in with his usual spiel:
'Never trust anyone, not even your dad.'
'That's terrible,' says Mrs Devison and everybody laughs.

Arriving feels like a great achievement
and the exhaustion from the physical exertion and fresh air
is a warm one
like we've been out in life
living it,
surviving it
and tired for the best reasons.

22

Near the end of term it's sports day.
Jess is away, she hates running
(must be the only thing she can't do).
The bus is full of exhausted, post-barracking athletes,
full except for one seat
and you're not allowed to stand.
One seat is left beside
Tony Bancini,
the eldest son of Jess's feuding neighbours.
I catch a close-up of him
before sitting and facing directly forwards.
Olive skin, huge brown eyes, long thick lashes,
a forelock of hair which he flicks off his left eye
and a scar on the side of his lip.
No one calls him a 'wog' because they're scared of him
and also because he's hot.
They say he crashed a motorbike once,
has a six-inch pin in his elbow
and the school would like to expel him
but he kicks all of their goals.
Our legs touch.
He's wearing white soccer shorts,
I pull my leg quickly away
and stare at the seat in front of me.
He calls his mate,
'Eh, Steelo!' (He leans over me.) 'Scuse us,' he says,
and passes a lighter and a packet of Tally-Hos across the aisle.
An electrical volt goes through me.
I think it goes through him too because
he is suddenly very quiet and still
like me.
We both stare through the seats in front.

Eventually he says,
'So what's a girl like you doing in a school like this?'

I look at him and say as casually as I can,
'What's a girl like me?'
He looks at my face, into my eyes, right into my eyes.
Something inside me slips like a Dali clock.
We both turn back to look at the seats in front
and try breathing.

When I finally walk to the front of the bus
I turn back to see
him staring at me,
slightly nodding with the threat
or promise
of Unfinished Business.

This feeling is monumental
but
of course
I can't tell Jess.

23

It feels like a year
before Monday
when I can get back on the bus.

I've cleaned my saddle, helped fix a fence,
greeted two new horses, mowed the front lawn
and learnt Lady Macbeth's speech about her damned spots.

Lots of distractions but
all I have thought of is
Tony Bancini.

Sunday night now and Dad's about to leave for Melbourne.
We're watching the news.
Pipstar is mimicking the Thatcher woman,
'The lady's not for turning.'
Dad asks, 'Who wants to be Australia's next PM?'

We all look at him blankly.
'You know you can achieve anything if you try hard enough.'
'No they can't,' says Bigstep. 'That's an unrealistic expectation.'
This turns into an argument
about who is and isn't trying hard enough
around the house
which falls backwards on Bigstep
because Dad's used to the hygiene of operating theatres,
the precision of nurses
and an exceptionally organised, house-proud first wife.
'Well, if you don't want to do it,
then organise a cleaner,' he says,
putting more than the usual grocery money on the table.

I wish he didn't have to drive to town.

Mum calls.
She tells me I should look out for another parcel
with nice stamps of tropical fish.
She asks about Pipstar before speaking to him.
'Keep an eye on him,' she says.
She asks how life is on the farm and
I tell her I'm kind of settling in.
'That's great, darling,' she says,
but you can tell, though she's happy for me,
she doesn't want me settling in too completely
for obvious reasons.

I thought it would be good to
celebrate something with her.
She was getting so upset whenever I was upset
which made me even worse to the point where
Dad suggested we limit the calls.
But I can't bring myself to tell her about Tony.
Instinct tells me not to
for some reason.
Yet.

She asks how it's going at school.
I tell her how the nice teacher, Mr Barley,
thought Christine was my mother
and how I told him,
'She's NOTHING like my mother.'
Because of the way I said it, he sat me down and told me
if I had any difficulties with having separated parents
he'd be happy to meet for a chat.

Mum surprises me with her response.
'Darling, that's private,' she says.
'Not everyone understands about divorces.
It's best to keep private talks in the home.
People might make judgements.
You don't really want people talking about your private life.'
'Oh, okay,' I say, but I'm not sure who in the home
she expects me to talk to?
Pip takes over the phone
and I return to the table
to try and finish my overdue homework.
Midstep is reading *TV Week*.
I glimpse a picture of the Iranian hostage crisis.
Know the feeling.

I open my exercise book
trying to remember Pythagoras' formula
but I'm thinking about how much Lady Macbeth
must have really loved her husband
and how Bigstep and Dad never seem to touch,
at least not in front of us
even though they got married.
He's off commuting to patients and concerts and hunting ducks.
She's saddled up with her hair in the breeze of her dream.
and when they're together
they're still kind of apart.
It's like they're
separately
sharing a life.

Midstep looks up at me staring at her.
'What? What?'
'Do you think it's a marriage of convenience?' I ask.
She looks down to see which celebrity couple I'm referring to.
'My dad and your mum.
Do you think it's a marriage of convenience?'
She shrugs, a bit disconcerted. 'I guess.'
'Well,' I say, 'do you think it's very convenient?'

Before bed, I begin a poem in my journal:

The Marriage of Inconvenience

Only I can't finish it because
I'm not sure how it ends.
Maybe the whole poem is in the title.
Or, maybe some poems take twenty-two years.
So instead I write
everything I like
(love) so far
about Tony Bancini.

24

He's not on the bus on Monday
or Tuesday or Wednesday or Thursday.
Why does he miss so much school?
On Friday
at last
on the homeward-bound
a glimpse
but Jess calls me to her seat
and I hide the fact that
after he winked
my heart just dropped
like a bowling ball
and rolled all the way down the aisle
towards him.

'I wish they'd shut up,' says Jess,
about the chanting racket in the back seats.
'Who?' I ask and turn around, so glad for the opportunity.
Tony and Steelo are having an arm wrestle.
'Bloody Bancini sisters and their mob.'
They're barracking for him.
(I'm barracking for him.)
'They worship their brother and put on a show
on the rare occasions he actually comes to school.'

The girls at the back point at us.
Jess quickly turns back and grabs my arm.
'Don't look,' she warns.
But I'm transfixed.
Tony looks at me and salutes.
I grin.
'Turn around!' says Jess, yanking my arm.
She's shaking her head,
'I told you their dad threatened my dad with a shotgun.'
I nod. I know.
'Tony's on probation. Three strikes and he's out.
Hope it happens soon. Good riddance.'

She changes the subject
to my great disappointment of the day
which is her great achievement:
she got the lead in the musical.
I don't know why I'm upset. I really can't sing.
'It can be quite fun in the chorus,' says Jess.
I don't answer.
'Well, don't worry,' she says, 'they alternate.
Next year they'll do a play and you'll be cast in the lead.'
'Hey, congratulations anyway,' I say with mixed feelings.
She says, 'He wrote the part with my voice in mind.'
(With more than your voice in mind, I think.)
'He said we'll have to do lots of rehearsals.'
No doubt. 'Well, that's great,' I say. And that's all I can say.

I think I'd be more generous if there wasn't this
problem of her being in the way between
me and Maestro Bancini.

I notice Midstep up the front of the bus
in the daggy seat next to the driver
staring out the window
as if we were still moving
even though we stopped to let out the
redhead kids to meet their redhead parents
at the gate of their farm with their redhead cows.
She might be into
popular culture
but after almost a year
she's still not overwhelmingly popular here.
She won't make the necessary changes.

Before I step off the bus
I turn back to wave at Jess
but really to look beyond her
where I see not only him
but his sisters and friend
all checking me out.
I get off in a rush
nearly tripping.

Midstep and I
wait in the bus shelter
for Bigstep to collect us.
A piece of corrugated iron roof
has half peeled off
making the sun
flash through
whenever the section lifts in the hot north wind.

'How was ya day?' I say, trying to strike up a conversation.
'Same,' she says, staring out for her mother
then kicking a patch of sandy dirt over and over.

'Wanna smoke?'
She screws up her face like I stink.
'Ya gotta make a bit of an effort to fit in,' I say.
She looks at me like I suggested she turn into a cicada.
'No point,' she says. 'Not my tribe. Never will be.'

The pale blue Volvo arrives.
Bigstep's mascara is smudged. Why does she wear it?
Horses don't care and my Ugly Stepmother's pretty without it.
'Is Dad able to come home tonight?'
She nods with visible relief,
perhaps more to get a break from us than to see him.
It's good she's not vain
but her casualness
about everything
sharply contrasts
the proficiency of my mother.

I get in the back beside Pipstar and Littlestep.
I should sit in the front
because I'm the oldest
but I have to hide the smell of smoke.

'Lucy, before I forget, there's a parcel for you in the dickie seat.'
I reach over to see it has twelve tropical fish stamps
and Mum's unmistakable handwriting.
'I forgot to mention it yesterday, sorry.'
I turn to my brother,
'Wouldn't you imagine that a parcel from our mother
would be something we'd want straight away?'
'Now, now,' she says, gently.
'Just open it,' says Pipstar.

It's wool. My favourite smoky blue colour.
I catch the scent of Mum's perfume.
Breathe it in.

Bigstep pulls the car into the drive and stops the engine.
'What is it?' says Pip.

I hold it up. 'I didn't know Mum could knit,' I say.
'Me neither,' says Pip.
Curious as cats, Bigstep and Midstep turn around
to perve at my hand-knitted, polo-neck jumper.
Everyone looks at it as though an alien landed in the car.
(Maybe because it's 37 degrees.)
'Looks like she had trouble,' says Midstep pointing,
'in a couple of spots.'
'Nice blue,' says Pipstar.
'The colour suits you,' says Bigstep.
As if my mother would choose a colour that didn't?
'But,' she says, 'polo-necks always make me feel strangled.'
This gives me the feeling to strangle her
but I don't.
'Must be hard,'
she says,
'knitting in the tropics.'

25

Back at the ranch
on Doglolly Hill,
Littlestep is in her usual position
on the lounge room couch
beside an empty tub of
Streets vanilla ice cream,
with her face in another book.
You'd think she'd put on weight easily
like Midstep and me
but ice cream is ALL she eats.
I don't know why but I feel the urge
to interrupt her peace.
'Haven't you finished all the Enid Blyton range by now?'
'Yes,' she says, recovering a little from the interruption,
'I'm reading them all again.'
I repeat what Electric Shock said
when she saw me leave the library with a pile of plays:

'Dork.'

I sneak up to the roof
to get some perspective
on how this is going to work,
with Tony hardly ever at school and
Jess, a major obstacle.

Through the chimney
I can hear the Steps all chatting around the lounge
and, faintly, Bigstep's new Dire Straits record
on my favourite song
'Where Do You Think You're Going?'
Have to admit she's got cool taste in music.

'I'll never fit in here,' says Midstep, 'and I don't want to either.'
I'm trying to listen but Dad's Scary Canary,
all diesel noisy, pulls up in the drive.
He gets out of the car with some difficulty.
Back pain, I suppose, and exhaustion.
Friday afternoon traffic.
'Me neither,' says Littlestep,
her voice frozen from too much vanilla ice cream.
Dad slams the car door.
'We've had enough of everything here. And Lucy's such a bitch.'
'Now, now.'

He collects his bag from the boot
and his satchel and his case of instruments.
I'm glad she got a cleaner.

'Please Mum?'
'Are you sure?' says Bigstep.

He drops his jacket, trying to carry too much in one go.
Goes to pick it up,
stops half bent,
leaves it.

'Well then, it's settled,' says Bigstep.
'If you really want to leave, then so be it.'

I can't believe I've just heard this.

'I'm hooooome,' calls out Dad.

I quickly get down
while they're all in the lounge
and head off
to the furthest paddock.

What's she gonna do?
Pack up all the horses and all of us and just leave?

I walk and walk to the furthest boundary fence,
where I watch the old Red Rattler clang on past.
A girl who looks like me in one of its windows waves.
At me?
The train sends off its hoot like a long, stuff-you fart
and screams its way towards Sydney,
where I no longer wish to run.
I have changed what I wear,
how I speak,
what I eat.
I can smoke a packet a day.
I can read the mood of my horse and
almost get him to do dressage ballet.
There's Jess in her cosy farmhouse
where any time I can visit and
next year I'll get the lead in the school play.
I'm doing well at school again,
maybe better than at Grammar.
And every second of every day
I'm thinking about
Tony Bancini.
It's almost the end of the year –
I survived.

How can we pack up and go,
when I only just arrived?

I come back for dinner,
hide for a minute, to suss out the situation.
Bigstep's album is playing over again.
I can hear the song
'Follow Me Home'.

The house smells of a roast
and the table's set
but nobody's at it.

'Where've you been?'
'We were about to send out a search party!'
'Just walking,' I say.
'Please don't do that without letting us know. You gave us a fright.'
I get a small twinge of pleasure in the fact that they noticed.

Dad has cooked paprika duck.
A poor creature from out of the freezer
that he shot on his last trip with quivering Katie.
She was trained to retrieve birds alive
but ate every one of our chickens.
She pretended, with a white feather on her nose,
that she had nothing to do with the massacre.
'She isn't suited to farm life,' said Bigstep,
who made Dad give her away
so this dinner is a challenging reminder.

Dad proudly carves the duck with the precision of a surgeon.
'Ehr,' says Littlestep, spitting out a mouthful.
It lands like a cockroach onto the plate.
'What's that?' She picks something out.
'Just a small pellet,' he says, 'nothing to get fussed about.'
'And it's crunchy,' says Midstep. 'Yuck.'
'Don't complain. Think of the starving millions.'
'But it's crunchy,' she says.
Pipstar spits out a mouthful too.

So do I. Not pellets. Something gritty.
'Yuck.'
'Yuck.'
It's the paprika spice – it's not paprika spice.
It's the red sand I souvenired from our Ayers Rock visit.
Sacred earth –
we ate it.
Poor Dad slides the duck off the platter and into the plastic bin.
The Steps are laughing but
we aren't finding it funny.
My brother thinks he will die.
'We've had enough,' says Midstep. 'Did Mum tell you?
We want to go to boarding school, at Grammar.'
'Don't they make you eat slops?' says Pipstar,
who recently watched *Oliver* on TV.

'Do you want to go to boarding school too, Lucinda?'
'Boarding school? Are you kidding?!'

I sneak out for another walk. It's dark.
There's a moon on every dam.
A fish,
or something,
comes up to swallow one of a trillion stars
and the whole universe wobbles.
A distant cow farewells a day
that will never be reclaimed.
A horse snorts and stamps the ground.
The insects hum a deeper sound slowing the earth
for its night-time turning.
Nope, you don't experience things like this in town.

Part Two

1

We are sitting at a round glass table
in a serviced apartment in Melbourne.
Mum's here for the holidays to see us.
Pipstar is on a camping trip
for the first three days,
with two of his old Grammar friends,
so I've got Mum
all to myself,
for once.

We've just come back from seeing
The Blue Lagoon.
I wish I was Brooke Shields.
We've got the same eyebrows and hair
but she's an awful lot prettier. She's stunning.
She hasn't got a Jewish nose and she's tall.
Mum says her Paradise
isn't quite like *The Blue Lagoon*,
but similar.

Mum looks great.
All tanned and healthy and slim and fit
though there's something sad
blended into her face.

Her photographer friend is doing a series on
Mothers and Daughters.
She decided not to include us
because we're all back to front.
Mum looks 1980s mod
and I look like I finally got found at Hanging Rock –
Miranda's European half-sister.
It's probably good.

Mum shines like a TV star in the presence of a camera
but my efforts at a wistful mysterious expression
make me look like I'm going to be sick.

'Should be ready,' she says, smelling the air
and heading into the kitchen to check the cake.

I look around the unfamiliar room:
sterile decorations, except for the pieces of
colourful wrapping paper
from my very belated birthday gifts.
A summer dress, an Indian skirt,
coconut soap, pineapple body cream,
a pair of sandals, handmade shell hair combs,
a handmade basket and a book,
Don't Stop the Carnival by Herman Wouk.

I follow after her into the small kitchen
which smells almost homely because of the cake.
Then I see it.
'Where's the other half?' I ask,
staring at the thin overcooked slice in the baking tin.
'That's it,' she says. 'It didn't quite rise.
I don't know what went wrong. It isn't my kitchen.'
Does she even have a kitchen any more, I wonder.
'Shall we call it
Mum's-where's-the-other-half chocolate cake?'
'Yep,' I say smiling at her enthusiasm, 'that's the right name.'
'I'm sure it tastes just as good. You sit down and I'll bring it in.'

She comes in with a tray
holding two tall iced coffees
and the 'Where's-the-other-half' cake
with exactly fifteen tall candles
which I have to blow out in one go
or I think I'll get jinxed.
(That is, if I'm not already.)

'Happy birthday, darling,' she says, and hugs me.

And it's all nice, even the cake
but it's also a little pathetic,
just the two of us
in this strange place
two months after my birthday,
looking through the glass table
beneath the cake
at our ungrounded feet.

While we're eating I decide to tell her about Tony.
I've got so much to tell because no one else has heard it
but the more I describe him the more she bites her lip
and frowns.
Finally she says, carefully,
'Yes, I guess I can understand a kind of
animal magnetism.'
I'm not sure this is complimentary.

I tell her about the horses
(she's never ridden)
and I tell her about the school play next year
and how I'm sure to be cast in the lead.
'I hope I can come and see it,' she says.
So I tell her when the play will be on and
she starts clinking the iced coffee spoon around
like she lost something important
somewhere between the ice blocks.

I take a big sip and a stupid blob of ice cream
lands on my nose.
I know she still considers iced coffee a treat,
seeing as we didn't used to be allowed to drink coffee,
so I don't tell her how much milk doesn't agree with me now,
especially since I saw where it came from.

And I don't tell her about Jess –
my famous-singer-new-best-friend.
I don't know why.

Perhaps I'm scared she won't react the way I want.

There's a pause between us –
like maybe we don't know each other
so well
any more.

'So when are you going to come back properly?' I ask.
'I don't know exactly,' she says, sipping, sipping…
'Why? Why don't you know exactly?'
'Woy… Woy… Darling, it's "Whyyy".
You're starting to speak like a country bumpkin!'
I drink the whole rest of the freezing coffee and eat more cake.
'Hey,' she says, 'save some room for your special dinner.'
'Are we having honey chicken?' I ask.
'No,' she says, 'this kitchen is hopeless.
I thought I'd take you out somewhere really special.'

We sit on the couch side by side.
'Do you really like them?' she asks.
'Yes, I do, thanks.'
And I do. I've so missed new clothes and the dress is really pretty.
Not quite the latest fashion in town but hey,
I don't live in town.

'Why don't you try them on?' she says.
'Okay.'
I pick up the clothes to take them to the bedroom.
'You can change in here,' she says, 'I'm your mum.'
There's a frozen moment.
I wish I hadn't drunk all that cold milky coffee.
I don't want to undress in front of her.
She hasn't seen my body for ages.
It's different now.
I'm no longer her little girl.
It doesn't belong to her any more.
It doesn't feel right.

I can feel as I leave the room
that she doesn't like this realisation.

'Oh,' she says,
when I come back in feeling strangely self-conscious.
'Looks lovely. What do you think? Do you like it?'
'Yes, I do. It fits. And the sandals are nice. They fit.'
They won't fit in stirrups or striding through long grass
and they won't keep the bull ants out but they're nice.
'Thanks.' I give her a hug and a kiss.

I sit down again, wondering how we'll fill the time before dinner.
She hates television, even though she worked on it.
'Want to go for a walk?' she says.
'Sure,' I shrug. I don't really. Walking is not the same in a city.
She looks at me. I look out the window at the power lines
draped across a dull sky.
We don't move.

'Mum,' I say, 'why do you stay in Paradise,
if it isn't really paradise
and every time you talk about it you cry?'
She says, 'It's a terribly difficult situation, darling.'
'What do you mean?'
'I wish I could explain it,' she says,
getting all caught up in her throat,
like she knew this was coming,
'but I don't think you'll understand.'
'How do you know if you don't try?'
'Oh, darling, one day, I promise,
I'll be able to tell you the whole story. I just can't right now.
It's too complicated. Too upsetting. For all of us.
Your father and I made an agreement not to discuss it.
(He's *my* father now. No longer her husband. She's disowned him.)
'I don't want to put any more burden on you than there already is.'
I look at the coloured wrappings wondering how that works when
not knowing is the biggest burden.

'Let's just say it was in the hands of the courts,' she says,
adding this as though the little extra information is forbidden.
Then I can see she's holding back tears.
I don't want to upset her.
I don't want to ruin our very special yet
terribly short time together
especially as she's trying so hard to make it so nice.
'Okay,' I say, 'let's go for a walk.'

We head to the park and along the oak tree path
that provides shade from the dry heat of summer
and see kids play on swings,
kids in families, still together.

I tell her about the big music gig going on soon at Broadford,
the one organised by the Hell's Angels bikies.
'By who?' she says, really interested.
'The Hell's Angels,' I say quietly.
'You wouldn't go to that, would you? That'd be really dangerous.
Oh, promise me you won't go to that. Is Dad letting you go to that?'
I shrug.
'Promise me you won't.'

She puts her arm around me.
'I've missed you so much.'
Me too, I want to say but no words come out
even though I have
missed her
terribly.

We sit down on a bench
looking at the upside-down girl on the monkey bar
with her hair touching the ground
just like Mum's favourite photo of me taken at that age.

'Do you still think you want to be an actress?' she asks.
'Not think – I know – I will!'
She smiles and half tilts her head like I'm sweet.
But I'm not sweet, I mean it. This is my life.

'Well, guess what? In the next holidays,
I'm going to try and get you a place
in a special drama careers development week.
They prepare young people for drama schools,
like NIDA and Victoria College.
'Wow!' I hug her. 'Really?'
(NIDA is where Judy Davis went! And Mel Gibson!)
'It's very hard to get a place but I'll do whatever it takes.'
'Yaaay!' I yell out.
'Shhh,' she looks around at the normal mums.
'Thanks!' I say and hug her again
and this moment is the highlight
of the whole holidays.

2

Back on Doglolly Ranch
there are four of us in the dressage lesson:
Bigstep, me and two ladies who keep their horse on our farm.
Arnie, our ex-Olympic three-day-eventing instructor,
has got us working on
the rising trot, the sitting trot and the extended trot today.
'That's a hell of a lot of trotting,' I said,
already sore in my mind before we started.
'Best place to start,' he answered, tapping his crop on his leg.

White Sails can't do the extended trot
where they stretch their legs out in front like ballet.
You have to get a specially trained horse
who understands dressage signals for that,
so I have to do extra practice at the
sitting trot
which, let me tell you,
is not a walk in the park.

If you get it wrong,
it hurts.

You have to try and
'become one with your horse'
(or at least with the saddle of your horse)
so there's not too much bumping around.
I think the inside of my calves have
already lost all their hair
which is good because
I'm too embarrassed to ask Bigstep for a razor.
It's getting tricky, trying to borrow hers.

I look over at Pip
sitting in the tray of the ute
which I learnt to drive last week
'so I could take rubbish down to the tip'.
He's intensely focused on pushing the buttons of his
electronic game that he got for his eleventh birthday.
Alien Invader is accompanied by beeping sounds
which drive the rest of us crazy.
Whenever we're asked to 'halt' the horses
I can hear it, even under my hat.

Pip doesn't care about any kind of trotting.
I hope he makes some proper friends this year.
It's quiet with the girls at boarding school.

I look at him
lost
in the game
where you have to try and kill as many aliens as you can
in the shortest space of time.
Nice example for young people.
No wonder the world's in a mess
with stuff like that war in Afghanistan.

'Concentrate!' says Arnie
turning on his boots
in the centre of our arena
in the midst of a halo of dust.

'Heels down, sit tall, look straight ahead.'

But it's hard to concentrate…
Tomorrow we go back to school. Year eleven.
I'm going to get involved with EVERYTHING I can, like debating, drama, tennis and dance classes.
I'm going to be the actor who auditions with the most skills.
And maybe I'll go down in a few school records.
I've got all these plans in my mind but the main thing is
Tony.
Will he be on the bus tomorrow? At last?
If I don't see him tomorrow
I'll die of longing.

'Okay,' says Arnie, 'now return to a walk on a loose rein.'
Sails hears this instruction before I do.
'Annnnd, come into the centre.'
We circle him.
'Halt.'
We let go of our reins.
The horses' heads droop like on a released spring.
They have a patch of sweat on their hot necks.
We pat them. 'Good boyyyyy.'
'Now,' says Arnie, looking straight up at me.
'You could be good.
You could be a very nice rider but not if you don't concentrate.
You have to commit to working very hard.'

I missed the first one but
maybe I could audition for the sequel of
'The Man from Snowy River'?

3

Jess and I are in our favourite seats halfway down the bus.
Everyone kind of knows they're ours by now.
She missed the morning bus and then we had sports trials.

What she doesn't know is that I saw him at lunch today,
in the equipment room. I was putting away the racquets.
He was behind the door like he'd been waiting for me to arrive.
The room was really stifling;
smelt of baseball gloves and batting pads and other sporty stuff.
He was holding a skipping rope. He said quietly,
'Welcome back.'
I had to squeeze past him to reach the racquet shelf.
'Missed ya,' he said.
On my way to the door
he looped the skipping rope over my head,
around my back
and pulled me towards him.
'Got you now,' he said.
We were almost touching,
I looked up
and he kissed me.
I got a free-fall melting hot feeling.
He let the rope drop.
'I'll be seeing ya,' he said
and walked out trailing the rope behind him.

When I got my brain, lungs and heart back,
I came out into the blaring sun of the quad,
glowing like I'd been painted with radiation
but nobody asked me any strange questions
which was good because I had
plenty for myself.

Jess is chatting but sometimes I turn back
to catch a glimpse of Tony.
He keeps talking to Steelo
then turns to me
really fast
and winks
then turns back to Steelo
like nothing ever happened.

His mate doesn't even notice
but his sister, Katerina, she knows,
I'm sure.
She even winked at me once,
I think,
from the very back seat.

One time Jess turns back to look
at why I'm turning around so much.
'What is it?' she asks, trying to work it out.
'Nothing,' I say.

I look out the window
at the long dry grass by the side of the road
in the faded paddocks of the farms we pass.
They said on the news it's been the driest summer since 1915.
Nobody's paddocks or lawns are green.
But I'm glad to be away from town
where the world was filled with
fake colours.
Glad to have made my decision
to be with Jess
and the horses and Tony
and all this fresh air.
I would never have got the lead in the Grammar school play.
The school was so huge I was just another statistic.
In a small school you get more attention
and I'm sure I'll do well here at HSC.

Besides,
I don't feel connected to
my old friends at Grammar any more.
In the holidays I went to a Toorak party
and sat on a beige suede couch all night
watching the fashion show.
Might as well have worn my jodhpurs.
I told Charlotte and Annabelle about Tony.
'A *pig* farmer?'

'How do you mean, Italian?
As in pizza shop? Or the Amalfi coast?'

Today I put my name down for the extra curricula activities
so I can be cast in any part and become the kind of actor who,
in Jess's words, will 'boost the Australian film industry'.
Living here will be my diving board into
My Brilliant Career.

'You didn't ask how my holidays went,' says Jess.
'Huh?' I jump out of my imaginings.
'How did your holidays go?' I ask.
'I'm in love,' she says.
I look at her and can tell by her face that she means it.
'Who is it?'
'Who do you think?'
For a minute I have this horrible feeling it's Tony,
but that's stupid because
the Harfords have the Bancinis on a lifelong blacklist.
'I don't know. Who is it?'
'Zed of course!'
'Oh yeah, that's ol' news,' I say.

In the background,
I can hear Tony laugh.
I badly want to turn around
but I can't,
it's too risky.

'I kissed him,' she says.
'You what?'
'I kissed him. Zed.'
'You what?' I say. 'Bullshit.'
'Yep, I met up with him in the holidays.'
'That's crap.' Everyone has a crush on a teacher
but it's not like you actually *kiss* them.
And your teacher certainly never kisses you back.
I know she's sweet sixteen but it's illegal to be with a teacher, I think.

'He's left.'
'What?'
'Are you deaf today? He's not coming back.'
'You're joking.'
'No. He's moved back to Melbourne.
He invited me to record a song.
I told Ma I was staying with my brother *but*
actually I stayed the whole night with Zed.'
'What?'
'On his couch.'
'My God,' I say. 'I can't believe it. Really?'
'We recorded all day long and had dinner
and did more recording and I was exhausted and then
we kissed
on the couch
before he went to bed.
I didn't sleep a wink at all because I'm totally in love.'
'God! Are you sure he doesn't just want you for your voice?'
'No, no, he wants all of me. I can feel it.'

Loud laughter from Tony at the back of the bus
lifts everyone's heads up and
snaps us out of our conversation.
I turn back to look at him quickly and grin.
Jess tugs me back, leans in close and whispers like a warning,
'Hey, did you know he's been expelled?'
'Who?'
'Bancini,' she says, gesturing with a distasteful expression.
'What?'
The bus approaches my stop.
'What?' she copies. 'Yep, finally they kicked him out.
Caught him smoking out of bounds again but this time
someone called him a wog and he took their bag and burnt it.'
'I thought they needed him for soccer.'
'Not any more. Half the time he was away anyway.
So many suspensions. Typical Bancini.
All the same. Goodbye and good riddance!'

I'm finding it hard to swallow this news.
'Luce,' she whispers quickly as I'm getting up,
'I've got so much more to tell you
about how I'm so crazily unbelievably in love
and what he said and did and everything. Tomorrow!'

I get off the bus without turning around.
The old rickety thing revs on past and I
see he is looking out the back window grinning.

How will we meet
if he's not coming to school?

4

I was nearly seen
getting up on the roof this afternoon.
I have to be more careful.
The tiles are still hot from the sun all day.
Luckily there's a breeze
and some clouds putting me
in and out of
shadows.

We haven't had rain for a while.
Everything's dusty.

Pipstar's clarinet practice is leaking up through the chimney.
He keeps hitting the same wrong note
and then starting again.
Apart from practising music,
he just comes home from school
and hits a ball against the wall or
plays rugby with make-believe players
made of our couch-leather bolsters.
Or murdering Alien Invaders
or if he's tired, it's TV with *Astro Boy* and *Shazam*.
He wants to be with his Grammar friends –
says there's no one here he gets on with.

I think there must be bullies. He won't tell.
It's a pity he hasn't developed a liking for horses.

I open up my red-bound journal.
I like how it's starting to feel thicker with the writing.

Dear Journie,

I sent off the application form to the Drama Careers Development Week. Mum also wrote to them. HOPE AND PRAYYYYYYYyyyyyyy!!!

Haven't seen him for 2 whole weeks now. It's driving me crazy. I finally told Jess (I had to tell someone) that I liked him. 'You can't be serious,' she said & laughed & I laughed too, so she didn't think I was serious.

I have to practise my laughing. I've read it's one of the hardest things for an actor to do authentically.

Racking my brain for a way for us to meet.

A kookaburra lands on the gutter
at the edge of the roof.
I thought kookies had no colour at all
but this one has brilliant blue feathers
on the side of its grey-brown wings.
She swoops down to the lawn
and comes back up with a worm.
Disgusting.
I have a phobia of worms. I'd rather die than eat one.
It makes me dry retch.

Dad keeps complaining about his sore back from bending over his patients. Pipstar said he should tie them up and operate vertical.

The more I'm into horses, the better I get on with Bigstep. I bet she's upset that her daughters abandoned her horsey dream. Thank the Rural Gods we've found something in common.

5

We had a dance class right after school today
and now we're waiting by the fence
for Jess's sister, Stacey to collect us.

Jess's mum doesn't drive.
Bigstep said if I wanted to take up dancing
I had to arrange after-school transport.
It clashes with the pack-up after her jumping lesson.

Jess joined the tennis team with me
but thank the Gods
she's not as good as me at something.
She's not bad but she looks a bit unco when she's serving.

'Where is she?' says Jess.
I shrug.
'Do you think we can sneak in a cigarette?'
'Wouldn't risk it. Better just wait here.
She might think we got a lift with somebody else.'

Having Jess's sister collect us is cool.
I'd love to ask her privately
about the wedding that didn't happen.
But I get the feeling you can't.

Jess swings a long leg
over the fence
then the other one
and sits
like a huge bird looking out.

At tennis training at lunch today
we had a row of boys
watching
because she was wearing a short skirt
and her legs go 'all the way to the ground'.
But she didn't have eyes for any of them.
She only has eyes for Zed.
Both of us are in love.
But the ones we love are invisible.
And mine more than hers because
even Jess cannot see.

6

Just when I'm going crazy,
tossing and turning,
trying to sleep but
thinking so much about
Tony –
at one a.m.
I hear a car
slowly crunching up the gravel drive.
We're not expecting visitors. It's spooky.
My room is nearest the carport
and is separated from the main house
by the breezeway, so
it's a long way
from the telephone and from Bigstep –
though I think if she saw me being murdered,
she'd calmly say, 'Now, now,'
like she said the day I had a brawl with her daughters
and Midstep bit me.

The car engine turns off.
My heart is beating so much I can't breathe very well and
my mouth is open so I can hear everything better.
I hear footsteps, then they disappear.
Should I scream to warn the others?
The footsteps return, closer. They stop.
Then a stone,
or something,
plinks on the glass doors.
I'm like a rabbit in a spotlight.
Then the fright of my life – a whisper:
'Hey, Luce.'

It's him!

I open the other door into the breezeway
and see him through the flyscreen.

We both
scream
in total silence –
then muffle some crazy laugh.
'How did you know I was here?'
'Took a risk. Took a guess.'
He points downwards.
'These are your school shoes, right?'

I sneak out
in my blue nightshirt
trying not to creak the flyscreen door
and wake up Pipstar or Bigstep.
I grab my jacket hanging off the hook
and put on my gumboots – the fastest option –
and we sneak around to the back of the house
near his car (or somebody's car at least).

'Nice place,' he says. 'Fucking palace!'
'Who owns the car?' I ask.
'Stole it. From me ma.'
'Jesus,' is all I can say. And I'm not religious.
He lights us both a cigarette.
'I had to see ya,' he says, inhaling deeply,
then blows three perfect smoke rings
into the quickly dissolving breeze.
The way his mouth makes the circles is sexy.
'Did you have to see me too?' he asks.
I grin, 'Yes. But this is really extreme.'
'That's me. No-holes-barred-Bancini.'
'Fuck,' I say again and inhale too deeply
so the smoke might never come out.

It is cool outside, but I'm so freaked out
I'm not feeling any weather.
I've noticed I'm shaking but that's more from the nerves.
'You okay?' he asks.
'Yeah,' I say, 'just freezing. I was warm in my bed.'

'But not sleeping.'
'No, not sleeping.'
'I knew it,' he says.
He sits on the low brick wall that holds in some half-alive shrubs
and pulls me close towards him so I'm standing between his legs.
'Ya sure you're okay?'
'Yeah.'
'Ya trust me?' he asks.
'Yeah, I'm just a bit cold.'
He pulls me closer and holds me there
with his hands behind my back.
I hear a horse snort in the dark.
It's got to be Bigstep's Pirate,
who's kept in the front paddock.
Horses are really curious.
If you sit in a paddock long enough
they'll come and check you out.
It's good that you can talk to them but
lucky they can't talk back and tell all your secrets.

'Ya trust me?' he says, again.
'Yeah,' I say, still shaking,
I think from the cold now as well as the shock. I'm not sure.
His hands drop below my jacket and onto my lower back.
I'm worried he'll notice I haven't got any underwear on.
'Missed ya,' he says.
He smells nice. He's warm.
'Me too,' I say and look away
but I can't see any horses
or anything much
to warrant looking away for very long.
We step on our cigarette butts. I'll hide them tomorrow.

I start worrying about what it's like to kiss a girl with braces.
Even if he's experienced at kissing, no one around here has them.

His hand slides down. Lower.
'Hey! No wonder ya fucken' cold!'

I'm so glad it's dark because he can't see me blushing.
He looks away at the invisible horse
then back at me
with that serious-business face again.
He whispers, 'Ya trust me?'
Why does he keep asking me this?
Is he going to do something terrifying
or is he nervous and kind of stalling?

We are stone-still for a minute,
then he
pulls me
even closer
and kisses me
and keeps kissing me
and the braces don't matter at all
as he keeps on kissing me
for ages.
It's warm
and wet and soft and
all dissolving and
while he kisses me,
his hand lifts up my nightshirt.
I feel hot.
He touches
closer and closer
where no one but me has
been before.

Something rustles in the grass –
gives us a fright which
separates us.
We come up for air
and breathe and laugh.

I don't care what will happen next.

I'm scared and it sounds really crazy but I do, I trust him –
this guy with the ten-inch pin in his arm
from his motorbike accident,
with the scar on his lip, expelled from school
who's rocked up here before dawn having stolen his mother's car.

Yeah, for some reason I trust him.
'I wanna give ya something,' he says.
Part of me is feeling like sure, give me everything.
I've dissolved and all the hard edges and thoughts and fears
have disappeared,
like the horses in the night,
the night mares,
and melted into the
warmest place
I've been for the longest time.

He puts his hand in his jacket pocket
and brings out a box.
'Open it later,' he says, 'not now.'
And he kisses me
again,
with his tongue and his
soft full lips and he
smiles and
winks his sexy eyelashes and
lets me go and says,
'Whatchya doing up so late, girl?
Get back ta bed!'

I watch his mum's car
sneak off down the drive
without its headlights on
until it winds its way down the rolling road
and switching on its lights
disappears over the hill.

7

I open the box.
I wouldn't have opened it up in the breeze
if I'd have known what it was.
The wind takes it –
my dandelion flower.
So all I've got is the box.
But I'm pretty certain he loves me.

I go back to bed but I do not sleep
for the next two weeks.
Every sound in the night is him.
But it isn't.

Poem: Teenagers
Teenagers live in Antarctica
Starved for physical affection
Nobody's touched us much
Since we were little
No wonder we get icy-brittle
Wary of other icebergs
Starving to belong
Like some white continent we broke off from
And lost

8

Jess and I are doing well in the after-school dance class.
We're learning a choreography to Blondie's 'Heart of Glass'.
I liked the teacher until she said,
'Oh, you'll never get into drama school – it's really competitive.'
She'll be really, really sorry she said that
down the track.

We come out at dusk
and it feels like it's going to rain,
which would settle a whole lot of dust.

Stacey isn't here yet, but guess who is?
He's sitting on the school fence. Smoking!
That's where we normally sit and wait
but we can't.
Jess whispers,
'Look the other way and just ignore him.'
My heart is beating fast.
It starts to spit with rain.

'Love the dance gear,' he says.
I'm kind of frozen.
The other kids are hopping into their parents' cars and leaving.
'Don't suppose I can scab a lift?' He grins.
Jess looks at him like,
why would I let an escaped convict into my sister's car?
You wouldn't want the wind to change on her face.
He says, 'I was heading home with Steelo but
he had to drive his dad to the hospital.'
'Can't you just get a cab?' says Jess.
'A cab for twenty ks?
Do you guys milk money from ya cows?' I laugh.
I know her dad would kill her but I ask nevertheless.
'Couldn't he just get a one-off lift? It's raining.'
Jess looks at me like she's going to get her dad to kill me.
We all look around at the empty school
and the grumpy gum trees
dangling their low branches around.
He throws his cigarette butt on the damp ground.
It continues to smoke by itself a moment
till the rain fizzles it out.
Then we wait.
Stalemate.

Stacey turns up in her burnt brown Datsun
beeping the horn.
Jess practically runs to the car
but I get stuck in no-man's-land.
'You coming or what?' she says.

'Go on,' he whispers to me. 'I can walk. Don't worry.'
Then he yells it out to Jess and Stacey,
'THANKS FOR NOTHING!'

'Are you okay?' asks Stacey. 'Did he hassle you girls?'
'Tell ya later,' she says.
'Why? What happened? Tell me now.'
'Later,' says Jess, silencing her.
None of us talk for the rest of the drive.
The windscreen wipers whinge back and forth,
out of time with her radio, which has bad interference
that crackle-crackles through the
'Ride Like the Wind' song.
The news reports the botched-up job
of failing to rescue the American hostages
as the sky hangs low over the long grey freeway
and in between Jess and me.

Dear Journie,
  How can I possibly keep Jess as a friend if I'm trying to be with Tony?
  How can I go out with Tony if we can hardly be together?
  How can I go out with Tony and still be respected at school?
  What's pig farming got to do with acting?
  What do the questions matter if everything rational is totally unclear?

9

After the silent drop-off
I enter the main house and call out 'Hello' to no reply.
Pipstar is asleep in front of *Gilligan's Island* –
that crazy bunch of misfits trying to
act like a family in order to survive
(know the feeling).
But Gilligan has just set fire to the shelter.

My brother looks so sweet when he's asleep.
I wish I could be like a mum for him
but I can hardly be like a mum for myself.

Lying there,
he looks like he needs a family.

Even though it's Friday night, Dad isn't home again.
His back is so bad now that driving is quite painful.
He might have to have an operation.

Bigstep has left my dinner in the turned-off oven.
It's her boiled white rice specialty mix
with a whole lot of canned ingredients
including pineapple this time.
I give it a miss. Even if I were hungry…
God I miss Mum's honey roast chicken.

I can hear Bigstep in her room on the phone
and the monotonous sound of rain.
The drought relief is good for the country
but not my for my secret boyfriend.

The heating is on for the first time since last winter
and something really stinks.
The smell is coming up through the floor ducts
like something died.

I go across the breezeway to my room
which doesn't have stinky heating,
though the downside is it's cold.
I sit on my bed and look at his empty box.
I've never been in love before. Not really.
Is this it?
Why does it have to be messy, confusing, difficult?
Is this why they call it 'falling'?

All I can think of is Tony, walking down the highway in the rain.
Holding a cigarette cupped in his hand so it doesn't get wet.
Walking beside the speeding trucks like in some James Dean movie.

I practise performing the Brooke Shields advertisement
about her wearing nothing under her Levi's jeans.
Thank the Rural Gods I've got a bedroom to myself again.

I start scribbling away in my journal to get the thoughts out of my head.

How could Jessica do that? Is she really someone I want as a friend? What do I like love about him?

Pros	**Cons**
Sexy	*Expelled*
Beautiful eyes	*No transport*
Courageous	*New best friend hates him*
Funny	*Something dangerous?*
Strong, rugged, rough	*Rugged, rough*
Gentle	
Knows me, Sees me	
Wants me	
Something strangely dangerous	

The pros list is longer which is a big key.
And I'm not sure which side to list some items on.

I do the scene in front of the mirror…
but jeans don't look so sexy on me.
And I get the fright of my life because
there's a knock on the glass door.
I nearly break the glass ripping back the curtains.
I rush to open the side door into the breezeway
and stare at him through the fly wire,
'Well, aren't you gonna let me in?
I just walked twenty ks in the rain for you.'

He stays almost the whole night
in my single bed –
we do
every kind of kissing
and dissolving into
some other world,
another whole planet of
hotness and wetness and
bodies entwining
and tongue-desiring
and closeness that feels like

we've fallen through into
a great oceanic expanse
of infinite depth.

We nearly even go all the way
but slow down, he says,
easy does it,
all the time in the world, take it slow,
we're not ready for that yet,
though I feel hungry,
starvingly ready.

Who'd have thought
the toughest guy
in the whole school
would be the gentlest guy
in my bed?

He doesn't ask me
any more
if I trust him.

When he leaves
before dawn
it's like he's peeling my own warm skin off me,
like my heart's going to be unprotected and freeze.

I strike a diagonal line through the Pros and Cons list.
How am I going to see him? What are we going to do?

10

Saturday morning and it's Pipstar's clarinet
that keeps me from sleeping in.
My first thoughts are a downer.

Dear Journie,
   Jessica hasn't spoken to me for two weeks. Not since the car-lift debacle.
I can't stand it. How can I survive at this godforsaken school, without her?

& her friends? How are we going to get famous together – apart? How can I go on torturously waiting for Tony to maybe turn up in the dark of night & all the while not tell anybody about it?

I go outside in my nightshirt and
see Pip on the front lawn at the patio table.
He's used a box of Dad's duck-shooting cartridges
to stop the sheet music from escaping with the wind.
I yell at him, 'I WAS ASLEEP!'
He looks at me, with the pipe in his mouth
then looks at his watch then keeps playing.
'Do you have to play the same old stupid notes over and over?'

He plays the sequence again
but it squeaks
which defies the defiant purpose.
He throws the clarinet on the lawn.
It falls apart in two pieces.
It doesn't break, it comes apart
but it looks like it's broken
which is probably the effect he wanted.
He strides around the far side of the house.

On my way to get a cigarette
(I've taken to smoking before breakfast),
I go via the hall in the main house and
check the keys on the hooks that hang on a rack
beneath Dad's hunting shotgun.
It's the Volvo keys that are missing
so she must've gone into town,
which gives me more time.

I sit at the table where Pip was playing,
torn between burning his sheet music
and apologising to him.
I can hear him playing handball against the wall again.
Over and over.
God, can't he get some friends?

Then I see myself
reflected in one of the million glass doors of our house
and I realise
I don't have any either.

I finish my cigarette.
Put his clarinet back together and take it to him with a 'sorry'.
He keeps hitting the ball against the wall until finally he says,
'I don't care. I don't even like the clarinet.
The tunes are really stupid.'
'You don't have to continue,' I say, enthusiastically.
'If you don't want to.'

He throws the ball
so hard against the wall
it bounces back
across the lawn
down to the fence line
and into the start of the
long, dry-grass grass.

'Of course I don't bloody want to. I hate it.'
'Really?'
'What do you reckon?'
'I dunno. I thought you liked it.'
'It was cool when I wasn't the only one
in the whole school who played an instrument.'
'I play the piano.'
'Not any more.'
It's true. Where's our piano?
'And I hate catching the train by myself,
down to Melbourne for the lesson.'
'Yeah, me too,' I say, 'to get my braces tightened.'
'And when I get there, the old Hungarian bag says,
"Darlink, You reeely mus prrrractise."
But everyone hates me practising.'

'No, they don't,' I say, realising that 'everyone'
has now become
me.

'Well,' I say, 'let's tell Dad it's too much.'
'No,' he says.
'He'll understand.'
'Yeah,' he says, 'but you don't.'
I open my hands out, welcoming an explanation.
He sits on the upside-down rubbish bin
that he uses as a cricket wicket.
'Because it's the only way I get time with Dad.'
'You serious? Is that the only reason?'
'Yep.'
We both look at each other a moment.

'After the lesson, he picks me up, asks me all about the lesson
and I go on with all the B flats and C sharps like one day
I'm gonna play in the Melbourne Symphony Orchestra
and he's thrilled to the eyeballs
and then we go and have
Chinese dinner together.
And lychees and ice cream.
And I stay the night in his medical rooms
with the smell of Pine-O-Cleen on the lino
and the phone messages waking me
and the plastic kidney on his desk
and the skeleton freaking me out in the dark –
but I get him all to myself
for one whole night a fortnight.'

I don't know what to say.
The tragic story makes me want to light up
another cigarette
but we hear the icy blue Volvo coming up the drive.
I throw the dead butt as far as I can
and hide my cigarette pack.

We look at each other,
stuck,
strangely hopeless, helpless,
like we need some kind of
outside force for,
I don't know...
a rescue?

'So who was that guy here the other night?'
'What guy?'
He rolls his eyes,
picks up his clarinet and goes to collect the ball.

'Lucindaaaa!' calls Bigstep.
'Come and help with the shopping please. I've got pink-iced buns.'
Pink-iced buns are nice 'n' all but why does she never ask Pip?

11

I'm on the roof next to Empty Ness,
who's creaking around in the autumn wind.
It's hard to light cigarettes up here, which is good because
it's true they're kind of addictive.
I liked them better when I thought I didn't need them.

The paddocks are bright with the light of the full moon.
The horses and fences are ghostly.
The dams are silver shapes hovering like space ships.
I feel like I'm in a classic black and white movie.
I wish I was in a classic black and white movie.

I open my journal. Switch on my torch and write.

Dear Journie,
    He hasn't come over for nearly 3 weeks. No sign at all. I'm going mad. WHERE IS HE? Did he crash a bike? Did his dad really hit him with a '4be2'? Is he seeing somebody else? Is he like Dad? Has he worked out I'm not someone to stick around for?

I'm not sleeping well. It's all interfering with everything; my homework, my tests, my riding, tennis, debating, dancing, acting… I can't be this exhausted when they cast me in the lead. It could ruin my future career. Having a boyfriend shouldn't be this hard. Should it?

I miss Jess. And all of her friends. She's the only one I can really talk to.

To ward off the turmoil, I review the list of rationalisations I wrote last night:

- *After I confessed my feelings, Jess gave me an ultimatum. 'It's him or me.'*
- *This love affair has to be secret, from everyone; school, family, friends. Energy-consuming. Hard to maintain. Lonely.*
- *Transport & communication issues.*
- *Pig farmer vs actress. He has absolutely nothing to do with my future career, i.e. cannot understand it, support me, or join me in it.*
- *You have to make serious sacrifices for a dream. Sybylla did.*
- *Farm boy vs city girl.*
- *'Wrong side of the tracks.' Not that it matters to me, but could get tricky, especially in other people's eyes, e.g. Mums, Dads…and I guess they'll know soon since Pip found out.*
- *Can't concentrate on anything else. I even fell off my horse for the first time while imagining us escaping together.*
- *Maybe he's having an affair – already – or might soon – like Dad.*
- *If he really knew me, he'd leave me.*
- *He might die in a bike accident.*
- *He might leave me first.*

I've got a headache from so much thinking.

'Lucy?'
I lie low. It's Pipstar.
'Lucy?'
I don't know what he wants me for. Poor kid.
But no one can know my hiding place.
It's the only place in the world I have to myself.
He'd be sure to slip out the secret, even by mistake.
Plus I need to think. I'm stuck.

It'd be great to run all this by Pip
but of course he couldn't understand.
'Lucy! Luuuuuuucy?'
His voice is fading as he heads around
the far end of the house.

Something's got to give
and maybe the obvious thing,
the hardest thing,
is Tony Bancini.

That is,
if he hasn't left me
already.

12

Bigstep brings home another new horse.
Shimmering Fire.
She's a bay Anglo-Arab,
recently trained by Arnie in the art of dressage.
She's about three hands taller than White Sails.
Falling off Sails was scary enough.
I love Sails but he is like a rescued kennel dog
beside this pure-bred red setter.
She's flicking her dished face up and down,
her fine mane is tossing around
she's snorting, moody, stamping the ground
like a prima donna.

'You'll be riding her soon,' says Bigstep,
trying to hold the Arab still
and beaming with pride and joy at her new purchase.
'Me?'
'Yes, for dressage. For showing.'
I look the horse in the eye.

For a second she stares –
dares me,
then tosses her head in the sky
as though she'd rather be up there flying
with unicorns.

Apart from feeling terrified
to ride this unworldly creature
I'm also furious
to be told
again
what I'm going to do next
by someone who isn't my mother.
'No, I'm not.'
'This is an incredible opportunity.'
'So?' I say.
'What do you mean, "so"?'
'Don't you speak English?'
'Now, now, no need to be rude.'
'I'm not riding this crazy horse.'
'You'll be fine. She's just anxious from the travelling.
It's all unfamiliar. They're a little bit nervous by nature.
It's typical of the Anglo-Arabs. Fiery.
But she's beautifully trained. You'll love her.
Just wait till you experience the difference.'

It's hard to tell if she's excited about giving me
the ride of my life
or if the whole investment is about owning
a horse who can win ribbons.
The more ribbons they win,
the better the reputation of your horse stud
and the more they're worth later as breeders.

'Why don't you ride her then?'
'Oh no, showing's not for me.'

The Arab turns on the spot
flicks her tail across my arm.
She's volatile but undeniably stunning.
'Shh shh, c'mon now,' says Bigstep – to the horse, not me –
and leads the fine specimen off to her new grassy kingdom.

I get back in the ute, take the rubbish down to the tip.
I sit on the edge of the gully, light a smoke and
look up at the dusky sky with the huge moon already rising.

I take out the note
from my pocket again
that was passed to me
in the bus today
by Tony's sister.
She smiled at me
and winked,
like a sister.

I will be their at midnite. TB

Then in different writing, added, I guess, by Katerina…
Hoowwwlllll!!!'

13

The moon looks heavy
as if it would fall
and create a devastating crater.
As if it was watching me
before the fall
as a warning,
as a target.

I have reread and reread my list of rationalisations.
I am ready.
Waiting at the top of the driveway.
I'll make it quick and clear like the summary
of the third speaking debater.

The more I rehearse it, the more I believe it.

But I look up at
Empty Ness
and see her open face
receiving the dark
like a silent scream.
Am I doing the right thing?

Then I see a dark figure
walking up the road inside our property
with the glow of a lit cigarette zigzagging around
like a firefly.

I didn't expect him to *walk* here.

I brace myself for the task at hand.
Revise my key points.
He will understand.

He climbs the thick rails of our lawn fence,
jumps down onto the grass
and walks up the hill towards me,
stopping once to stamp out his cigarette.
Arriving, he feels both pockets then says, grinning,
'Long time no see.'
I can't withhold a smile
but my jaw is grinding tight with the task ahead.
The weirdest thing is all I want to do is
hug him.
But it's over. It's too difficult now.
And it can only get more difficult.
I have to get out now for all my reasons and
before he sees who I really am
and leaves me.
If indeed this is not what he already came for.

'Long time no see,' I say, like he did.
'Do I get a kiss?'

I stay where I am. Shrug.
'Shy,' he says, 'are you? Did you forget me?'
'No,' I say. 'Where've you been?'
'Long story,' he says, obviously not about to tell it.

The new Arab canters restlessly across her new paddock,
strangely lit under the bright moon.
I get the feeling that horse will never properly arrive. Anywhere.

He comes towards me, leans in to kiss me but I can't.
Not with my speech in the pocket of my mind.
He looks at me. 'What's wrong? Is it your step-mum?'
I shake my head
'Your ol' man?'
'No.'
'The horse?'
'No.'
'Me?'
I shrug.
'Come and sit down.' He takes my hand,
leads me to the brick fence that surrounds the flower garden
where we were that night when he asked me if I trusted him.
Now we sit side by side.

'So…' he says, 'let's sort out our situation.'

A tide of panic
rises in me.
He's not going to leave me first.
No way.
'I have to talk to you,' I say.
He waits a moment.
'Well, here I am.'
I say, 'I don't know if it ever really started but
it has to end. It's over.'

It comes out a bit abruptly
But at least I've said it, clearly.

I wait for his relief,
his 'glad you said that because that's what I've come to tell you…'
but he doesn't speak
at all.
Doesn't even light up his cigarette.

'Bought you a present,' he finally says,
taking a small velvet box out of his pocket.
My heart sinks.
I shake my head, receiving it only because I
don't know what else to do.
I hold it out in front of me for him to take it back.
This is not how I thought this would go.

'Open it,' he says.
I lift the lid. The moon makes it sparkle.
A ring, with three tiny dot-sized stones,
the one in the middle so bright it must be a diamond.

'I can't,' I say, feeling terribly sad all of a sudden.
'You don't like it?'
'I love it.'
'Try it on.'
'I can't.'
'Please.'
It fits my middle finger.
I'm not sure if that was the finger it was meant for but it fits.
Must've cost him a fortune.
I don't see how I can go backwards on
everything it took for me to make my decision.
'I can't keep it,' I say. 'I meant what I said.
I'm sorry, it's all just too hard.'
I try to revise my rationalisations,
but my heart is dragging across the ground
like the moon
harrowing the paddocks with its sickly green light.

He takes out a cigarette. Doesn't offer me one.

'It's the Harfords that done this, right?'
'No, no, it's not.' My reasoning goes up with the smoke.
'It's yer ol' man then.'
'No.'
'And his tosser lady.'
'No.'
'I'm not posh enough, is that it? A pig farmer.
A wog boy, kicked outa school?'
'No!' I say. 'Nothing like that. Really.'
'What is it then? Did ya meet someone else?'
'No! It's just so hard. I mean, it's not like I want to do this,' I say, sounding pathetic, feeling awful.
'Please understand. It's not that I don't want to be with you.
It's just that I can't. We can't.'

I give him back the ring in the velvet box.

'So that's it then?' he says.
I can't answer.
'You sure about this?'
'Yes,' I say, trying to be strong.
Thinking of my career. My social life.
My sanity. My survival. My need to be in control.

'Well, fuck it,' he says and stands up,
stamps out the cigarette
and begins to walk down the lawn
towards the dark stained fence.
His back is a frightening sight.
His anger is scary.
I didn't imagine it going like this.
Nothing like this.
He climbs the fence.
I have an ache
like I'm losing
a lung
or something essential.

On the top rung
he throws a second leg over
in the haunting glow
of the bright night
that is hiding nothing.
He calls back, 'You fucken' won't forget this!'
He spits, then jumps down into the long grass
and strides off into the dark.

I feel a sickness
like the sea just drained
out of the ocean
and my ship fell over sideways.

14

I look back over my rationalisation list. My eyes blur.
This morning the list looks about as rational
as a plan to remove kidney stones
with pliers.

Dear Journie...
 I keep playing the Dire Straits song 'Six Blade Knife' about all her emotional blades cutting up his heart.
 I just didn't think to factor in the feelings. I didn't imagine the hurt. The anger. I didn't factor in the gift in the velvet box. No, I didn't factor in anybody's feelings. His or mine. I feel like my veins are bleeding with sadness. Flowing with some kind of black pain like the flood the country needs. It's morning now but I'm still sinking in the dark. I thought I'd be calling Jess to celebrate getting our friendship back but if it wasn't for her, maybe this wouldn't have happened. I need her shoulder to cry on but how can she be sympathetic? I HATE myself. What have I done?

15

When I get on the school bus
there's a hissing sound
and nobody talks –
unusual.

I see Jess but she doesn't look at me.
She doesn't know.
I realise the hissing is coming from the back of the bus
and is orchestrated by Tony's sister,
who's incited a gang of year ten girls
to join her.
They are all looking directly at me,
except Katerina who looks directly
through me
with dagger eyes.

Others in the bus
check out how I'm handling this
then get on with talking.

I sit frozen, staring at the seat in front.

Next thing, with the seeming excuse of passing something
to a mate up the front,
my arm is aggressively bumped by Katerina.

'Sit down please,' says the bus driver.

Before she heads back she leans over me,
whispers coldly,
'Nobody treats my brother like that. Slut. You'll pay.'
I keep staring at the seat in front.
Do they have Mafia in Australia?

After a frozen mile or three I hear
'Hey, Gonzo…'
I don't react.
'Psst. Move over.' I'm nudged by Jess.

The back-seat gang hiss again.
'Sit down please,' says the driver.
'What happened?' she whispers.
The pain starts leaking out of my eyes.
'Tony,' I say. Then I can't even speak
until three more bus stops.

She rummages for a tissue.
'What did he do to you?'
'Nothing.'
She shakes her head. Worried.
'He did *nothing*,' I say. 'It was me.'
'Oh.'
For a minute I completely hate her.
But I don't want her to get up and go.
I just got her back. I need her.
What I would like right now is for myself to disappear.
She puts her arm around me and keeps me here.
The back-seat bus-bitches hiss again.
'Don't worry,' she says,
'Whatever you did, you did the right thing.
And we'll all stand by you.'

I stare at the seat.
There's a whole congregation inside me
booing and hissing at myself.

At recess and lunch I hang with her friends,
all raw and pathetic with nothing to say.

But by the end of the day
it's a relief to at least have Jess and her gang on my team.
School was a bit of a Darwinian desert without them.
Now it's even more dog eat dog but at least I'm in a pack.
I only wish I could cry about him on her shoulder.
Anybody's shoulder.

16

Dear Journie,
Still feel the heavy ache in my chest. I wake up every morning half under water. How long will it take to go away? No sign at all from him. Don't expect it but still listening for every sound.
Katerina & her girl-gang are making life hell. Thank the Gods for Jess & her friends. Like when there's dolphins around, there's no sharks. At least, that's what Mum said.
Today we had the auditions for the school play. I keep going over & over the lines I had to read – trying to remember how I said them. You'd be amazed how many ways you can say the same words. I LOVE you, I love YOU, I…love you, etc. Just the choosing can be exhausting. I don't know if I got it right. I couldn't decide, even in the middle of the audition.

I try it all the ways out loud again.
Listening for the right, most truthful one.
I wish I'd said these words out loud to Tony.

17

Weekends are such a relief,
being away from the firing line
of the back-seat bus-bitches,
like hyenas who try to catch me off-guard in corridors
when Jess or her friends are not by my side.

Even though we're wearing windcheaters,
we're lying on the trampoline with baby oil on our legs
trying to absorb the last of summer.
It's the clearest day, not a single cloud to obstruct our blue view to infinity.

The breeze is blowing our hair around and we're singing
and half bouncing along to the old song on 3XY – 'Cold as Ice'.
She suddenly stops at the peak of the chorus,
about our love being sacrificed,
catching me, out loud and off key.

'Definitely stick to acting,' she says.
I hit her on the arm.
After the laughter she says out of the blue,
'I want to quit school.'
'Yeah,' I say, 'who doesn't?'
'No,' she says, 'I mean really.'

I sit up. 'What? You're only in year eleven.'
She nods. Looking resigned. Factual.
I glance across the fields.
Everything's the same as before except
the horses have moved to different positions.
'Why?'
'I want to earn money, like my brothers and sister.
I want to live in Melbourne. I want to be closer to Zed.'

'You can't leave at year eleven!'
'Why not?' she says.
'Your parents will be furious.'
'Why? Earning money would help them, like the others did.
Only thing is, Mum wants me to stay close to the farm.'
'What about your education?'
'For what?'
'University.'
She shrugs. Shakes her head. 'It's not for me.'
'Why not? What about the school play?'
She shrugs. I'm in shock.
Nobody ever considered the option
of leaving school early at Grammar.

I'm grasping for straws…
'What if it doesn't work out with Zed?'
'It will.'
I look at her like which planet do you live on?
Relationships don't last.

I play the last card. 'What about me?'
It's the only one that gets an energetic response.
She sits up. Gives me a hug.

'You'll be fine. I'll ring you all the time.
Come up and visit you on weekends.
You're gonna finish your HSC, get into drama school
and boost the Australian film industry.'

I see something move,
behind a clump of trees, down near the first dam.
It's probably just a horse or a shadow.
but everything in my peripheral vision is Tony.

'Cheer up,' she says, offering me a cigarette. I take one,
even though Bigstep will be back soon from Kilmore.
Whatever.

Three magpies who've been trying to harmonise
as badly as me
in the nearby eucalyptus tree
are suddenly silent.
One glides down to the fence post near
where Tony climbed the fence.
Then the bird takes off.
Birds are so free. Birds have it easy.

'So let's change the subject,' she says,
even though we were finishing our smokes in silence.
'Something I've been meaning to ask… You still a virgin?'
'What?'
'You heard me, Bignose.' She kicks me with an oily foot.

'Guess what?' I say,
'Dad's offered to get me a nose job for my next birthday.'
'Bullshit.'
'No. He knows I hate my nose.
And surgeons like chopping things.
He's already got rid of my tonsils and adenoids.
What do you think?'
'God, Luce, it's not that bad.'
'It is when you're trying your whole life
not to sit beside anyone in profile.'

'I'll still love you, Gonzo.'
'Yeah, but will the camera?'
'Ugh,' she says. 'That's extreme. I wouldn't do it.'
I turn side on and pull back my hair to highlight the problem.
'But apparently it really hurts and afterwards
not everyone notices. And,' I add,
'Barbra Streisand managed to get famous with hers.'
'Yeah, exactly,' she says, 'but only because she could sing.'
'Shut up about the singing!'
'Anyway, Bignose, on a more interesting note,
you haven't answered my important question.'
'What?'
'You know what.'
'What do you think?'
She shrugs. 'Lately I'm not sure. There's stuff you haven't told me.'

My brother comes over. Climbs up on the trampoline.
'No, Pip. Don't bounce.'
'I'm not.'
'Get off.'
'I'm not bouncing.'
'So what are you doing?'
'Nothing.'
'Can't you see we're having a private conversation?'
'No.'
'Well, we are.'
'Well, I can tell when I'm not wanted.'
'Good.'
Jess says, 'Sorry, mate. Girls' business.'
He gets down and wanders off. To nowhere.

I tell her what Miss Wardlow, the vice principal said
and I hold my nose, to copy her voice.
'"It must be so much harder for your brother
because he's younger and doesn't understand."'
'Yeah...' I said sarcastically, 'understanding makes it much easier.'
'Don't worry about her,' says Jess. 'She wouldn't have a clue.
She's ancient.'

'I thought you were supposed to get wise with age?'
'Well, it obviously doesn't happen to everyone.'

The wind has picked up and clouds have covered the sun.
We sit up, put the towels over our legs to stay warm
and look out across the paddocks.
'I'm not gonna let you quit school,' I say.
She smiles. Brushes the trampoline net.
Throws off a twig that's landed there
and a few fire-coloured gum leaves.

'So anyway,' she says, eventually.
'Do I have to dig it out of you? Have you done it?'
I turn it around, 'Have you?'
'Maybe.'
'Maybe,' I copy.
'Really?'
'Nearly.'
'Nearly or really? Have you or haven't you?'
I pause but can't help grinning. 'Nuh. You?'
'Nup.'
'I knew it.'
'Me too. But,' she says, 'let's from now on
make out that we have done it, okay?
It's so totally uncool to be a virgin.'
'Okay.'
'And let's make it a plan to not be virgins
as soon as we possibly can.'
I nod.
She gives me a handshake but I'm not excited.
In fact, it makes me feel really sad.
I was nearly not a virgin.
And there's nobody else in the world I want to kiss.

18

I call Dad as soon as I get home from school.
'Who's calling, please?' says the nurse.
'Lucinda,' I say, 'his daughter.'
'Rick? It's Lucinda, your daughter.'
As if he doesn't know Lucinda is his daughter.
And who the hell calls my father 'Rick'?
Her hand muffles the speaker. 'Shall I say you're asleep?'
It's weird having a stranger
manage your relationship with your father.

Dad has really gone downhill.
He must have because
why would you have a nurse look after you
before you've even had your slipped disc operation?
Maybe all the playing around – the dodging here and there –
was a bit of a strain?
Maybe the stress occurred long before all that.
Like when he arrived
and was bullied for having an Austrian accent
and being short and Jewish
even though he'd never been to a synagogue before.
Or maybe the impact was even before that when
as a boy
he listened to Nazi boots marching past his bedroom window.
How can you live
a normal life
after all that?

Maybe that's why
he has trouble being
monogamous?

'Hi, darling,' he says softly.
'Sorry it took me a while to get to the phone.'
'Hi, Dad. How's your back?'
'Not too bad,' he says, which isn't true
or he'd be here with us much more often.

'How's things?' he asks.
'Not too good.'
'What's up?'
'I got a dud role in the school play.'
'What's that?' he says, over Beethoven's Ninth Symphony.
'Can you turn it down a bit?' I ask.
'I said I got a dud role in the school play.'
'Never mind,' he reassures,
'all the parts are important or they wouldn't be in it.'
'Not this play,' I say. 'It was written by one of the teachers.
Some of the characters are just in it so that everyone gets a go.'
'Well, even the spear holders are important in an opera,' he says.
'In an opera they all sing,' I say. 'My character's the biggest dud of all.'
'Well,' he says, 'it's not the end of the world.'
What kind of line is that? It's *my* world.

'Your wife was just as helpful. She said, "Oh well,
can you take the rubbish down to the tip please?"'
'Well, she can't do it all on her own,' says Dad.
'You have to help around the house while I'm out of action.
Are you helping?'
'Why don't you ever stick up for me?' I say.

'Come on, chin up. It's not that bad. Just try again next time.
Some of the best in the world had to struggle.
Things aren't so bad, in the scheme of things. You could be in Ethiopia.'
I get off the phone as soon as I can.

It's true.
I've got a pretty amazing life. A life that looks really pretty.
But just because you've got pretty things
doesn't mean you can keep your chin up
because it's hard to keep your chin up unless
you're in the life you want to be in and you're feeling good inside.

I head up to the roof.
The sky is low and grey today. It matches how I'm feeling.
It's getting cold. I'm getting a cold.

The two new agisted horses have been galloping back and forth
in their paddock, all disturbed, like me
and the Arab, Fire, goes crazy in the wind.
Just watching them makes me feel trapped.
Empty Ness is trying to keep her one big eye on both.
She definitely needs an oiling.
The fireplace smoke gets in my eyes and
smells like it must be from somebody else's cosy home.

I can hear the stupid *Looney Tunes*.
Pipstar's moronic again, in front of the TV.
He doesn't want to do anything lately.
I'd like to go and cheer him up but today I'm even lower.
It'd be kind of handy if he was someone I could talk to
and vice versa, I guess.
Maybe I should've been nicer to the little Steps.

It's cold and overcast but I thought that
sitting on the roof with a little perspective
and Empty Ness
might help lift my spirits.
They must be too heavy.

I hold the cast list over the chimney and let go
but the wind lifts it up and it flies off over the roof
across the lawn and over the first paddock.
I wonder if it caught a spark on the way.
The grass is really dry and Dad is always so worried about fire.

Yesterday after school, I saw Bigstep out riding alone.
She nearly sprung me smoking.
We saw each other across the creek and both did a kind of salute.
Two lost cavalry soldiers
on different hills.

Dear Journie,
  Jess got offered a great role but here's the irony of it all – doesn't matter because guess what? She's leaving. I got no role at all so it's a double tragedy.

My team's winning the debating rounds. I get the highest points. So why didn't I get a good role in the play? What the hell is wrong with them? I don't want to play myself. I don't want to be me. Haven't they noticed my passion? Dedication? What does a girl have to do around here to get noticed?

Thank Mum & the RGs for the Drama Careers Week in the holidays. The professionals will get what I've got to give.

19

It's the Wandong Wingding –
Second largest truck 'n' country festival in the southern hemisphere.
The event of the year around here. Everyone's going.
Not necessarily for the country music.

I told Jess, 'Today's the day.'
She knows what I mean.
Today's the day when I do something about it.
Enough of this pretending.
You have to take control of your life.
If you want something to happen, you have to make it happen.
I may not be cast in the lead of the play
but I'm casting myself in the lead of my own life.

I've borrowed this beautiful navy blue rayon dress from Bigstep.
She doesn't know.
It's swish-full of swirling material that makes me feel all sensual
as I stride along in my R.M. Williams boots.
I like the contradiction.

The paddocks are packed with cars and bikes and caravans
and tents surrounding the football oval
all underneath the larger tent of another infinity-blue sky.
There's a big crowd mulling around in front of the old wooden stage.
Some sitting, some lying, some wandering.
Dust is haloing everyone.
I see hundreds of cowboy-hatted, flannelette-shirt and boot-wearing
boys –

plenty of testosterone to choose from.
But I can only have eyes for one.

He's the best-looking guy in our school. Everyone's in love with him.
He has 'romantic lead' looks. And charisma.
His real name is Brett but between Jess and myself,
we nickname him Rhett from *Gone With the Wind*.
He has an identical twin
who's not quite identical because
for some Darwinian reason
he's not as attractive to me.

I chose Rhett because he's
experienced and available
since splitting up with Sandy.
I don't want anything to go wrong.
Keep it simple – in order to make the successful
rite of passage to becoming a woman.
None of the nightmare of
'falling in love'.
Just the mission –
the mission position to graduation beyond being a girl.
And of course I need 'making love' in my knowledge as an actor –
not to mention the cool points I'll get at school for doing the deed.

Jess thinks that choosing Rhett (if he's willing)
is a great idea
even though she thinks we should really be 'going 'round together first.'

Up on the stage
some country dude is wailing on with
'Bye Bye Love'.
The atmosphere feels like something is going to happen,
if it hasn't already.
Like when we arrived, there was a commotion down at the creek –
someone said it was a Hell's Angels stabbing.
Apparently they don't usually come to a 'soft gig' like this
but there's no missing all their Harleys here today.
If Mum knew, she'd kill me.

We all sit around,
everyone drinking beer under the flirty dusty sun
and debating whether Lindy Chamberlain is innocent or not.
I hardly cry in public either, but it doesn't mean I'm guilty.
What I notice is the sad human fact that
seeing someone else's troubles makes you feel better about your own.
Maybe that's why the news is all bad. It's reassuring entertainment.

Stevie Maclain is looking at me with his kind eyes.
Handsome in a sturdy way. Like a bushranger or a safari guide.
He flicks his long strawberry blond hair off his open face.
It's a pity he's not for me. He's too nice.
He might want you married yesterday. I'm only fifteen.

By the time we all pile into Nick's dad's caravan
for the passing around of the joint,
I'm completely focused on sending the vibes to Rhett.
Even if I wasn't scared of losing control,
I need to concentrate – as in, not be off my face
though there's enough smoke here to lose the whole plot and punchline.

They're all talking over each other in long waffly monologues
about nothing at all,
while I listen to 'Desperado' (the song about the fences)
which is wafting across from the main stage.

There's an older girl, Kate, who's moved back from Melbourne.
She smiles at me from across the van.
And there's Tina, the prettiest girl in the school.
She says in a delicious fairy floss voice,
'This is Nimbin strength spliff.'
Jess winks at me in slow motion.
She's humming along, still with me in my mission
but also disappearing a little with them.
And if they don't open a window soon, I'll be cactus too.

Stevie's the only one who remembers each round
to not pass me the joint.

Rhett has been getting all my unspoken messages.
He puts his arm around my shoulder
as though to rest a casual hand.
This must be some kind of boys-club clue
because the others all pile out of the van.
Kate winks on her way.
Stevie passes last and says, 'You okay?'
'Yeah,' I say.
Then we're left alone together, Rhett and me
on the crummy foam-rubber excuse for a mattress.

We don't waste too much time
(this is good)
about getting on with the deed – getting on with my mission.
Some kissing and then our clothes are coming off
while still kissing
(which is also good because you can kind of hide).

Rhett doesn't say too much. 'Got a condom?'
(As a matter of fact, I did organise that.)
And I guess he can tell this is new for me by the fact that he says,
'You a virgin?'

I look out the small caravan window.
It's not exactly a palace or a bubbling brook under a willow tree
but I see some kind of currawongy-type bird fly by
reminding me
of the beauty of country life.

I get the hang of it quickly and then
the whole caravan
is rocking
but not so much from us as from his joker mates outside.
Rhett asks me his final question, 'Did ya want that?'
And I realise to all of his queries I've answered, 'Yeah.'

When everything finally stops we get up from our
sticky mess
and pull on our dusty clothes unglamorously.

He opens the small caravan door and we face the glaring light of the
very public afternoon.

'Me and Bobby McGee' is being sung on the main stage.
A sad song, really. Not quite right for the momentous event
I expect to experience next –
that is, how it feels to
Not Be a Virgin.
How it feels to have finally become a woman.

Squinting,
I look for Jess
and see her sitting on someone's esky smoking a cigarette.
She is gazing up at the Joplin-copy singer.

I walk with Rhett, subtly trying to catch Jess's attention,
back to where the rest of the gang are hanging out on the grass.
They are getting ready to go to Tina's house for the afternoon
because her parents are shopping in Melbourne.

The way Rhett walks off
with his arm around Tina's shoulder
(the prettiest girl in the school)
makes me feel
queasy.
But no point getting sentimental now –
I got what I wanted.
Achieved the mission.
And now I've got to get down to the
serious business
of revelations to feel.

Jess taps my shoulder
'You all right?'
I jump a little, 'Yeah.'
The Joplin-copy sings something about a
ball and chain.
'You did it. Didn't you…' she says flatly.
'Yeah,' I say, sounding a bit distracted.

'How was it?'
I shrug.
I can tell she's waiting eagerly for details. For feedback.
I'm just trying to focus so that I can have
the graduation feeling.
I'm hearing the song,
about the weight on her shoulders…
about the chain and the ball…

After a while I say out loud
the thing that's going round and round in my head:
'I don't feel any different.'
She looks at me, our eyes meet with a mutual sense of disappointment,
like we bought something and it didn't get delivered.
Then for a while
we just listen to the heaviness of the song.

20

The smell of fried onion and toast is wafting through the lounge.
Yummy except it's my brother's latest fad – cooking –
same thing every day for breakfast, dinner and lunch.
While he's dishing the onion onto the toast, I ask,
'Wanna come down to the tip with me?'
'Nuh.'
'Y' sure?'
'I'm having lunch,' he says, like I'm really stupid.
'I mean after.'
'Nuh.' He shakes his head, turning the onions.

The kitchen's a bit of a mess
from now and from breakfast and from dinner last night.
Bigstep went to Melbourne to see her kids and her parents.
She's driving Dad back up here tomorrow.
It's the first time we've been left alone for a night.
It's scary
but we don't care. It probably won't make much difference.

'I heard Jess has quit school,' he says with a mouthful.
'Yeah,' I say. 'I heard you quit clarinet.'
'Yeah,' he says. 'Phew!' A bit of onion lands on the breakfast table.
'Not worth it any more. Dad's not up to going out.
And besides he's always grumpy.'
'That's because he's in pain.'
'So why doesn't he get a doctor-mate to fix it?'
'I think he will, but it's a big job. You wanna be sure you need it first.'
'Believe me, he needs it. Like your nose.'

I decide to try and share some kind of dialogue
about the concerns I have for our situation.
'Do you think they have a good marriage? Dad and Bigstep?'
He shrugs. Keeps eating. 'Who cares? Long as they're happy.'
'But do you think they're happy?'
'Who cares?' he says and cuts some more toast,
forcing an onion ring off the plate.
'Are you happy here?'
After taking his time to swallow, he says, 'Nothing I can do about it.'
'I really miss Mum,' I say, at least trying to connect emotionally
on the subject of our shared condition.
'C'n you pass the sauce please?'
I reach for the Rosella.
Trying to be lighter, I ask him, 'How's school?'
He busies himself with the sauce, paints with it like a signature.
'Seems like you don't want to talk much?'
'Hello... You're ruining my lunch.'
'Sorry,' I say sarcastically. Nothing like bonding. 'So how is it?'
'What?'
'Your lunch?'
He stuffs the last of it in
(how come he stays thin?)
and stands holding his knife and fork
like he's about to conduct a symphony.
'Couldn't've cooked it better myself!' he says
and waltzes back to the TV room.

I drive to the tip with the stinky rubbish piled in the back.
There's certain things you can't easily throw out
like some feelings, but I try, with every bag of putrid rubbish.
And when the tray in the back of the ute is clear
I experience a convenient sensation that feels like
'whatever'.

21

Jess's mother's renovated the tiny storeroom behind their house
and made it into a beautiful miniature bedroom
with pale pink curtains and floral camellia wallpaper.
But poor Mrs Harford –
Jess is still going to move to Melbourne to live with her brother.
She got a job in a jewellery shop starting next week.
She knows nothing about jewels but says, 'I'll be dealing in diamonds.'

So this is the last weekend staying with Jess
before she leaves me here
in the wilderness.
We've lit some incense so the little room
doesn't smell of our cigarette smoke.
Apart from the tragedy of her leaving
I will have to quit dance classes
because I won't have a lift any more.
She says I should make up my own dance for the school concert
or maybe even for art for HSC next year. It's not a bad idea.

We're applying blue nail polish,
resting our cigarettes in the lid of a jar and
listening to Joni Mitchell sing about clouds.

I snatch a peek out the storybook window down towards the dam
where the Harfords' ducks
swim daringly close to the Bancinis' mid-water fence.
'Once they got through and the ducks were almost stew,'
she once told me.

It's so weird to be
so close to him
and at such a crazy distance.
I keep telling myself I made the right choice.
I try not to let her see me look out that window.

'Did you hear about toxic shock syndrome?' she says.
'Yeah, terrifying.'
'Makes you not want to use tampons.'
'I know,' I say.
'But I'm not going out wearing surfboards,' she says. 'I'd rather die.'

We try to work out why winning tennis and debating
and ribbons for dressage on Shimmering Fire
and gaining cool points for Not Being a Virgin
and all these achievements
aren't making me wondrously happy.
But actually, it's not that I'm feeling unhappy lately,
it's more that I'm not feeling anything much at all.

22

I'm in my bedroom
with Rhett's twin brother, Timbo, or nicknamed 'Twin Two' by me,
when I hear a knock on the bedroom door.
At first we ignore it, it's hard to be sure –
the music is loud and everyone's into the party
and we're trying to get into each other.

I've heard a few cars coming up the drive but
Bigstep's not bringing Dad back until Sunday night,
so there's no concern about that.

Another clear knock on the door.
'Piss off,' says Twin Two Timbo, a little pissed himself
and gets back to some sloppy kissing
which doesn't quite fit my mouth.
Quite a different technique from his older brother
(older by two minutes).

Suddenly the music's switched off and everyone goes quiet.
There's a louder banging on the door.
'Lucinda?' There's no mistaking Dad's voice.
Before we have a chance to get our clothes on, the door opens,
'What's going on in here?'

The worst part is
Pipstar's with him and he looks more
disgusted
than Dad.

23

After I clean up on Sunday morning
I head sheepishly across the breezeway through the lounge,
through the sound barrier of some symphony
hotting up for its grand finale
and towards the kitchen.
Someone's left a pack of squashed-fly biscuits
out on the breakfast table.
I'm staring out the window eating my seventh one for breakfast
when I think I hear a rat in the walk-in pantry.
When I brave myself to open the door I nearly die from shock –
I'm not alone –
what I see is
the frightened eyes of
a crazy kid from the farm next door.
I'm not sure whether to
close the door and lock him in
or scream and run
but he's out before
I work it out.
Outside and running.

He's one of the strange neighbours we call the Crazies.
They're the only neighbours we have
but they've bred more people than horses so it's plenty.

There's a rumour at Pipstar's school
that they drowned all their kittens
in a hessian sack in the dam.
Maybe you go mad
year after year
driving horses round in circles.

I'm trying to work out what he's stolen
but all I can see is a few fallen Honey Smacks.
Maybe he's got a taste for dry cereal like me.
Does that make us both extra hungry, or crazy?

This explains the other strange noises I've heard lately.
I was beginning to think it was the Aboriginal ghosts
we called up in that séance at Christmas
when Bigstep's hair caught on fire.
Spooky though to find someone in your house.
Someone who easily got into your house.

The visitation is useful, however, as a distraction.
I announce the morning's discovery
with great dramatic flair but it works only briefly.
Dad's in pain,
so his sense of humour is
tarnished.
And taking time off work really isn't his thing.
Bigstep is also moody today
which seems bigger than my misbehaving.
I mean it's not as though she had to clean things up.
After we discuss the plan to meet with the kid's father,
Dad gets down to the business of reprimanding me for last night.
I know it's going to be a serious conversation because
he's turned his radio off.

We're in the kitchen and I don't know why but he's
hand-washing the dishes.

He looks out every now and then
at his 500 acres
that he hasn't seen for a while
as though he's wondering what possessed him to buy them.
'What's wrong with the dishwasher, Dad?'
'Nothing.'
'Would you like me to do the dishes?'
'No,' he says.

'Now firstly,' he starts, 'do you think that's good manners?'
It's hard to answer. In my world,
heading off to the back room at a party is the thing to do.
It means you're getting things right.
'Good manners?' I say, enquiring.
'To be mucking around like that
in the room next door to your guests?'
'I guess not,' I say politely.
'Because that's what I found you doing last night. Right?'
All I can think to say is, 'Correct.'
Way too much detergent. The soap suds are halfway up his arms.
It's kind of funny, his angle on it – kind of unexpected.
It's the social aspect he seems to be worried about,
not my gallivanting around –
or the fact that my brother just happened to be
an inappropriate witness.

He's stacking the dishes without a rack.
They're covered in bubbles and keep slipping off each other.

'Did we give you permission to host a party in our home?'
Home? I'd like to say. Call it a home?
'It wasn't really a party. People just kept turning up.'
He looks at me, holding his dripping arms just above the bubbles.
'Do you think I was born yesterday?'
(Parents ask so many questions you can't answer.)

He tries to stack the colander
but it keeps falling off the pile that's too high already.
The bubbles are dangling daggily off his arms.

'Did you apologise to your guests?'
'Oh,' I say, 'yes.' Like, right, sure – are you kidding?
'Well, that's good then,' he says,
stacking, stacking, then letting the water out,
trying to dissolve all the bubbles.

I'm waiting for the 'Secondly,' or maybe we're up to 'Thirdly,'
but he says, 'So now we can get onto the main business.'
'Right,' I say, being cooperative.
'Now,' he says, rinsing, rinsing, dish by dish
from the washed stack back to the other side.
'Now the business I want to discuss with you is…'
he clears his throat, 'contraception.
Have you thought about that?'
'Contraception?'
'Yes, you know what it is?'
'Yes.'
Aha, at last. It's my birds 'n' bees chat.
I'd like to say, 'Not a moment too late!'
but of course it's so many moments.

I suddenly feel profoundly enthusiastic. This could really go my way –
I've been wondering how I could broach the topic myself.
Doctors can write prescriptions!
'Yes, Dad, you want to be really careful.'
'Correct,' he says (copying me).
Rinsing, stacking, now back again to the other side,
for no purpose except to elongate the activity.
'Now maybe I can help you with that,'
he says, rinsing the colander a second time.
It's gleaming, like that awful ad for Palmolive detergent.

He pulls off the gloves like a professional surgeon
leaving his arms smelling of stinky rubber.
'Shall I dry them?'
'No,' he says, bending to put the gloves under the sink with a groan.
'Now I want you to come with me.'
So I follow him to their en suite bathroom.

Bigstep leaves just as we arrive, in a waft of freshly sprayed Rexona.
'I'm going to feed Pirate and Fire,' she mutters.
Apparently those horses need a special diet
beyond grass. And a perspiration-free feeder.

Pip calls out 'Dad?' and approaches.
'Just a minute, son,' he says, 'give me a minute.'
Pip gives me the evil eye. 'Who was that guy?' he asks.
I mouth the words, 'Shut up.'

'Sit there,' says Dad and gestures to the unmade bed.
Already lying there is his spooky back-brace
With white ribs like the skeleton of a torso.
From their bathroom he
brings back a black doctorish sponge bag,
and sits with it on his lap. He slowly unzips it and
pulls out a box of
Trojans.
He must have kept them since he was eighteen (circa 1948)
because the box looks like the first condoms ever invented.

He seems a little disappointed that
in my expression,
his treasured Trojans have not turned out to be the ultimate gift.
(Was he keeping them for Pipstar?)
It's all kind of sweet and I'd like to hug him
but I don't want to upset his credibility.
I brace myself to
a) not laugh and
b) ask for a prescription.

After some necessary discussion
which I think I handle most efficiently,
defending and justifying my underage request,
eventually I leave their room with a nice piece of paper
that will protect me in the process of becoming
an experienced woman.

24

I was looking forward to getting home from school today
but there's still the bus trip.
With Jess gone,
the back-seat bus-bitches are 100 times worse
and not just on the bus.
They hiss when I pass them and today
Katerina spat on the ground before me.

Apparently Tony's gone missing
and his disappearance is,
according to her,
all because of me;
'You'll fucken' pay for this, bitch.'
But I'm already paying.

I pray to the Gods he's all right.
Is it my fault?

I move a few seats down towards the front,
away from where I used to sit with Jess.
The closer you sit to the driver, the daggier your reputation
but the safer it gets.

Bigstep is not at the bus stop.
I wait a while, feeling nauseous because of the Pill.
It's the same every day. Urky.
Some price to pay for the confidence
in reassuring
both myself and some guy
of the safety of our adventures.
And if I forget to take one
it's a whole month of queasiness wasted.
It's also supposed to help with my period pain but so far
it hasn't.

Eventually I start walking home.
Better than sitting and waiting. She'll see me on the way.
It takes me about fifty-three minutes to get up to Doglolly House.
And her dirty blue Volvo's gone.

I walk in, dump my bag and stand in the pantry for about a year,
looking for something I can eat that will take me away from here.

Sitting at the breakfast table, halfway through the Mint Slices,
I see Dad at the patio table with his radio companion
and his other friend, his duck-shooting gun, which he's cleaning.

I go out to see him.
'Hi.'
He doesn't hear me.
'HI!'
'Huh! You gave me a fright! Be careful, I'm cleaning the gun.
I wonder if Dad's going deaf because of the gun or the music.
'Hey…listen…shhh. Do you know this piece of music?'
I shake my head because
a) I don't know the music and
b) the quiz drives me insane.

He closes his eyes and conducts a little
with the gun-cleaning pipe in his hand.
I reach for the radio. Turn it off.
'Hey!'
He goes to turn it back on. I grab the radio.
'Christine didn't pick me up from the bus stop.'
'Oh no, really? How did you get home?'
I put the radio down. Point to both my feet with both my hands.
'Oh, darling,' he says. 'I'm sorry. If I could drive…
She was going to pick you up after they came back from the vet.'
'Whatever,' I say.
'But that's the first time you've had to walk home, isn't it?'
'Yep. And the last.'
'Sorry, darling. She must've been held up. C'mon, sit down,' he says
and resumes cleaning his gun.

'She's really doing her best, you know.'
'So am I.'
'Well, I know. That's good. I appreciate it.
I really need you to pull your weight,
especially as I have to have this operation.'
My heart sinks in a wave of nausea.
I was hoping it would get better all by itself.
'Soon?' I ask and he nods, with resignation.
I hug him and say, 'You'll be back on the tennis court in no time.
And up the rivers shooting ducks.' He smiles, uncertain.

Deflecting, I say, 'The Pill makes me feel sick.'
'Does it, darling? Maybe you need to try another kind.'
'Are there different kinds?'
'Yes. Yes, I'll look into it.' He drops the shotgun brush. I pick it up.
'So I'm going to need you to watch Pip while I'm away.'
'I always do.'
'I won't be able to come back to the farm until after rehabilitation.'
'How long's that?'
'Well, it's a big operation. A few weeks, I'm afraid. If all goes well.'
(What if it doesn't?)
'Can I rely on you to help me hold things together for a while?'
'Sure. Of course.'
'To chip in and help Christine as much as you can?'
'Yeah, course.'
He puts down the gun. I get a crazy thought, to pick it up.
Somehow use it.
He packs all his equipment away, very neatly, like a surgeon.

'Will she drive us down to visit you or will we have to come on the train?'
'No. Of course she'll bring you down, whenever she can.'
I nod. Uncertain. Uncertain about every aspect of this news.
'Will you be all right?' I ask him. 'Seriously?'
'I'll be fine. I'm in very good hands. The best in the country.
No need to worry at all.
Now, pass me that radio, will you?
How could anyone switch off the Brahms Piano Concerto?'

25

Up early.
There are small clouds
resting down in the valley
above the dams
as though they had
fallen
from the weightlessness
of not carrying enough rain.

We are preparing Shimmering Fire
for her first show at Seymour.
Nearly an hour's drive with the float.

The transition from doing dressage
on White Sails to Fire was terrifying at first
but you know what they say,
'Once you've driven a Porsche, you can't go back to a Honda,'
or something like that.
Not that I don't love Sails,
but trying to get him to do flying changes
is impossible.
I still ride him around the farm
but all the dressage lessons have been on Fire
since I braved the extra hands up to ride her.

I got up in the dark and since the sun first rose this morning
I have washed and groomed her.
The sun is still low in the sky and the early spring air is crispy clear.
All the molasses, barley, sunflower meal and lucerne and exercise
has worked a treat.
She is shining enough to live up to her name.
I have plaited her mane and sewed the plaits into
a neat row of baubles along the proud arc of her neck.
I have painted her hoofs black with Show Shine polish.

Bigstep has got the float ready and
Fire is all nervous and excited
like me.
I'm only going in two events
so it's a lot of work for a tiny bit of competition time
but that's no different from going on stage.
Exhausting, exhilarating, terrifying.

Arnie said Fire had a better chance of winning
with me on top
which was good for my ego
so ironically now
I'm living out Bigstep's dream.
And Bigstep is thrilled to pieces that
her prized horse is ready for showing
and her prize step-brat is at last up to the task.
If the horse starts winning competitions
I think Fire will become more valuable,
especially for her foals.

Bigstep brings her over with the enticing bucket of feed
to lure her into the float.
Why any horse trusts a human to get in a float is beyond me.
'I think you should walk in first. Shim loves you. Ready?'
'Yeah,' I say, nervously, securing the last protective leg bandage.
'Are you sure?' she asks.
'Yeah,' I say again, more firmly.
Bigstep smiles, then gives me (not the horse) a pat on the back.
'Let's go then.'

It's a weird feeling.
I don't want to be living out her dream but I'm excited as hell.
It's true, I wouldn't be given this opportunity without her.
Around the horses, she's extra nice,
which makes it impossible to refer to her as my
'cruel stepmother'.

I collect my navy blue jacket
with velvet elbows, my matching velvet riding hat,
clean beige joddys and R.M. Williams boots.
My hair's already neat like Fire's. Matching plaits.
'So we're right to go?'
'Yep,' I say, suddenly feeling guilty. 'Do you wish you were riding?'
'God, no,' she says, 'I'd be much too nervous. I think you're brave.'
We get in the ute and she switches on the wipers
to clear the dew from the windscreen.

I check behind. Fire is nodding.
She's probably just checking the headroom space
but it's a 'YES' all round
for the three of us who are
well and truly in it together.
And 'you gotta be in it to win it'.

26

Alas, just because you're in it
doesn't mean you'll win it.
This is also true for the compulsory electoral competition.

Bigstep's driving Dad into Kilmore to vote. I just want a hot pie.
I think Dad's going for Malcolm, the 'crazy grazier' farmer.
He doesn't look like a real farmer to me, any more than Dad.
He looks like the dad of a Grammar school friend.
I say, 'Fraser sounds a bit up himself.'
'He's misunderstood,' says Dad on his fully reclined seat.
'Pity Hawke's not running,' says Bigstep.
'Yes, Hayden's a bit of a wimp. But at least he's not Jo Blow.'
'Or Reagan,' says Bigstep.
'He was an actor!' I say.
'Yes, we know.'
Their banter turns into a heated debate about who stands for what
which makes me wonder what I stand for and where the fuck I belong.
I sneak out my journal in the back seat to examine the issue…

Which party should I belong to? Both sound fake. Kids choose the same as their parents but mine disagree. Which class am I in? They say we don't have them in Oz but I'm not sure. Am I now a private/public school girl? Don't even belong to a proper family. Feel like a piece of flotsam. Dad escaped the Nazis but has never been to synagogue. Parents married in an Anglican church but don't believe in God. I'm not even proud to be Aussie. We're invaders. We're Convicts from Down Under. Skin is white but I sunbake to get brown. Feminist yes, but no party/church/tribe for that and if there's a glass ceiling let's smash it. Feel like a piece of plankton, a free-floater, a tiny star in the Milky Way, reaching for a sun in eclipse. Could I belong to Hollywood?

27

It's a barn party.
I've only been allowed to go on one condition:
that I get picked up at 11 p.m. Cringe.
Jess is up for the weekend.
She arrived here before me and is warding off duelling suitors.
She hardly flirts at all any more but the boys find her more fascinating.
I feel like I have to *act* fascinating to get the same kind of attention.
Is it being blonde and having long legs or is she just nicer?
Or is it because she's unavailable now?
Or maybe it's my nose? Or my braces?
Speaking of which, I had them tightened on Thursday.
Might as well tie me to a truck and drag me along by the teeth.
I've only consumed what fits through a straw
for the past forty-eight hours.
Consequently, I feel slim tonight
which is something to be said for the
agonies of having to be a metal-mouthed brace-face.

Spring certainly hasn't warmed the night air yet.
It feels damp outside but country folk don't feel the cold,
especially after a few beers.
Pity I'm not a country folk and I don't drink.
I spend my life trying to be in control of

uncontrollable things.
Why exaggerate the dilemma?
But I'm freezing.

Jess throws a plastic cup of Fosters beer
all over a guy who keeps putting his arm around her.
'Dickhead,' she says.
There's a bit of an argument after that.
She's much more prudish since she committed herself to Zed.
Next she'll be talking marriage.
Where I come from, you don't talk yet about getting married
any more than you'd think about leaving school.
In my particular case,
I'm not thinking about getting married at all.
Well, at least I think you should save some hassle by
missing out on the first one
and skipping straight to the second one when you turn forty.
You want to get it right.
You don't want to walk your kids through all the step-shit.
That's if you have them at all.

Some guys are taking bets on who they think killed JR –
in this American soapie ranch show that everyone's watching
with plastic women totally caked in make-up.
I don't care who killed him.

I find myself down the hill with Twin Two Timbo.
I guess you could call him my second best.
Now I can confirm they are
definitely not identical.

The grass is long and prickly so it's
lucky I'm on top.
We are experimenting with my first sixty-niner,
which is challenging on a slope,
and also when your partner is a good foot taller than you.
I'm acting like I do this all the time, but why would you?
It's tricky.

Twin Two isn't bothered at all.
Not even about the lethal aspect of my braces.
Or the fact it's the first chewable thing I've had in my mouth
for forty-eight hours.
And he's drunk enough to not notice the prickly grass.

Echoing over the paddocks is the party crowd and music –
'The Nips Are Getting Bigger'.
I'm finally getting the hang of
the position
when I hear the sound of my name, over the music, in the distance.
I stop moving a second to listen better.
'Whatsa matter?' he asks.
'Shh,' I say.
He says, 'Don't stop. Keep going.'
'Shhhhh,' I say, which you can't say while keeping on going.

Three or four people are calling out for me
but the voice that stands out is Jess, 'LUUU CYYY!'
It can't be 11 p.m. yet?
Next I hear my name being called by someone more familiar.

Getting up, I practically stand on Twin Two
and dress as fast as I can in the dark.
My undies are missing.
'What's wrong?' he asks.
'Dad's here,' I say.
It has a sobering effect because apparently if I'm under sixteen
he's up for carnal knowledge.

I arrive at the top of the hill, heavily breathing,
to see the barn all lit up like something out of
Close Encounters of the Third Kind.
I can hear the car's distinguishable diesel panting
and I discover that, sure enough,
the glowing illumination of the barn
is caused by Dad's Yellow Peril, with its headlights on high beam.

They have driven the car right into the barn
and left the engine running.
Cringe factor 12 out of 10.

Jess looks at me like 'You're about to die a death from stoning and
I don't know how I can save you from execution.'
I walk to the car's passenger window behind which Dad is fully reclined
while an audience on hay bales spectates in ecstatic silence,
except for the song which plays out softer and softer…

Dad's electric window slides down like a professor's glasses.
(Nobody else has electric windows around here.)
A whole lot of Stravinsky escapes
and blends in with the party speakers, now blaring out
Sherbet's 'Howzat',
a song about getting caught in the act.
'Get in the car.'
The party animals join in for the stupidly timed lyrics.

Driving off,
I turn back to see Jess's hand in a frozen wave position
while the crowd get on with revelling
in hysterics.

Bigstep drives on
seriously
leaving the dirty work to her husband.

The radio news goes on about Fraser's re-election
even though unemployment is increasing and inflation is inflating
and then more about the IRA hunger strike
and Saddam Hussein and his war in Iran.
Cheerful.

Dad, with some painful difficulty,
turns around to look at me in the middle of the back seat.
I put my seat belt on – something righteous and lawful at least.
He shakes his head slowly, looks down at my shirt, points and says,
'Missed a button.'

28

Dear Journie,
  I'm on the roof tryingto writen the dark forgot my torch. It's after midnight. They think I'm asleeep. Eerie up here but peaceful. Only a half moon but there's still a bit of aglowaround and the stars arefantastic. Can almost touch the Milky Way...
  Bigstep & Pip came to the finalperformance of the play tonight. She let me borrow her beautiful skirt to wear afterwards but we rushed home and nobody really saw it. Dad was in too much pain to evencomefor the drive. Sitting is his worst position. Pip fell asleeparound the time I came on stage & Bigstep said, 'Lucky I didn't blink. I would've missed you!' Very funny.
  It wasn't my best night because the Backseatbusbitches hassled me so much before I went on with their 'break-a-leg, slut' that I forgot 1 of my 7 lines & had to make it up.
  Can't wait to get to the Drama Careers Week that Mum got me into where professionalswill help identify & nurture my talent.
  PS. This journal will be so interesting whendown the track my biographer can analyse my trajectory.

I stop writing when I hear their arguing voices
coming up through the chimney.
She says, 'Why do I have to look after them on my own?
They're *your* children.'
I block my ears and look into the night. Not a soul driving up the road.
I start humming Tony's favourite song, 'Ride like the Wind'.
Apparently Tony's still missing and so is Steelo's bike.
I imagine him speeding down the white lines towards Tasmania.

Rural Gods (I say to the sequined sky),
Please don't let him have another accident.
Please let Dad be all right and come home soon.
Please bring Mum back asap.
Please look after Jess.
Please look after Pipstar.
Please deal with the back-seat bus-bitches.
Please don't let me fall off Shim again.
Please let the drama careers week people recognise my talent.

29

School holidays at last.
Mum's flown back and rented another apartment and car.
She's driving me to the first day of the drama careers week. Yay!
Pipstar's in the front seat trying to steer the conversation his way.

The tutors are professional actors.
I hope we get the girl from *Picnic at Hanging Rock*.
'God, I wish I could have played Miranda,' I say.
'But Miranda was pretty and tall and blonde,' says Pipstar.
'Thanks.'

Mum's driving is out of practice.
I guess there's no cars on her island.
She gets tooted outside the Victoria Market
for cutting off the cab who was trying to pass us.

She took even longer to get ready this morning. Longer than me.
She had a spaz when she saw I'd shaved my legs.
'Who said you could do that?' It was like she owned them.
And she wouldn't let me wear my boob-tube top.
She got quite upset, which threw me.
All week I planned what I was going to wear.
I already felt a bit weird in something figure-hugging
but I took a risk to look good.
She said, 'You look like Tottie Goldsmith!' She's this
'society' girl
who gets photographed looking stunning wearing next to nothing
in the South Yarra nightclubs. (I think her dad even owns one.)
I would not mind looking like Tottie Goldsmith
but Mum made me feel so tacky and cheap
I probably won't wear the top ever again.
It's not like I've even got a cleavage.

But Mum's got extra cleavage today
and she's wearing her beautiful perfume,
the one that I can still faintly smell on my blue jumper.

She says she's excited to introduce us to Jacques tonight.
She's picking him up from the airport.
I'm thinking 'Great, another step-parent.'
My brother asks, 'Are you going to get married?'
'Well…' she starts to say.
'Will he be sleeping in your bed?' Mum doesn't answer.
Pipstar says, 'We found a boy in Lucy's bed but he wasn't sleeping.'
I kick the back of his seat. He's pretending to be five.

Mum says, 'Lucinda…'
Pipstar grins eagerly at the lecture tone in her voice.
She looks at me through the rear-vision mirror
as much as she can while driving (badly).
'Lucinda,' she says, with the utmost sincerity,
'darling, it's really important – you must make sure
that the first boy you ever make love with
is someone you really love.'
She glances at me,
into me.
'Can you promise me that, darling?'

It's hard to lie to your mother,
especially my mother,
but hell, where has she been?
Where was she to tell me that
before it was too late?
'Sure,' I reply, swallowing truth
like a pill without water.
Too much to explain. Way too much to explain.
Pipstar twists around and looks at me again
like he can't believe what I've turned into.

Someone I really love.
Novel idea.

Someone you really love
might leave you.

30

The first day was
amazing.
All these fascinating people
with talent.

A girl with a long dark plait of hair arrived with a *sun* umbrella.
She wore a floral skirt and lace-up sandals and
got to work on the role of Juliet.
We all had to offer suggestions.

A boy called Jason with a British accent played her Romeo.
They were perfect
together.
I wish I was her.
(With him.)

We did acting exercises, like carrying invisible trays
and the girl who imagined that her tray had handles
was seriously praised.

The tutors watched and took notes.
At the end they will prepare a report
to recommend us for the drama schools
and a career in the performing arts.
I took home the drama school application books
and I've just about underlined everything on every page.

Mum seemed anxious when she picked me up
but was glad I was in a good mood to meet
her tall dark handsome Frenchman.

My first impression is that
he really is tall dark and handsome.
To be honest, if my husband was having affairs,
I would have gone for him too.
My second impression is that he actually seems nice.
My third impression is that he adores her.

It's like there's a magnet pulling them together
and their eyes are all sparkly like in the cartoons.

After dinner of sautéed steak in garlic, cream and white wine,
with yummy sliced, fried butter herb potatoes,
he cooks Pip and me some pancakes, or 'crêpes' as he calls them.
He flips them almost as high as the ceiling
and lands almost all of them perfectly in the pan.
Mum is just beaming with pride and relief.
We like him
and our 'precious time together' is going exceptionally well.

His accent is strong.
He teaches us 'comment allez vous' and 'très bien merci beaucoup'
and accidentally when one pancake slips out of the pan, 'Ah, merde.'

He wears an open-neck shirt with a sexy silver chain.
He smokes Dunhill cigarettes and smokes them all suave.
The packet looks nice but they're really strong.
I stole one to try the flavour.

I go to bed early to learn my lines for the acting piece tomorrow.
I can hear Mum talking and Jacques laughing his deep French laugh.
Mum has many talents of course but the best one is
(when she's not upset)
she's funny.

In the morning
I go to the bathroom to have my shower and
accidentally walk in on Jacques while he's in the nude.
We both get a hell of a fright
saying 'sorry' 'sorry' and all of that.
It's really embarrassing for us both.

Later I hear Mum and Jacques in the bedroom
having a whispering argument.
I'm about to sit down to croissants and jam
when Mum comes in all serious about the rules of privacy and respect.
'Always knock first,' she says.

'It was an accident,' I say. 'I didn't know he was in there.'
'Always knock first,' she says again,
like I was in some kind of terrible danger or criminal breach of the law.

We head off to day two of my drama careers week.
She says goodbye to Pipstar but she's a bit upset with Jacques.
'I love you,' he says, like something out of a movie.

31

Friday afternoon. The course is nearly over.
We have a minute of silence for the thousands of souls
who've died in the Italian earthquake.
It's kind of hard to imagine their horror when they're so far away
but the ceremony of silence is quite profound.
I'm not entirely sure if my tears are for
the tragedy of those people I didn't know
or the fact that this course is ending
or maybe for all my upsets of late
or all the upsets of all humans since the beginning of time.
Maybe a combination.

We have to perform our audition pieces but first
an actress called Liz performs a poem called
'Daddy' by Sylvia Plath.
She puts so much emotion into it that
some of us cry again (like me).

I've chosen one of Mum's favourite plays:
Murder in the Cathedral by T.S. Eliot.
I've worked hard to make sense of the funny language,
unsuccessfully,
but the poetry of it sounds good.
Maybe it's not the best piece for me really
but at least I won't be another Lady Macbeth or Ophelia.

I get stuck deciding how to say a line while delivering it.
I'm thinking about it technically too much to convey the meaning.
It doesn't help that I know that I'm doing this. It makes it worse.
But I remember the lines and I get to the end all right.

The last thing is a debrief of how we all experienced the week
where I finally feel like a member of the right tribe.
Oh God, I want this so much –
my ticket of leave, my ride to freedom, the doorway to my true self,
the gateway to my independent, respected, valuable, stimulating,
meaningful life.

Mum picks me up. We head to the Ringwood station to pick up Jess.
Mum drives us to the ice-skating rink as a kid type treat because
tomorrow is my sixteenth birthday.
Jess gives me the new Dire Straits album, *Making Movies*. Perfect.

Mum helps us order our boots and jokes while we lace them up.
Jess whispers to me, 'Your mother is totally, stunningly beautiful –
even more than your ugly beautiful stepmother,'
which is a bit of an overstatement
but it makes me proud.
Later she says, 'You're so lucky. She's so funny. She's fantastic.
She's like a friend. Not like a mother at all,'
which in a sense, for better and worse, I have to agree with.

We can't skate
but we have a good laugh
trying.

Mum sits in the icy stalls, waving whenever we look up to her.
She's so closely watching me hug the rail
around the edge of the rink,
around and around
as though each round is making up for a month of
missed contact.

Jess tells me all about Zed,
how it's hard for them to find time to meet and write songs together
with work and going home most weekends as her mum isn't well.
'We'll work it out,' she says. 'Anything's possible
when two people are in love.'
But I wonder if it is two people.

I tell her all about the careers week, and what Mum said,
about loving the first man you sleep with.
I tell her my horrid epiphany:
'You can't sleep with someone
for the first time
ever again.'
She gives me an idea: maybe I need to go back to Rhett.
Give him a chance to be with me, more meaningfully.
It's not like I gave off an 'I'm available' message.
Maybe it's not such a crazy idea that he'd actually want me?
Novel idea: a regular proper boyfriend.

Back at the station, Jess says, 'Thanks, Mrs Smeaton,'
I grab her arm, shake my head; she ain't Mrs Smeaton no more.
'Don't worry about the "Mrs",' says Mum. 'Lovely to meet you too.'
Jess gives me *and* Mum a hug. All the judgements she had of her
not being around
have melted in the skating rink
due to Mum being such an 'attractive, wonderful, witty, smart woman'.

'That report'll be great,' she says.
'Your daughter's going to boost the Australian film industry.'
'Good luck with Zed,' I say.

Mum says, 'She's a lovely girl.
A lovely uncomplicated country girl.
She obviously loves you very much.'
Is 'uncomplicated' a compliment?
Whatever. I take it as such
because I wish I could be more like Jess.

32

Mum has cooked my favourite dinner for my birthday:
honey roast chicken,
potatoes sliced and baked and sugar mint peas.
Crème caramel for dessert with extra caramel toffee
and a 'where's-the-other-half' chocolate cake.

I can't play my new album because there isn't a record player
but Mum has a small cassette player
she bought duty-free for Pipstar and me
which right now is serenading us
with her new favourite Charles Aznavour song, 'She'.

The Happy Birthday song overwhelms Aznavour for a minute
and after the candles are blown out
Jacques toasts my sixteenth year with some French champagne.
He says all French children drink wine and champagne.
Not that I'm a child.

'I wish you a wonderful long life, ealth and appiness.'
With his accent, he drops the aitches,
which makes my brother laugh and copy Jacques.
'Elth an a-penis?'
'A-ppiness' says Jacques again.
'A penis!' repeats Pip
and it goes back and forth while
Pip tries to coach him: 'H – h – happiness.'
'Hhhhh…a-ppiness…'
and the best thing is
the feeling
of all this 'appiness around.

33

On the way to Spencer Street Station,
Mum parks outside Freemasons Hospital
and walks us as far as the nurses' station
then tells us she'll wait for us in the visitors' lounge.

We're very familiar with hospitals
but usually because
we're hanging around
while Dad 'does his rounds'.

It's the day before his operation
and he has to be rested
and checked for everything first.

He looks small in the bed in a room with three other patients.
He could have a room on his own but he doesn't like being alone.
It's strange to see him lying down in a hospital gown
instead of racing around in a safari suit with a stethoscope.

At first he doesn't notice us because he's staring up at the telly
and also wearing earpieces for his radio.
John Lennon's just been assassinated.
I don't like Beatles music but it's still a big ugly shock.

'Hi, Dad,' says Pip.
'Oh, now look who we have here,' says Dad, removing his earpieces.
He has a Band-Aid on his arm and his hair is a bit ruffled.
'That's nice of you to come and visit your poor ol' Pop.'
We kiss him on the cheek. But I'm a bit careful so as not to catch
golden staphylococcus, which is apparently easy to get in hospitals.

A nurse comes in and Dad smiles warmly,
the same way he smiles at waitresses.
'This is Angie,' he says. (Trust Dad to get the prettiest nurse.)
'And she's doing an excellent job of looking after your dad.'
She smiles sheepishly at him. We're not introduced.
He's a little distracted. Perhaps they've got him on premeds.

He reaches out for the nurse's arm.
'So I'm still first off the rank tomorrow?'
'Yes,' she says, 'at this stage, definitely yes.'
'You'll make sure of it, won't you, dear,' he says with a wink.
It's weird.
I'm used to him flirting with nurses from a more vertical position.

Pip talks with him about cricket
and Dad talks about when he trained in Liverpool,
where the Beatles are from.
I don't feel like talking but things get quiet
so I mention the drama careers week.
'Sounds wonderful, darling. You'll be walking the boards in no time.'
Then dinner arrives at afternoon tea time. Go figure.
Grey meat, mash and a dull-coloured carrot and pea mix.
It smells like aeroplane food but looks much worse.
We wish him luck, a strange thing to wish a doctor
who's probably relying more on experience and expertise.
'I'm in the best hands in the country,' he says.
No doubt.
But just a sneeze
and a slip of those hands
could make him a paraplegic.

34

It's Thursday and after school, I finally talked
Bigstep into going to the post box in Kilmore
to see if my drama careers week report's arrived.
I told her I'd go on a hunger strike if we didn't go there today
but given my record for overeating
I'm not sure if she believed me.

It's been like waiting for the gold pass to the life you want to lead.
I've got it on the table, I'm enjoying the suspense
before announcing the contents to Bigstep and Pip after dinner –
which contains the usual blend of easy ingredients.

I'm playing my *Making Movies* album,
the song 'Tunnel of Love'.

I was going to read it to Dad on the phone
but he's been delirious since Monday.
When I finally got through to the recovery ward
he thought I was Bigstep.
Still, it's a tremendous relief to hear his slurry voice
even if it's filled with the waking morphine nightmares of
cockroaches crawling over his hairy chest
and goldfish in the catheter bag.
We're celebrating the fact that he's
a) alive
b) almost got his brain in order
c) not a paraplegic.

So the letter rests unopened and ready as the big treat after dessert.
Thankfully dinner takes about as long to eat
as it must have taken to prepare.

I know all the words. I'm softly singing in a dream,
about how she left
and for some reason
he doesn't follow her,
when Bigstep says, 'What are you going to do if the news isn't good?'
I could kill her for saying it out loud
because I've managed to keep the thought buried all week.
'It *will* be good,' I say.
She says, 'Sometimes you need to prepare yourself just in case.'
Talk about a wet blanket. A bubble pricker.
That's what you call a 'glass-half-empty' thinker.
Thanks for the faith and belief.

She gets the ice cream and the dessert out of the freezer.
It's another frozen Sara Lee cheesecake.
It's crap food and it's not crème brûlée but still delicious.
I'm focusing on that and the music to distract myself,
about Romeo and Juliet
and the time not being right.

As she's scooping the ice cream, I decide I can't wait any longer.
I trust the professionals have got who I am.
I need to prove her doubts (and my doubts) in me are wrong.
I need to celebrate my future.
But just in case, I read it to myself first:

'…although Lucinda shows a strong empathic ability for accurate character analysis, she seems to have difficulty losing herself in a character, i.e. believing in and expressing herself as somebody else… There is a lack of confidence, certainty and immersion in her performance… As a result of these observations, we do not recommend that Miss Smeaton pursues a career as an actor. Her passion and perception, however, may indeed lead her towards more authorial or directorial roles within the performing arts…'

I look at Bigstep and Pipstar's waiting faces.
Then I run off
down through the paddocks
and as far as I can
until I totally run out of breath.

Part Three

1

I've moved to the front seat of the school bus.
Totally uncool
but I can't stand the trip any closer to the back-seat bus-bitches.

Apparently Tony eventually came back
from his disappearance
in one piece.
And this time without any '4be2' beatings because
he's bigger than his father now and threatened to burn down the house.

This year my brother comes with me to the high school.
I had an unfulfilled hope that the back-seat bus-bitches
might have quit school or something
but he's already witnessed the way they treat his big sister.
He lies low and plays pocket-sized electronic games,
killing as many widgets as he can.
He sits with this boy called
Ryan Hayes
who has a permanent grin and the look of a plan
in his darting green eyes.
The kid can't sit still. It's like he's on speed or something.

We get off the bus to the hisses of the back-seat bus-bitches.
Pipstar's new mate gets off here too
though he lives closer to the next stop.
'Hey, Smeato,' he says, 'don't forget the jar.'
It's like I don't exist.
The kid runs off bowling a stone like a cricket ball and then
both of them yell out 'Howzat!' and laugh.

We wait for the faded blue Volvo. Bigstep is late as usual.
Three million crickets are screaming around in the
long dry grass.
Heat seems to lift off the road in a tangible fuzzy layer.

'What's the jar for?' I ask.
'None of your beeswax,' he says.
'C'mon,' I say. 'Don't keep me in suspense.'
'Hayzo's got a plan. That's all.'
I don't pry further. Just glad he's finally got himself a buddy.
I ask, 'What do you think of the high school now?'
'Better than the baby school, I s'pose.
But compared to Grammar, the facilities are shit.'

We watch two cockatoos chatting and picking at things
as they hop-walk down the railroad tracks.
'Looks like the Little Steps,' I say.
He shrugs, 'Sorta.'
He sure doesn't speak like a Grammar kid any more.
'It's kind of quiet without them,' I say.
'Big house.'
He starts playing noughts and crosses
(both sides)
in the dirt with a stick.
Then he gets to the point of his reserve:
'So what did you actually do to Katerina's brother?'
I'm like, 'What?'
'I saw him that night on the fence.'
I look at him. Searching for what he's seen.
'I had nightmares he was going to come back and kill us.
What made him so pissed off?'

A ute goes past
really fast,
leaving us breathing into our sleeves
with our eyes squeezed shut to avoid
dust asphyxiation.
Their crazed border collie,
loose in the back of the tray,
goes barking into the distance.

'He wanted to be my boyfriend,' I say, 'but it wasn't a good idea.'
'So why were you so upset?'

'Well, bad ideas are sometimes what you want most.'
'Who's your boyfriend now?' he asks.
'No one,' I say, thinking of Rhett and how it'd be nice
to have a real boyfriend soon.
'Well,' he says, 'plenty to choose from round here.'
I'm not sure if he's being sarcastic or judgemental or
funny or concerned but I just let it go as I see our pick-up arriving.

It'd be nice for us to sit in the dickie seat
for old time's sake
but the back is full of saddle gear and molasses tins
and anyway
those cute old days
are over.

The smell makes me feel ill.
Nothing new since I've been on the Pill.
They're all the same. A constant state of low-grade nausea.
I think I'm going to quit it. What's the point?
Wait till it's worth it for a real boyfriend.

Bigstep seems depressed.
'What's the matter?' I ask. It feels uncomfortable
to have your only care-giver in a morbid state.
'Huh?'
'You seem very quiet.'
'Well, your father's taking his time to recover.'
'It takes as long as it takes, doesn't it?'
'Sure. Could do with a little assistance, that's all,' she says.
'Are you going to go down to look after him?'
'No,' she says, defensively.
'I have to look after the horses...and you.'
(In that order.)
'Besides, he's got that nurse who seems to be doing
an excellent job of that.'
I give Pip the suspicious look but his face is just
worried about Dad.
I tell him we'll call him tonight.

As we near our farm, one of the neighbours' pacers
comes around their track.
I try to see if it's one of the Crazies working the horse.
They're very rarely at school.

'Chris,' asks Pip, 'is that the same nurse who looked after Dad
before the operation?'
Bigstep nods.

We're pulling into the driveway.
The sign on the gate is the name of our farm: Yarrimbah.
But someone has recently shot a hole through the 'a'.
'How long's that been there?' I ask.
'What?'
'The hole in the sign?'
'Don't know.'
'Yarrimboh,' I say out loud.
'Rhymes with bimbo,' says Pip, 'the Bimbo from Yarrimboh.'

2

Dear Journie,

I was going to give up smoking today but all I could think of all day at school was getting home to my stash & lighting up. It's starting to annoy me how the cigarettes control my mind. But maybe I'll wait till after the HSC year — it'll be easy to quit then. Maybe I'll just quit the queasy Pill now instead.

There are only 9 students who've come back to do HSC. It's going to be hard to get a comparison; to check how I'm rating across the state. Will I pass? Two of them are repeating (failed last year). 1 is Dewi, a lovely exchange student from Indonesia & there's a new girl, (she deferred a couple of years) Kate, who I met in the caravan at the Wandong Wingding. She's older than us & quite funny & the only 1 I can really relate to. It's great she also chose art. I just hope she lasts the year.

I've been assigned as the mentoring buddy for Dewi. I get to see first hand again how some kids treat anyone new or different. She has dark skin and struggles with English which is even more disturbing to some than a 'posh bitch up from the big smoke'. Why is being different such a threat?

Why don't parents remind their kids that none of us were here first? Why don't they remember that we all come from somewhere else? I try to be there to defend her but they wait to attack when she's isolated like in some kind of Attenborough episode.

I looked at the Drama School brochures I collected from the Careers Week. Maybe it's about tenacity & believing in yourself. Maybe I just need some confidence and some training. Maybe they just couldn't see my potential. Plenty have been wrong before. Dad was told he was a hopeless academic but he surprised the school by becoming a specialist doctor. I mean who'd have thought I'd be good on a horse? And now I'm in dressage shows. Nothing will stop me applying. Just have to pass HSC first.

I've asked the art teacher if I can choreograph & perform a dance for my art exam. He's looking into it. I'm looking into him. He's sexy.

PS. They released those American hostages who were kept captive almost as long as I've been kept here.

PPS. Acting can lead to great things. Ronnie Reagan is America's president. Just have to believe.

3

It's Sunday afternoon.
Kate's brother picked me up in his beat-up old Valiant.
He's dropping us over at Rhett and Twin Two Timbo's house
for a Sunday afternoon barbecue.

I'm just exhausted. On Friday we won
our school quarter-final tennis match against Shepparton.
I've got two essays due and I was up really late last night
working on the choreography for my dance.
Our art teacher says he's all for something original but
if I don't come up with the concept soon
then I might have to submit something regular –
like a painting. He said it like a warning.
He knows my paintings look like a three-year-old did them
but not in the same way as Jackson Pollock.

Kate says it could be easier to choose a
less demanding project
but the truth is I'm not really good at regular art.
I tell her I just need more time.

Maybe I'm going to have to cut some extracurriculars, like tennis.
Anything not directly related to the performing arts.
Tennis has really helped me belong to the school
but there's probably not that many acting roles that demand it.
She says, 'And you could cut out debating.'
'The school would kill me,' I say. 'Mr Barley would be in tears.
It's the first time they've ever been winning.
And debating is like acting, sort of,
except for the fact that debaters have to be themselves.'

I'm thinking this through in a daydream like a zombie on the couch.
Then I look back to see Twin Two is looking at me
to see if I'm up for finishing off the job I started in the paddock.
But no, it's a real boyfriend I want now –
not an experiment.
Except the real boyfriend material – Rhett –
hasn't noticed me since I arrived.

Nick says hello by pointing an imaginary gun at me,
which everyone's doing this week since Ronnie Reagan got shot at.

The joint's been passed around so many times
we're all in a kind of fishbowl.
Dad says you should try everything at least once.
So I do. At least once.
And they've all been drinking while I'm just sinking
into some kind of weirdo bubble.

'C'mon,' says Kate, 'if you're going to fall asleep, then
you may as well be horizontal.'
I follow her into the twins' parents' bedroom and we lie down
on the mustard chenille bedspread.
It's nice to lie down to relax in the room with the blinds drawn.

She starts me
laughing
about Mr Mitchell, our groovy art teacher,
who wears handmade leather waistcoats
and encourages radical ideas.
We nickname him 'Mr Leather'.

Nick comes in and makes us laugh more
about other stuff and, frankly, soon
everything's funny.
Can't stop.
Nick is cracking us up.
I wink at Kate like, there's one for you…
Then guess who comes in too?
'Noisy bunch o' bastards,' says Rhett
and closes the door and lies – the six-foot sexy length of him –
right across the bed. Mmmm…
Here's my chance for us.

Nick tickles Kate to prolong a laugh for one of his jokes
but his tickling turns into kissing.
Rhett and I grin and act like we
don't know where to look,
then, almost as a solution,
he rolls over and
kisses me too.
I catch Kate's eye and we wink again and then,
with Rhett's hand moving up the inside of my leg,
he tells a joke which is so unfunny
that we all start to laugh
like a bunch of crazy kookaburras.
We muck around
until it all gets to be like a
slo-mo game of Twister.

I'm starting to feel weird…from the joint, I think.

The bedspread's getting all messed up
and I open my eyes to find
Nick in my face.
He's about to kiss me.
He's cute and all but he's not the one that I'm here for
so I turn away and find myself
face to face
with Kate.
There's a strange pause, then Rhett says, 'Ever kissed a girl?'
Kate answers by kissing me
and the boys urge us on
to keep going as long as we can.
I can tell he's looking
and liking the looking.
I can feel it all over.
Whatever turns him on…

Then everything's blurry with
clothes coming off and arms and legs
and different mouths
and the crackle of wrappers of condoms.
I close my eyes trying to hold onto Rhett
to be sure it sorts out in the
right configuration.
There's more twisting around and upside-downing
and after a while
it's hard to tell the difference –
it's just heat and heavy breathing
and gripping and slipping…
and I start to get crazy pictures of things,
like all of us on a merry-go-round
and I'm spinning and spinning and there's
Dad rising up from his hospital bed, spinning, spinning
and Bigstep flying a unicorn into the clouds…
and Pipstar riding a giant clarinet rocket…
and Mum morphing into an angel fish…

4

Dear Journie,
I feel sick and disgusting. Just hope it was all worth it – for Rhett & Me.

I'm sitting out at the patio table
supposed to be doing a heap of homework
but writing my journal first.
Summer is turning a sad corner.
You can feel the trees clinging to their green leaves
trying not to let them be bled into red and taken.

PS. I can no longer threaten hunger strikes. Bobby Sands died.

Bigstep's playing her new Van Morrison album as loud as a teen.
It's called *Into the Music*,
which today I am not.
The song is 'It's All in the Game',
which today I am not.

I'm exhausted. With everything. And all the study I have to do.
Just the thought of today's dressage lesson is killing me.
I put down my journal
and work on my dance costume
but I get distracted by rehearsing how I will tell the sports teacher
that I can't continue with tennis.
It's too much pressure.

Pipstar and Hayzo cross the lawn
with a box full of rags and jars and stuff.
'Where are you guys off to?' I ask.
'None of y' biz,' he says.
They head off down to the paddocks giggling.
Yeah…hilarious.

The last Van track finishes
and all you can hear are the distant shrieks of Pipstar and Hayzo
and the needle of our record player
which can't tell when the music is finished.
It gives me a fright when I look up to see Bigstep on the lawn.

'You've just thrown all your clothes in the laundry sink.'
'I can't do everything,' I say. 'I'm on overload.
In case you've forgotten, I'm trying to pass my HSC.'
'No need to be rude.
I was able to pass matriculation and still help my parents.'
I think to myself, you're not my parent, you're a stand-in.
'Maybe you could do a few less extracurricular things…
like tennis, or debating?'
(Interesting how she doesn't suggest the horse showing.)
'I've already dropped dance and our school is winning the debating.'
'Well…priorities is all I'm saying.'
'Like laundry? Some of us need extracurricular shit
if we're not dux of the school!'
She touches her forehead, brushes hair off her face
and heads off to restart the record.
Her parents are still happily married.
And I bet they all sat round the kitchen table
helping her with her homework.

5

I call Dad. He's in rehab.
It takes me twenty minutes and three nurses
to get through to the phone by his bed.
He's off the morphine but still drowsy on extra-strength painkillers.
'Hi, darling,' he says, sounding weak. 'How're your studies going?'
You can tell he won't handle an answer longer than 'good'.

I haven't seen him since the operation.
The only time Bigstep had time to drive me down
was midweek during school or last weekend
when I had twenty-four hours to finish three assignments.

He says he's going to have to lie flat for days,
on a sheepskin rug so he doesn't get bed sores.
'Angie gave me the rug,' he says. 'Nice of her, wasn't it?
Listen to this,' he says. 'What is it?'
Loud radio music blares in my ear.

'I don't know,' I say. 'DAD?'
He takes the radio away from the speaker. 'Could you hear it?'
'Yes.'
'You know it, don't you?'
'Maybe. Um, no.'
'Come on…it's Mahler's *Song of the Earth*.'
'Sounds sad.'
'Well, yes, but a marvellous work nonetheless.'

I'd like to tell him about how
scary it is
doing HSC
and worrying every day about passing.
And about how upset the school was when I quit the tennis team.
And how the other Pill made me just as queasy and I quit.
And to ask his advice about the back-seat bus-bitches
and how to best fill out the drama school application forms
(even though they're not due till September).
And about how stressful it is
keeping up with the research that goes into debating competitions
and the practice that goes into dressage
and the decisions about choreographing my dance
and the trials and tribulations of being Lucinderella and
living out at Whoop-Whoop on Doglolly Hill
with my not so Ugly Stepmother
without a licence to leave the property
and a budget for long-distance phone calls.
And how I'm keeping an eye on Pip
in the rare moments when I know where he is…
But who's keeping an eye on me?
And how horses are great to talk to but they
don't talk back
and who the hell is this Angie-the-nurse anyway…?

But I can't because
though I might be feeling
like I'm falling off a horse in slow motion,
it's like he's already fallen.

I figure you can't ask help from someone
who's already on the ground.
'Are you keeping an eye out for your little brother?'
'Yes,' I say, 'of course.'

6

As I ride out of the dressage ring
proudly wearing a large red ribbon diagonally across my chest,
I want to hug Christine for getting me to the stage
where I can win second place at the Kilmore show.
This is a luxury benefit really.
My original motive was to broaden my acting skills
and to go for a part in *The Man from Snowy River*.

Compared with kids who grow up with horses,
it feels amazing to be in this position. I only just started riding.
I'm so lucky to have my own horses
and to experience exceptional training with Arnie,
who thinks I could do really well if I rode full-time.
It's nice to feel good about myself for a change but
the problem is that I'd rather win an Oscar.

Bigstep is waiting just outside the entrance to the arena.
She's looking awfully proud of her prize horse
and her prize brat.
Fire and I are hot and sweaty, dying for a long drink.
It's unusually hot for April.
I pat her neck and ride her out on a generous long rein… 'Good girl.'
As I dismount, the first thing Bigstep says is,
'Pity your father wasn't here to see that.'
It makes me sad. And even though Mum can't tell
the nose from the rear end of a horse,
I wish she was here too. Neither know I'm competing today.

Bigstep takes the reins and leads Fire back to our float.
I walk beside her. A bit wobbly and shaky
after using all my concentration and leg muscles so intensely.

I'm kind of waiting for the congratulations.
'What happened with the flying changes?'
she asks, loosening Fire's girth.
'What do you mean, what happened?
I got second place!' I say, pointing to the ribbon.
'Yes, but you would have won! You know she can do them.'
I look at her like, isn't second place enough?
Then I say it, 'Isn't second place enough?'
'Of course, of course,' she says,
'I just wondered what had happened, that's all.'

The whole process of unsaddling
and packing Fire into the float
and driving home is tedious.
It's all fake conversation.
I just want to smoke.
Flying changes?
I just want to sleep.
For about a year.

Back at Doglolly Hill
with Fire free and naked in her paddock
and me showered and clean,
I feel wrecked and strange like I need something big.
Or even small. Like a hug?
I go looking for my blue jumper
to get a whiff of Mum's perfume.
All I want to do is lie down,
drink creamy soda and listen to my music.
I'm just not sure I can keep up the momentum
of all these activities, with the pressure of my HSC.

'Have you seen my blue jumper?' I ask coolly.
'Oh,' she says, flatly. 'It's in the laundry.'
She gestures with her head and picks up the kitchen sponge.
'There was a bit of a problem,' she calls out after I pass her.

I'm thinking maybe she soaked it in with my tennis whites.
Like my school winter shirt that went pink.

Washing isn't her forte. The laundry just isn't her zone.
But what I find is far worse than tennis blues.
'A bit of a problem' is the understatement of the century.
My jumper has shrunk to a suitable size for a poodle.

'What the hell did you do?' I come into the kitchen
holding the jumper's little arms out as wide as they will go.
'Did you put it in the dryer?'
'Oh, it went in with the washing,' she says,
as though it went in by itself.
'It mustn't be the kind of wool you can wash in the machine.'
I stare at her in shock.
She says, 'Never mind, we can buy you a new one.'
'I didn't even *want* you to wash it!' I throw it on the kitchen table.
It slides off, sulking onto the floor.
'Lucy,' she says quietly, 'it had begun to stink.'
'The stink was my mother's perfume.'
'Oh, I don't think so,' she says. 'Look, it's a shame, I'm sorry.'
'A shame? It's a fucking disaster!'
'Now now, no swearing please,' she says,
all calm and wiping the kitchen bench
gently, as though trying to avoid some ants.
But I've had it with being patient.
Even a domestic Neanderthal doesn't machine wash a woollen jumper.
How can you be dux of the school and do that?
'What the fuck did you do that for? Was it on purpose?'
'Come on now. Don't be silly. And it's not the end of the world.
It's just a jumper. I'll get you a new one.'
But here's where she's terribly, terribly wrong.
Missing the whole point.
Missing the person who's missing in my life and missing me altogether.
'Fuck your flying changes,' I say.
'It's all your bloody fault we live in this idiotic wasteland.
I'm NEVER riding your fucking horses again!'
I kick my miniature polo-neck across the floor
and it stops at the glass door,
staring out like a little dead dog that died waiting to exit.

7

The rains have finally come. Water is
running off the hard soil down the dirt roads,
making tiny rivers all over the place and
turning the paddocks into mud.
It's a relief to feel the sky let go
and to hear the earth drinking.
But I woke with the same old rainy-day dreads
and wrote some of them down.

Will Dad get vertical again? Will Mum return? Am I good enough for Rhett? What if I don't pass HSC? What if I don't get into drama school? Are my dreams unreasonable? What if I really don't matter at all?

I've written these questions before. The usual anxieties
like layers of dust
on an ornament left too long on the shelf –
starting to weigh it down.
I went outside in my nightshirt
and stood there
letting the rain wash the dust off all of these feelings
then I came inside
still feeling muddy.

I had breakfast accompanied by Van the Man,
singing 'Venice USA'
with its dooby-doo style chorus.
Going mad.
Need a break from the study.

When the sky took a pause in its crying,
I called Kate and bravely asked her to call the guys,
to invite them to our farm for a spin in the ute.
I want to show them a new trick that I worked out
(by accident)
the last time I drove the rubbish to the tip.

Getting ready for their arrival serves as a
fantastic distraction
from study and worries
but some of the confidence and enthusiasm
between the idea and its realisation
has now been lost.

We head out down the muddy road towards the first gate.
In the back tray, there is Rhett, Nick and Twin Two Timbo,
plus Pipstar and Hayzo.
Up front, beside me, Kate and Stevie.

In the wide open paddock along the flat,
I wait for the right moment
then turn sharp and accelerate
making the back spin out
and sending the ute into a 360-degree spin.
The kids yell out, 'Yeeehaaaah.'
I correct the steering, then line it up,
rev hard and turn so it happens again,
and the gang all go wild. Particularly Hayzo.
Then I drive forward for a while, building up tension,
in order to surprise them suddenly with the next one.

It's exactly as I planned
but it's like giving a little kid a wizzy spin,
the way they say 'more' and 'again'
when you've had enough.
The way they have no sense of the danger.
Pip and Hayzo are desperate for adventure
and my friends are
stoned
so it's only me
who suddenly sees the fun as
idiotic.
But I'm winning heaps of cool points
and hoping Rhett's impressed.

Down at the gully, I stop to let out Hayzo and Pipstar.
They're wearing gumboots and raincoats with hoods.
I hoot the horn as they head away from the car.
Pip waves without looking back
and Hayzo jumps in the sky and punches the air like
there's nothing better in life
than danger and freedom.

'Did you see what was in that kid's plastic bag?' asks Stevie.
'No?'
'What?' asks Kate.
'Porn mags and an airgun.'
'Oh, God,' I say.
'How old are they?'
'Twelve and thirteen.'
Kate asks him, 'Were you reading porn at twelve?'
'No,' he says, then adds, 'It didn't involve any reading.'

I hear 'C'monnnnnn' from the guys in the back.
They start banging the side of the ute.
I pick up speed again. What are the odds?
How many times can you spin a car without really losing control?
Then a thought crosses my mind: 'Who cares?'

8

I've been in my room, studying, since the fight this morning.
She banned me from driving the ute
because of the 'reckless' doughnut marks I left across the farm
and how 'seriously dangerous' it was
to put 'innocent' lives at risk.

My brother couldn't defend me to say it was
the highlight of his month because
when Bigstep and I have a fight these days
he puts on his TV headphones.
I like to dive into a mess, try sort things through
but he likes to disappear.

It's just what we do
though neither way
seems particularly
effective.

I wander out to get some lunch, hoping not to see her
but there she is on the patio
listening to Elvis Costello singing
'Accidents Will Happen'.
with a glass of red wine. At lunchtime.
And she's taken up smoking.
Maybe too much country fresh air
leads to this.

I'm hungry but I sneak back to my room without food.
I haven't got any spare energy to face her.

9

Now that I'm not riding, I just study all weekend
and work on my dance.
I miss the riding badly but visit Sails and Fire when Bigstep's out.
I secretly plan to get back into it as soon as the exams are done.

Stevie telephones to say he has something to tell me about Rhett
and could he pick me up for a drive.
'What about Rhett, I mean Brett?' I ask.
'I'll tell you when I see you. It's highly confidential.'
'Give me a clue?'
'Okay,' he says, 'he's totally swept off his feet.'
I can virtually hear my heart beating. Rhett!
I'm so overwhelmed with excitement that
I can hardly invent my good reason for
going out instead of studying,
which I insisted I had to do,
but I come up with the need-a-break-for-sanity syndrome.

She's probably glad when I go – even though it's a big house
and we are managing to keep away from each other
as much as possible lately.

Stevie arrives in his white panel van –
the one he rents out free to mates.
Bigstep says, 'You're not going out in that!'
But I tell her I am.
And what I realise, which is kind of cool
and awful,
is that she can't stop me.

He turns up the live concert Bob Marley tape,
'Get Up Stand Up'.
Everyone's playing him lately since he recently died of skin cancer.
'Ya gotta make the most o' life, don't ya think?'
'Too young,' I say, 'just like Janis Joplin and Jimmy Hendrix.'

He parks outside the Wallan oval. Gets out leaving the music on loud.

'Right, c'mon, let's have a smoke and a chat.'
He opens the back doors climbs in and makes himself really comfy.
I'm like, 'Just give me the story!'
'Well,' he says after lighting a spliff, 'I heard the goss
from the man himself and he's asked me to speak with you first.'
(I'm shaking.)
'As I said, he's totally swept off both his fucken' feet.'
I act like an innocent. 'Cool… Who is she?'
'He wants you,'
(magic words)
'he wants you to let him know if it's reciprocated first.'
'If it's what?'
'If the person he loves… loves him back.'
'Oh, okay, sure…' I say, grinning.
'Before he makes a move, if you know what I mean?'
'Course.'
'So how do you feel about talking to Kate first?'
'Kate?'

'Yeah, Kate, ya good mate.'
'Why would I talk to Kate first?'
'Well, ya dingo, to confirm she's equally crazy about Brett!'
'Kate?'
'Yeah. Don't act surprised!'
'No! Kate, of course, yeah.'

After that,
I'm so deflated
we share the whole joint together
and I hardly even hear him say
he's been wanting to tell me
he's crazy about me
and I hardly notice I'm
overlooking the Wallan football oval
in the back of his famous fuck-truck (for hire)
beneath green gingham curtains that his mother sewed,
lying on his foam mattress
and having sex with Stevie Maclain.
No, I hardly register I'm there at all
until the condom breaks.

10

Interesting how Bigstep can rewind a punishment
when it suits her.
I'm allowed to drive the ute again
but only to the tip.

The rain has been
incessant.
That early relief we all felt when it finally arrived
and quenched the earth is already forgotten.

The dams are full, the water troughs overflowing,
cutting rivulets into the grass beneath them.
The creek is a creek again, not just a crunchy gully.

'If you leave one questionable track on the paddocks,'
she says, threatening, warning...
But you can tell she can't think of something to punish me with.
What's she going to take away?
I've already quit everything fun in order to study.
'I'll tell your father about your smoking,'
she says, grasping at straws.
'I'll tell my father about *your* smoking,' I say.
She tries to look like, 'Whatever', but can't disguise some surprise.

When I drive past the shed, I get a hell of a fright.
The two boys jump out holding rakes like spears with a 'RAH!'
I stop the car, nearly getting whiplash.
My nerves are wrecked.
'Don't *ever* do that again.'
They start getting in. 'Not allowed, 'I say.
'C'monnn,' says Pip. 'She won't know.'
It's pissing down. She's not riding.'

They get in beside me. Hayzo is carrying a box.
'Off to do a bit of reading?' I say.
Hayzo says, 'Yeah, right, like we love to read in the rain.'
He turns to my brother who, from my quick glance,
appears to be blushing.
'Ya sister might have a little trouble passing her HSC.'
Have to silently agree.
'Wanna walk?' I say.
'Take it easy,' he says. 'Jus' kidding.'
'What's in the box?'
'Molotov,' he says, toasting the air.
'What?'
'Stuff, you know.'
'No? What stuff? An airgun?'
'What's it to you?'
'Is there some reason why you have to be so rude?'
'Nuh,' he says, giggling.
I get a glimpse of what it's like to be a stepmother.

Pipstar does the duty of opening the gate
through to the creek paddock.
He looks small in his full wet weather gear.
The car stalls. 'Good one,' says Hayzo.
'What is your problem?' I say.
'No problem,' he answers lightly.
'Do me a favour,' I say. 'Just don't get my brother into trouble.
He's got enough to deal with these days.'
'Why would I get him into trouble?' he says with an altar boy face.
I restart the car, drive through and Pip gets back in.
'Can you smell petrol?' I ask.
'Nuh,' they both say together.
I'm truly hoping I haven't stuffed up the tank
with that crazy driving I did.

I stop the car at the creek and see
they've built some kind of humpy shelter.
'Home away from home?'
'Yep. No visitors welcome.'
'Men's business,' says Pip.

'See ya, Rose,' says Pip, hopping out.
He's been calling me this since he heard me practising
over and over for the debating semi-finals.
'It's better to plant a cabbage than a rose.'
I'm the third speaker, arguing against this topic.
'You're a dreamer,' he said. 'You're sure to win that one.'
'See ya, cabbage,' I yell out.
'See ya, Rosie Big Nose,' says Hayzo, who
runs off after my brother, carrying the box.

At the tip, I turn the engine off,
relieved that the petrol smell's gone.
I stomp back and forth in my gumboots
and throw the bags into the tip one by one.
Maybe I need to let go of something else.
Debating takes so much preparation. Priorities?

I go back to the car and sit for a while smoking a cigarette,
with the engine off and the window an inch open.
'Please, Rural Gods, don't let me be pregnant.'
To distract myself, I focus on all the things I've been giving away,
like the riding, the tennis, the dance classes, the fun… Tony…
I hear a loud crack. It echoes up from the creek.
I should check on the boys, find out what they're doing,
but I've got 'personal problems' and a history test tomorrow
and I'm still getting all mixed up with World War I and II.
What's Hitler got to do with acting?
Besides, I'm not their mother.

Back at Doglolly House,
Bigstep is sitting at the kitchen table holding an opened envelope
and staring at the horizon through the glass doors.
There is a cigarette butt in the lid of the gherkin jar
and under that a packet of cigarettes.

No music.

'Rubbish is done,' I say.
She doesn't move or speak.
'Rubbish is done.'
'Okay, thanks,' she says, vacantly.

She puts the envelope over the butt in the jar lid, stands up in a daze,
looks at her watch and snaps out of the trance.
'Where are the boys?'
'Dunno,' I say.
It's weird to realise I've turned into a liar.
She looks at me like she's deciding something
horribly new and serious,
then nods her pale face like not finding the boys is okay.

'Are you okay?'
'I'm just going to have a bit of a lie down,' she says
and heads off to the bedroom like a ghost.

I sit in her warm seat
wondering if maybe I can start to smoke inside too.
I lift the envelope to check the cigarette brand:
Alpine. Pathetic. Well, we won't be sharing cigarettes.
I put the envelope back on the stinky butt.
It's unsealed and unaddressed.

Curiosity gets the better of me.
Inside are two opera tickets, past their use-by date but unused.
Also a packet of Interdent toothpicks, Dad's favourite brand.
A docket from a shoe repair shop in East Melbourne.
A Thank You card from a patient
and three Polaroid photographs.
Everything is pretty normal, for Dad,
except for the photographs
of this woman,
slightly familiar,
lying across the blue sheets
of an unmade bed,
smiling and
wearing no clothes.

11

It's freezing.
My teeth are chattering enough to loosen my braces
without the need for the orthodontist
to wrench them off my teeth today.
It's exciting but daunting. I'm sure it will hurt.
Will they leave marks? Who will I be without them?
Will the boys love me as much as they love Jess?

My train carriage has three open windows that won't shut.
It's still raining. The seats next to the windows are wet.
Drafty and cold but at least I get the whole carriage to myself.
Writing is hard because of the train's movement.
I brought my assignments but all I have done so far is
write in my journal:

Dear Journie,
 Freaking out – waiting for my period. Please, please pleeeeeeeeease...
Can you imagine? Christ! This is all I need.

Each time I get on this Red Rattler train
my worries get more complicated.

An inspector comes through to check my ticket.
She has no facial expression. 'Tickets, tickets.'
She's like a machine; stocky and hard and programmed on automatic.
I'm clearly hunting in my bag but she says it again, 'Tickets, tickets.'
This is another reason to work hard.
You don't want to end up in a job like this.
You don't want to become a sad automated nobody.

After she leaves my carriage, I get out my art essay:
'What were the Pre-Raphaelite Brotherhood reacting to?
Who and what influenced their work?
Why were they considered the first avant-garde movement?
Discuss using examples of the artists' work.'
But from Heathcote Junction to Craigieburn
I find I mainly stare out of the rainy window.
No better way than on a train to see life passing you by.
Visible time.

I find myself using the same words over and over again:
portrays, conveys, reveals, displays, illustrates, illuminates, demonstrates.
After a while, art essays get boring.

I read my *Vogue* magazine for a while but it's depressing. I want to be romantic, mod, street-wise, innocent, sexy, skinny, tall, all of them but the truth is I can't be any of them. Best not to look.

 Bigstep put an ad in the paper to sell 2 of our horses and one of them was Sails. Devastated. She says we have too many to manage. I know I'm not riding him but I talk to him and what about her girls' ponies? They spend most of their holidays in town with their dad or with her & her parents.

Is this the beginning of the end? I don't know why she thought Dad'd be different. Did she think he'd turn into somebody else?
   I'm getting picked up at the station by Angie, the nurse. Will find out if it's her, the one in those pictures without clothes.
   Ps. Mr Leather really believes in me. I so want to do well. For him as much as me. Sexxxxxyyyyyyyy.

I get off the train feeling bad that I didn't write any of my essay.

Compared with Wandong, Spencer Street Station is full of people.
Two bump into me. It's a shock.
I think I've developed a wider personal space.
I don't like people coming too close.
That's a benefit of living in the country –
not even an animal would bump into you
unless it really wanted something.

Her soft half-wave looks like a cross between
the Queen and an innocent kid. She smiles.
Yep. That's the lady on the blue sheets.

She looks nothing like Bigstep, though equally attractive.
Got to give Dad points for taste
and for not choosing young dolly bird clichés.
She has dark thick hair, dark eyes, olive skin...
but there's a kind of dreaminess in her expression too
that makes them seems tribally related.

I force a smile through the last of my metal mouth teeth,
cringing underneath,
and focus on the positive fact that she's looked after Dad.
I say hello politely just in case she's all right.
But in my heart, I don't want another stepmother.
My hello does not come out sounding nice.
'Gosh, you must be missing your dad,' she says.
What can I say to an upsetting question-statement like that?

I wish I could be like Mother Teresa, or the Pope
who forgave the man who just shot him
but maybe you have to wear long robes
and pray a lot
to be as consistently friendly as that.

12

I've just eaten two breakfasts in a row.
There's a pause in the rain this morning
but the sky is still dark.
Staring out the glass doors to some low clouds in the valley
and the grass is white with frost.
You can see the horses' breath.
When the phone rings I think it's going to be Dad
but I hear the extra long-distance beep beep beeps…

'How are you, darling? How's all the study?
Did you get your braces off yet?'
'Yeah,' I say.
'Oh, how does it look?'
'It looks better.' (It'd want to – after all that pain and cost.)
'Are you thrilled?'
'Yeah,' I say, like I had a personality bypass.
'Oh, darling, you don't sound very happy at all.
Are you stressed from all the study?'
'Yeah,' I say, with no mention of everything else –
including the horrifying fact that
I'm certain I'm pregnant.
I feel huge and emotional and nauseous.
My period is four days late. I hold my bloated belly.
If I tell her, what can she do?
If I tell her, she'll know it was definitely not
'someone I really loved'.

The weak sun is filtering through the icy trees and
there's mist rising off the dam.

'I wish I could just hug you, darling.'
Let's not linger on the impossible. I change the subject.
'I'm in the district semi-finals of the school debate on Friday.'
'Oh, how exciting,' she says. 'Well done! What's the topic?'
I guess that letter hasn't arrived yet,
the one listing every possible rebuttal.
Some of them don't. I should photocopy them at school
but I hardly even have time lately
to write them.
'That it's better to plant a cabbage than a rose.'
'Oh,' she says, 'I don't agree with that.'

Looking around, all I want to do
is eat everything in the kitchen.
I've already finished the dry packet of Coco Pops
and had four pieces of toast with chocolate spread.
I feel like a beached walrus,
all heavy, full of fluid, hormonal.
Unsettled. Like the tide is
dragging me out against my will.
It makes me want to eat
to anchor myself.

She asks about the dance I'm choreographing.
I tell her Pipstar saw me practising
and said I looked like I'd escaped from
One Flew Over the Cuckoo's Nest,
which he hasn't seen,
he's only heard me re-enact some of the Nurse Ratched scenes.
I suppose I can't expect him to appreciate contemporary dance.
Mum agrees.
'Is he all right?' she asks.
'He's got a new friend.'
'What? Sorry, darling, it's very windy here and the phone is echoing.'
'He's got a new friend called Hayzo.'
'Oh, that's good to hear, at last.'
'Yeah,' I say.
It's not the time to worry her with my concerns about him.

'And how's Dad?' she asks,
trying to get me to elaborate on at least something.
'Oh, he's much better,' I say. 'He'll be coming home soon.'
Though home isn't quite the word for it and I'm not sure when.
'He's been well looked after by his nurse,' I say,
unable to withhold an urge to colour the tone with a little sarcasm.
But I don't think I want to tell her what I know.
It will only bring up all the old painful stuff that caused her
to leave Dad in the first place.
'Sorry, darling, I didn't hear you.'
'I said he's being well looked after.'
The phone cuts out.
I hold it to my ear for a while
just listening to the engaged signal,
even joining in with the beeps for a while
before I hang up.

I forgot to ask her how she is.

I climb up on the roof with my journal in my bag
and my cigarettes and my torch.
Haven't been up here for a while with all the rain.
There's a strange glow in the sky as the sun tries to
force its way through the cloud ceiling.

Thank the Gods that Doglolly House has a roof.
Where do city people go to get perspective?

I've taken to rolling my own cigarettes
but have to prepare them
before I get out in the breeze.
The rollie is stronger than a usual cigarette
and without the filter, little bits of leaf stay on my tongue
but there's something kind of
earthy and real about getting directly to the tobacco
and it looks cool. More like a joint.
I figure I will smoke less because it takes more time
to roll them up.
So far, the theory isn't working.

After I light up I have a bit of a chat to
Empty Ness
and notice an aqua-winged kookaburra
perched on the gutter's edge.
Not laughing.
She cocks her head, looks at me.
I cock my head and look at her.
Talk about Cuckoo's Nest.

Dear Journie,

Bigstep sold another horse this week but thankfully not White Sails. No one replied to the ad. It feels like she's giving up.

Really don't know if I can pass. Having real problems with history & geog. Can't seem to retain facts re canopies of trees & dates of dictators. Thought I was doing fine but I'm not. Haven't passed the last 2 tests. The only thing I'm into is my dance. I have to stop eating. Mr L will see me in a leotard. Can't stop thinking about him (in every position). Nb. See recent dream in dream diary.

Ps. Please please please please please let me bleed.

Kookie leaps off the edge of the roof and swoops low
before rising up into the dark branches of the nearby gum tree.
There goes the closest thing I've had lately to a good laugh.

13

We sit in our debating seats facing an audience of
students, parents and teachers at Assumption College.
Mr Barley thanks the head of their English department
for welcoming us to the district semi-finals.
(There are drama scouts in the audience, he told me,
looking for actors to be cast in the
end of year combined school Christmas production.)

During his introductory speech
I feel the unquestionable dragging pain
that signifies my monthly bleed which is
wonderful
and awful.

'Your school has a reputation for producing
remarkable AFL players,' he says,
'but we're keen today to play you on the debating field.'
He turns back and winks at me –
his prize-three summary speaker.
You can tell he notices something wrong in my face because
he pauses then stutters a bit.

I don't know whether to interrupt, hold things up and
excuse myself now
and go stuff my undies with toilet paper –
or hope for the best until the debate is over.
I figure I could have half an hour up my sleeve
before an embarrassing dress-staining disaster.

Along with a nauseous cocktail of relief, fear and dread,
the pain is like someone pulling out my guts in slow motion.
It weakens me. Makes me feel indefensible.
The timing is horrid. I can't cope.
I'm convinced the Rural Gods think I'm a cosmic joke.
This is the last debate. After this one, I'm quitting.

I stay there and cope.
My two team members do an amazing job
of clarifying all the points we researched together then
I draw on every bit of courage and strength and conviction
and deep breathing tips that my mother gave me
and I defend our position passionately
like a president, like a barrister, like a poet,
until it's impossible to consider a single situation
where it might be better
to plant a cabbage than a rose.

We win more points than any previous team
in the history of our school debating.
I wish Mr Leather was here to hear it.
Or Mum. Or Dad.

The best part is, their head of English
comes up to me after and quietly whispers,
'You have a gift.'
I drink in his words like a blood infusion,
thank him and rush to the toilet.
Just in time.
There's blood, sweat and tears
and diarrhoea as my fears go down the toilet.
I come back to the hall. That's it. I quit.
Time to focus on my exams,
but I see the win as total proof that
I can achieve my dream.

14

Oh, my God!
Mr Leather has asked me to go to his house.
He says he wants to help make my costume after school.
He told Bigstep on the phone he'd drop me back home
but she has to come into Broady anyway later
to collect something from the vet.

He's being so supportive.
God – it occurred to me
on the way here that maybe he's the one
who's going to 'discover' me.
And he's been there right on my doorstep
the whole time.

The house he designed is really cool.
Leather lounges with suede cushions.
Natural rugs on seagrass matting. Naked wooden rafters.
There are two armchairs he made himself,
with leather roped to the wooden frames.

He says I can change in the spare room.
I didn't realise he'd actually want me to try it on.
'Yes of course,' he says, curiously.

'So we can tailor it to make sure it works.'
Eek.
We've roughly attached these gossamer pieces
of floating material along the arms.
He says we need to see it on to cut the right length and shape
to match the gigantic fabric backdrop wave I made.
It's all to create an effect so that when I dance,
all in white Lycra under UV light,
I will look like a crest of a wave on a moonlit night.
Well, that's the idea.

On the way to the spare room,
I get a glimpse of his bedroom.
There's a huge fur rug on the floor
and the far wall is all made of glass
inviting the tangled bush to come inside.
The king-sized bed has a quilt made of
large silk bronze and burgundy squares. Inviting!
What have I been doing with immature boys
in beat-up caravans and panel vans?

While taking as long as I can to change I notice a clay sculpture
of a naked woman beside the bed
and a bunch of dried flowers, almost see-through in the light.

But I don't want to come out to the lounge in my costume.
White Lycra shows every bump and curve.
It's meant to glow in the UV light
and be part of a flowing movement like
the froth of white waves in moonlight.
But in the daytime it's just me in a shiny leotard,
virtually naked.
I'm sort of used to being with boys in the dark.

There's a break in the rain today and his house is warm
but I still feel bleakly undressed.
The floating pieces of uncut fabric that I pinned badly
along the underarms of the leotard are pricking me.

'Okay,' he says, as I tiptoe out. 'Now let's have a look.'
He holds his arms wide gesturing for me to do the same.
I'm starting to feel like Jesus when he says,
'Okay, now, we'll have to lay it out flat and re-pin it.'
I cover as much of my body as I can
with the see-through fabric 'wings' and he asks me to
kneel down on the swirly handmade rug.
I feel totally weird.
'Might be best if you lie down?'
I go to lie face down and he says, nicely,
'Okay, so, might be better to lie on your back I think.'

Afternoon sun casts a streak of light across my chest,
embarrassingly
highlighting my undersized breasts.

'Arms out,' he says,
so I have to take the fabric away from its use as a disguise.
'Bit wider,' he says, showing me again, like a crucifix.

Then he kneels down
beside me.
I can hardly breathe.
If he knew what I'd written in my journal…
If he knew I'd imagined…everything…together.
But it's not like I imagined.
In the classroom I feel I know him well
but here, I realise I don't know this man at all and
it's broad daylight.
He lays out the fabric
slowly, so slowly, with care.
'So now we need to match the wings to the wave.'
He places the copy of Mr Hokusai's Japanese print
The Great Wave on the floor above my head.
He stands up and looks down with the marking pen
gripped in his teeth
and takes in the whole picture,
the picture and the whole of me.

Think of the print…
Think of the print…
Just think of the Japanese print…

Then he kneels down with his knee at my waist
and begins to draw the outline.
'You can breathe,' he says, smiling.
It's a good idea, except for the fact that I can't.
I seem to be having some kind of
out-of-body experience
while being well and truly stuck inside my own.
Think of the print…
of *The Great Wave*…
of Mr Hokusai…
No, just think of *The Great Wave*…

'I like the music you chose,' he says. 'Where did you find it?'
Glad for the change of focus,
I tell him it's by the composer who wrote the soundtrack to *Gallipoli*.
I tell him the piece was perfect because it
starts with the sound of the ocean
then builds into a fantastic crescendo
then dies down again,
like life…
and other
climactic
things.

I wish I hadn't used the word climactic.
Just think of the print…

'Very talented young lady,' he says. 'I heard about your debating.'
He stands again, almost over me
to check his markings align with the print
then, like an artist about to
use me as their canvas,
he kneels down and
leans in close.
I can feel his breath…

I breathe in deep for the first time – I like his scent.
Then, slowly, God how slowly, God…
(I have to close my eyes…)
he starts to cut around the edges of the delicate fabric
until about a whole year later when he says,
'There you are. All done.'

15

I ask Bigstep if I can call Jess.
STD calls cost more in the daytime, especially on weekends.
I wish she was out, though I know she checks the itemised bill.
'It's urgent,' I say.
She nods and says, 'Urgent…' like it isn't.
'Five minutes,' she says. 'You know what your father said.'

It doesn't make sense.
A bag of horse feed probably costs more than a half-hour call.
Is making a horse's coat shiny, more important than communication?

First I tell Jess all the bad stuff,
like the marathon study nightmare,
my fears about passing,
the horror of the back-seat bus-bitches,
how the farm isn't nearly as fun without riding
and about arguments with my Ugly Stepmum.

She tells me all the bad bits too,
like how Zed hasn't called for over a week
since the last time they tried and failed to record a song together
and how she hates the jewellery shop job
'Soooooooooooo borrrrrrrrrrrrrrrrrrrrrrrrring…'
And how she's worried about her mum
who's having all sorts of nasty tests and not getting any better.

Bigstep walks past, 'How long've you been on the phone?'
'About three minutes,' I say.
She frowns and says as threateningly as she's able, 'Two more.'

I have to waste a whole minute and a half
talking about useless stuff until I'm sure she's out of the lounge.
'But guess what?' I say. 'The best news is…'
'You got into drama school!'
'No, no, not yet, no… I'm *not* pregnant!'
'My God,' she says, 'what a total relief.
I mean he's nice and all but you don't want a red-head baby.'

I tell her it scared me so much I went back on the Pill
even though it makes me feel nauseous
and I don't even have a boyfriend.
I tell her Dad's coming home soon
and that I got a letter from Mum and it sounds like finally
she and Jacques will soon be coming to live in Melbourne.
'Your mum should just come back without him,' says Jess.
'It's your dad who should have left.'
I wasn't expecting my timed phone call
to go on this treacherous detour.
'You'd leave if your husband wasn't monogamous?'
'Wasn't what?'
'If he was unfaithful. Anyway, next year I'll be at the age where
the courts will let me live wherever I want.'
'But by that age, will you still need to live with your mother?'

After a silence that accentuates the weight of the valid question,
the precious time ticking by and the cost of the long distance call,
I say flatly, 'The other good news I've been wanting to tell you
is about Mr Leather and my dance.'
Bigstep walks through the lounge towards the kitchen.
'Okay, that's enough. Hang up now, please.'
'Come on, please, just one more minute…'
'No. It's peak hour. It's expensive. You know the rules.
I gave you five minutes,' she says, nearly at the door.
'Please, please, please!'
'Get off the phone now,' she calls out, 'or I'll disconnect it.'

I quickly whisper, 'Jess… I'm totally in love.'
'What?' she says.
'I'm totally in love.'

'Oh, my God. Did Rhett change his mind?'
'No. And frankly I don't give a damn. Brett is still with Kate but now, like you, I've found a man.'
'Who? Who?'
'I'll give you a clue. You know how you liked music classes? Well, remember how much I liked art?'
'No!'
'Yep.'
'You're kidding?'
'That's it,' says Bigstep, coming into the lounge.
'Isn't he married?' I hear Jess say.
'No,' I say, speaking fast, ignoring Bigstep.
'No mention of a wife?'
'None at all. Maybe if there was a wife, they got divorced.'
The line goes dead. She appears, holding the phone lead in her hand.
'No calls for a month. You know the rules.'

16

Dear Journie,

I've been working so hard on my dance.

Prince Charles married Lady Diana. We watched the fairy tale wedding on TV. All too good to be true. It'll end in disaster. But hey, she was just a kindy teacher. So yeah, anything's possible. Dream on!!! Speaking of dreams, here's last night's: Performing my dance – Mr Leather came out on stage at the end with a big bunch of flowers & kissed me. Hundreds were applauding then there was a loud ambulance siren & everyone scattered. Bigstep galloped a horse onto the stage trampling the strewn flowers & yelled, 'Your father's coming, your father's coming'…??? Dreams are weird. What are they for? A big psychic clean out?

Not sure if it was worth quitting the debating team to lower the stress & gain extra time to study. Especially just b4 the final. I can't handle everyone's disappointment. I've let down the school.

I like how Mr Leather's really silent about what's happening between us – as though it's all innocent & nothing's going on. The truth is, I know we both know we can't make a move until after I've sat the exams & am no longer a student & the whole thing is acceptable. But I have to admit, it's hard to study when all I can think about is lying on that swirly rug in his leathery house, completely naked.

17

I'm preparing to do my dance at the mixed talent concert
in front of the whole school as a rehearsal for the exam.
'A good opportunity to test everything out,' says Mr Leather.
'Break a leg,' he says, with a smile and a wink,
which is what you say to actors before they go on stage,
but Katerina walks past and hears it
and now all the back-seat bus-bitches are telling me to
'BREAK YA LEG, YA BITCH,' so I'm terrified
they might've cursed me to really do it.

I breathe deeply like Mum taught me.
I can see the enormous white backdrop wave
in the shape of Mr Hokusai's print
that I filled with padding to make it three-dimensional
and sewed onto an invisible wall of blue tulle.
It's magically lit by the UV lights
so it seems to be hovering
and about to break
in mid-air.
Exactly as I imagined it.
Excited.

This is for him, I say to myself.
I take my position in front of the backdrop and bend forward
as though I'm held like a foetus within the wave.
The Jean-Michel Jarre soundtrack from *Oxygène* begins
with just the sound of the ocean waves and then
my voice-over poem comes whispering through...

'Life
Ebbs and flows
Like endless waves
Washing against the shores

What comes always goes
Life ebbs and flows.'

And then I begin to move,
all in white, my arms flowing with the soft chiffon waves
and I dance so I feel all of the seven seas within me.

There is silence when I finish, for quite an eerie minute.
Then everyone applauds, generously.
A few people, including Mr Leather, even stand up!
Did I arrive in heaven?

Afterwards, I change into this beautiful white dress
that Bigstep let me wear.
Mr Leather is the first to meet me outside the change room.
He stands totally close, holds his hands out for both my hands,
looks deeply into my eyes and sincerely says,
'That was so moving.' Then he hugs me.

After interval, it's his turn to sing a soulful song about being alone.
I'm amazed to discover he has a really beautiful voice.
I fall in love with him even more.
We performers understand each other.

I go home on the biggest high
since my last birthday party
when Mum and Dad were happily together.
I don't even care that the bus-bitches
completely trashed what they saw.
'Piece of dunny paper waving under a streetlight!'
Et cetera.
You just have to 'hold onto your own',
'dance to the beat of your own drum',
or whatever.

I write about Mr L until two a.m.
I can tell you now
he won't be singing
sad lonesome songs for very long.

18

It's nearly midnight. Can't sleep.
I've written six pages in my journal.
The school year's nearly over and I can't wait to finish
and be with him and audition for Vic College but at the same time
it means the exams are really soon.
Can't believe how little time I have to study.
It's like a pressure cooker and the only release is my journal –
especially after Bigstep banned the 'unnecessary' phone calls.

The last thing I expect to hear is the crunch of gravel
as a car comes up the drive.
Scary.
Maybe this time it really is someone coming to kill us.
There may be more murderers in cities
but in the country, no-one can hear you scream.

Footsteps. I freeze and then,
'Luce?'
Christ!
I open the door and stare at him through the flywire screen.
He seems taller. Older. More serious.
I let him in, but what if it's actually
Tony
who's come to kill us?

We sit on my bed in a thick hot silence for a minute.
Everything's the same. Same but different.
'I've forgiven ya,' he says. 'Water under the bridge.'
It's a weird thing for him to say – like somebody else said it.
He looks around the room. 'You still got the box.'
'Yeah.'
'Got a new boyfriend?'
I shake my head, checking to see where I left my journal.
'Missed ya,' he says.
'Me too,' I say. 'Where did you go? Everyone was really worried.'
'Not everyone.'
He picks up the box. Studies it carefully. No dandelion.

'Had to get out of town. Had to ride.'
'Ride Like the Wind' we say together and laugh.
'Nah,' he says, 'just had to sort my head out.'
'I was worried you'd have another crash or something.'
'I did,' he says, 'in here.' He punches his heart.

I open the curtains but it's still dark so we can only see ourselves,
not the shape of the Great Dividing Range we know is in the distance.
'I never meant to –'
'Shh,' he whispers.
'It's just –'
'Wasn't meant to be. Wrong side of the tracks and all that.'
'No,' I say, 'that's not it. That crap doesn't matter at all.'
'Yeah, it does,' he says. 'Sooner or later that crap'll matter.'
'No,' I say.
He holds his hand up and shakes his head, 'Shh, don't worry.
I was outa my head. It was never meant to be.'
Although this feels somehow true,
I really don't like having it all dismissed.

'So how ya been?'
'Okay. Stressed. Your sister and her mates are giving me hell.
I get punished every day.'
'Really?' he says, smiling.
'Yeah. I think they want to kill me.'
'Loyal,' he says.
'Yeah,' I say, 'like the Mafia.'
'I'll have a word with her,' he says.
'Thank you. I'm trying to pass HSC before they kill me.'
'You'll pass.'
'I'm not so sure. It's been really, really stressful.'
He sits closer. Puts an arm around me.
'I'm really sorry,' I say. 'I never…'
'Shh.' He takes my hand. I melt a bit.
I'm not the girl I was before
but she's still in there
somewhere.
She must be.

It's all different now.
We're different but
he smells the same.

He leans in slowly
and turns toward a kiss
desire alive
I melt into his familiar taste
his thirst
our bodies
keen to dissolve
to be filled
to arrive
and I give him
everything,
all I can –
to make amends,
to bring back the
magic
that disappeared
the night he went over the fence…
We go to places I don't think he's been.
The places he really
deserved
much more than the others.

But all the
proficiency
feels meaningless
with the loss of the
innocent feelings.

I think he gets
the sense of it too;
the thing we had
and missed
and lost.

We lie for a while
afterwards,
still and
awfully silent.

He gets up and begins to dress.
There's no doubting the empty feeling
like a draught in a room that used to be airtight.

'Well,' he says later, zipping his bike jacket halfway up,
'I guess I'll see you round.'
'Yeah,' I say.
'Good luck,' he says, 'I know you'll pass,'
and winks
and leaves
with my scent all over him
and his all over me –
and he closes the door,
presumably for the last time,
leaving me with a feeling
more like the end
than when it ended.

19

Pipstar is washing black stuff off his hands
in our shared bathroom.
'Have you been down at the creek all afternoon?'
'Nuh, in the library.'
'Can you ever give a straight answer any more?'
'Yeah. That's what we call the hay shed.'
'I can only imagine why… You smell of petrol.'
'Yeah, from the motorbike.'
'You smell of smoke.'
'So do you.'
He keeps washing but the black stuff isn't coming off.
'You okay?' I ask him.
'Yep.'

'What's Hayzo got you into now?'
'Nothing.'
'Must be something.'
'What's it to you? Doesn't matter.'
'It might.'
'Look,' he says, 'you've got your life and I've got mine,'
which sounds weird but true
because once we were in
the same sinking boat
but now we're in two separate boats,
sinking side by side.
'Well, long as you're okay,' I say.
'Fine,' he says, 'best time I've had since we got here.'
He dries his hands, still black, on the yellow towel.

'So, Rose,' he says, as I'm heading out the door,
'which one have you got coming over tonight?'

20

When the rain stops, it really stops. Not a drop for ages.
The ground is lumpy in paddocks
and the earth has dried hard
where wheels made grooves
and horses stomped the mud.

I'm on the front lawn in my dance costume
practising for the exam.
Even though the concert went well
it's important to keep the performance in peak form.
The record is blaring out from the lounge room
and it feels good to dance outside on the patio stage
to the audience of animals, birds and trees.
Some days I wonder how I'll ever live back in the city.

I'm building the emotion of the dance to its climax,
trying to release some of the tension and fear
about the exams beginning next week
when the music scratches and stops.

I go inside and see Bigstep.
'Don't wreck the record! It's the backup for the tape!'
'I didn't. It was just too loud.'
'I'm rehearsing!'
'Oh, sorry,' she says. 'I didn't see you out there.
Anyway, they're bringing your father home any minute.
I don't think he'd like to arrive with all that commotion.'

I go back out on the patio. Sit at the outdoor table.
Light a cigarette, in full view, and wait.
Coming over the hill and along the road,
past the trotters going in circles,
I see an ambulance, quiet without its siren or lights.
A way to bring Dad 'home' more comfortably.
To bring him home horizontal.

I take a deep inhalation of the cigarette smoke
and blow it out across the fields.
'Put that out!' calls Bigstep from the lounge room door.
I take another drag, just stare at her numbly and blow it fully out.
'What are you doing?' she asks, exasperated.
I guess it wouldn't look good for her
if Dad saw she'd let me get out of control.
'Dad's here,' I say, casually dropping the butt to put it out.
Then I smile and say, 'He'll think it's yours.'

I get up to go and meet the ambulance.
Drift across the lawn like a white wayward angel nurse
in my ocean costume.
It's an emotional cocktail. I'm pissed off with Bigstep,
desperate to work on my dance, seriously needing to study,
relieved to have Dad coming home, anxious to see how he will be
and excited for him to see all the balloons we blew up,
the welcome home sign and to eat the cake we made –
it's got the ingredients of the tension here in it but
will hopefully taste okay.

Pip rushes over all eager and fidgety and curiously keen,
ignoring us as if with this arrival, order will at last be restored.

The two men open the van doors, 'Welcome home!' we all say
'Ah yes, home at last,' says Dad. 'I could eat a horse!'
But he looks pale and frail and queasy and concerned. It's frightening.

They help him onto the single lounge bed
that Bigstep has set up. She's put the TV beside it.
'I can walk,' he says, reassuringly,
'but the less agitation after the long drive, the better.
I'll be right in a couple of weeks.'
My brother is staring bewildered
like they brought home the wrong Dad.
This isn't the man he goes duck shooting with,
the man who taught him tennis and snow skiing.

'You look like an angel darling. Did I die and go to heaven?
Could you get me a glass of iced water please darling?
And Pip, could you find my radio please?'
Pip points, 'It's there!' But it hurts Dad to turn so Pip reaches for it.
It dawns on me that at the busiest scariest time of my HSC
we'll need to be angels for Dad,
and apparently doctors make the worst patients.

21

I had to get out of the house.
I've come down to visit White Sails.
Bigstep and Dad were having another argument
about who gets to play what music and when
and money and other stuff.
At least she's got someone else now to bust her boiler.
She threw the accounts book across the lounge
which knocked the marble sculpted face off the coffee table
onto the fireplace bricks and cracked it.
Reminded me of the teapot that broke
all those years ago on the kitchen floor.

I'm sitting in Sail's paddock.
Right beside a patch of new daisies.

He's taking a while to come to me,
even with two carrots and an apple.
I begin to thread a daisy chain
and start reciting dates for the history exam
but I get them mixed up, which scares me,
so I start reciting names of painters
from different art periods.
Renaissance, Neoclassicism, Impressionism, Cubism and so on…
Then I try to get them in the right order.
There's no doubting that studying for HSC
drives you a little crazy.

Eventually Sails comes over,
and munches conscientiously through each of my gifts,
leaving slobber on my wrist.
'Missed you,' I say to him and immediately remember
Tony saying the same thing.
I try to shut the whole experience out of my mind.
'As soon as my exams are over, we'll go for the longest ride.
Yeah, maybe we'll ride all the way to Sydney.'
Sails nuzzles me, looking for more apples,
then gives up and starts munching grass.
'You're lucky,' I say out loud.
'All you have to think about is eating.'
He's swishing his tail, munching, munching.
'It's not like you're harbouring dreams for the Grand National.'
He snorts.
'Why do some people need something grand to live for?'
He pauses a moment, looks at me, then continues munching along,
step by step, sniffing for greener and greener grass.

Sometimes I wish I lived in a country
where there were no magazines
and you didn't have to do anything special to matter.
Where you could just carry water on your head,
wear colourful clothes
and make beads.
(So long as I wasn't hungry.)

22

It's the night before the first exam. English.
I'm reading all my practice essays – the good and the bad.
Pipstar barges into my room saying Mum's on the phone.
I run across the breezeway into the lounge, past Dad,
who is all propped up, reading and listening to a piano concerto.
I pick up the phone. 'Mum? Hello?'
'Hi, darling,' she says, faintly beneath the crackly line.
'Dad, can you turn it down please?'
'What?' says Mum.
'Eh?' says Dad.
'TURN IT DOWN PLEASE, DAD.'
'No need to yell. Okay, just a minute.' He tries to reach it.
'Hang on,' I say to Mum and go and sort Dad's radio.
I return to the phone. 'Sorry. Hello?'
'Hi, darling. The call's quite expensive. Is everything all right?'
I catch my breath. Reflect on the question.
Is…everything…all…right…?
'Hello?'
'Hi, yes.'
'First exam tomorrow, isn't it?'
'Yes,' I say.
'How are you feeling about it?'
I notice Dad is looking at me.
I don't really want to share this conversation.
'Okay,' I say, lying.
'Do you feel ready?'
'Ready as I can be.'
'You can only do your best,' Dad calls out.
'Shh,' I say, 'I can't hear Mum.'
'What, darling?' says Mum. 'I'm terribly proud.
You know that, don't you? I didn't even sit matriculation.
I wish I did but I went straight to work.
I think you're wonderfully clever and brave
and I hope the whole week goes really well.
I want to wish you a huge good luck, darling.'

'Yeah,' I say, 'I think I'm gonna need it.'
'Breathe deeply, darling, before you go in
and go to bed early, okay?'
'Okay.'
'Let me know how it all goes? You don't have to write.
I'll call you again on Sunday, with a surprise.'
'What?'
'Sunday. I'll let you get back to the study now. Love you.'
'You too,' I say, quietly – a little self-conscious in front of Dad
due to the tricky issue of divided loyalty.
The line cuts to the engaged signal.
I hang up, like I'm letting go of a lifeline
that I might need tomorrow.

'How is she?' says Dad.
Yeah, like he really wants to know.
I shrug. 'I don't know.' I really don't know.
'Still planning to come back to Melbourne soon?'
'I don't know,' I say. Have to keep my composure for tomorrow.
Can't lose it tonight. Need my strength. Change the subject.
'What are you reading?'
He shows me the page of his medical journal. Something gory.
'Urgh,' I say, 'How do you do that anyway? Cut people open?'
'With a scalpel,' he says and smiles.
I look at him, try to work him out.
I guess you've got to be a bit odd
to be able to
slice open
live humans
and fiddle around inside.
'I miss it,' he says. 'But won't be long.
Be back on my feet in no time. Pass the radio would you?'

23

It's my third exam.
I'm at the first desk in a row of eight,
down the middle of the auditorium.

I guess in some schools there'd be hundreds of desks
like in a Dickens boarding school.
Only four desks are filled today.
English was the only subject that all eight of us were sitting.
Dewi, the Indonesian girl flew home early. I don't blame her.
I wish I was at the back. The last person can see everyone.
The first can only see the teacher,
unless you hear an unusual noise
and can get away with turning around to look quickly.

I swear the clock's second hand overhead
is moving slower than regular seconds.

I have period pain. Good timing.
I think people get compensation for hardship. Not for this.
Or maybe they do but I was too embarrassed to ask
as they might think I'm the pain.

I'm soooooooooooooooo exhausted.

Even with only four of us, the intensity in here is thick.
Amanda Stamford drops her pen.
Jane Godwin has to ask for
permission to be taken to the toilet.
She never lasts a class without a visit.
The only relief is when Michael O'Connor farts.
These small events are profound in here
amid the hovering silence of exam conditions.

English went well. Even though I hardly slept the night before.
The free creative essay section offered a miracle question:
What do we need the most – the hammer or the rose?
Of course I could use my rose–cabbage debate
and, thank the Rural Gods, I flew through it.
Today's history is not so lucky.
I'm having trouble with the question:
Does a dictator manipulate a nation
or is the nation ripe for the dictator's message?
Explain, with reference to Hitler and World War II.

All I know is Dad and his family
were not ripe
for Hitler's message.

Even if you wanted to, there's no way you could cheat.
Too much space between the desks.
And anyway, it's not like mathematics.
In English writing there's nothing definitely right or wrong.
I never expected to pass Geography, even though I know soil erosion
but I really need English, Literature, Art and History.
Please, RGs – help me!
I squeeze my lucky shell, reflect on Dewi's personal hell
and get on with what I think about human ripeness for dictatorship.

24

Dear Journie,

Final examination on Friday. The 1 that matters the most to me.

Sooooooooooo exhausted. Can't see the wood for the trees. Everyone wished me 'break a leg' but I'm so tired I might really do that.

Guess what!?#$%+*@!# The district HSC art work will be displayed this year at Benalla High school – so the judges only travel to 1 place to examine them. Because my art is me (!) I have to travel there to perform my dance. It's quite a drive so… Mr Leather suggested to Dad & Bigstep that I STAY THE NIGHT in his house. (As in… stay the night!!!) It's for 2 reasons. (Well, only 2 that he mentioned, ha ha…)

1. So we can get an early start there &

2. So we can record the music on his equipment, making it compatible for their examination hall.

I'm so nervous, not only about the performance but (oh, my God) staying the night… Do you think he'll want to do it B4 I've finished school? Like even on the night before my performance??? Imagine doing it with someone reeeeaaaaallly experienced? Oh, my God!!!

25

Lying on the single bed
in Mr Leather's spare room,
staring at the bright light bulb of the lamp
beside the bunch of dried flowers – 'Honesty' he called them.
Eleven p.m… Waiting… Waiting…

Nope… He's not on his way back from the bathroom.
Or bringing the champagne up from the cellar.
He's not here at all. He's gone out to dinner.
An anniversary dinner.
With his wife.

Jess was right.
He's married.
'Happily', it seems.

She's stunning…
Slim, gracious, soulful, sexy, interesting and smart.
I hate her. I hate this naked clay sculpture of her beside the bed.

Was it all in my head?

'Every year I love her more and more,'
he said, after he introduced her.
I nearly threw up
except my throat was so choked I could hardly inhale.
He talked me through the recording equipment
(couldn't listen to a word)
and showed me the spare room.
'You should get a really good night's sleep,' he said (yeah, right)
and then they left. Together.
So fucking together.

If all that wasn't horrid enough,
I seem to have
scratched
the record.

It keeps catching at the same place.
Now I'm just numb, staring at the rafters
of their arty-farty leather-bound house.

I feel sick and bleak.
Bleak and sick and empty.
Like I got my whole life wrong.
Like I really fucked up.

Seventeen minutes past eleven.
How much anniversary dinner can you eat?

There won't be any time to sort out
the crack in my record.
I decide I'm the crack in the record of my own life.

I feel like ripping up their quilt –
strewing the feathers and the Honesty across the seagrass floor
but they're so 'alternative' they'd probably come home and like it.

I hate myself and I've
run out of rollies and the
bastards here don't smoke.

26

Driving north to Benalla.
Really hot day – 'a stinker,' as they say.
The grass is yellow already and it's only spring.
We constantly drive towards a mirage of water
hovering above the highway ahead.
His old blue Celica doesn't have air conditioning.
'Cars are just things to get from A to B.'
My shirt is sticking to the seat.

Mr Leather is chirpy, even after 'fine French champagne'
and a late night.
They didn't turn out their light until one thirty-seven a.m. –
you can guess what they must've been doing.

At least he fixed the record. It only needed a clean.
Made me feel like a loony for getting into such a state.
I suppose he thinks I'm moody today because of the exam.

He's acting like a total innocent.
It can't have been all a delusion. Can it? Am I that blind to reality?
And if I am, what does that mean about every other thing?

I ask him to please stop in Seymour at the service station.
It's not that I'm desperate to go yet,
it's just that I might be
later
when there isn't one
and anyway, I need a break – from him.

Nervousness
is only a small component
of my oil spill of emotions today, which include:
disappointment, frustration, humiliation, confusion, despair.
Plus I didn't sleep at all.

I thought on the trip
we'd be getting to know each other better and savouring the flashbacks
but his wife might as well be here in my seat
and I might as well be locked up in the boot
with a bag over my head.

I try to keep up appearances – my usual flirty stuff
that let him nickname me in class
'the wicked, wicked woman'.
But I can tell you my heart's not in it.
My heart's not even in the car.

I ask him to stop again at Euroa.
He says, 'But you've just been.'
'Bit nervous,' I say.

The next place we stop is an ice cream shop in Violet Town.
'Australia's best,' he says.

It's not the best thing before a performance
but maybe it's just what I need.
Like a kid on a long drive.

I try to do some sexy things with the way I lick the ice cream
just so he can see what he's missed out on
but you have to lick fast in the heat
and it doesn't look as good.
When I finish it I remember that
ice cream is made of cow's milk.

Just past the Baddaginnie sign
we virtually have to pull over into the emergency lane
when a gang of Hell's Angels on Harleys go by.
The noise is deafening.
I wish I could just jump ship.
Hop on the back of one of their bikes
and ride off into the sunset
never to be seen again.

The Benalla High School receptionist
has one eye that doesn't keep up with the other,
and hasn't a clue who Mr Leather is.
But after three calls some elderly teacher
comes along to welcome us
and directs us to bring our gear to the foyer of the hall.
There are art works from all the district's students
displayed everywhere,
mostly hideous
which makes me feel more confident about my dance.

I'm the only student presenting a live performance.
Why couldn't I do something easy like a drawing?
Why can't I draw?

I'm taken to the school library
to wait,
while Mr Leather examines the other works
and sets up the hall for my dance.

Two and a half hours... Alone... Hell...
I fill three exercise books with writings about
everything that's been going on in my life
until my hand is hurting.
Every few pages I go to the toilet.
Queasy. No lunch.

I don't even get to see
the stage
before I'm examined on it.

The thing I write a few times is
IT BETTER BE WORTH IT!
I better get an A for this.

Finally, I am called to get into costume.
The gymnasium change rooms at the back of the stage
smell of sweaty shoes and something sweet, like banana.

As I'm changing I'm trying to psych up
into imagining myself as a white gossamer wave in the moonlight
but I feel more like a fat shiny lychee.
It's thirty-eight degrees. There are sweat marks under my arms.

When I walk out ready in costume,
I see my backdrop is
hanging there in its nice familiar position but
something feels wrong.

Beneath the stage
there are seven judges
sitting side by side behind two trestle tables
in the middle of the hall.
I can see every one of their freaky faces
including Mr Leather's.

At the school concert
I couldn't see
anyone.

It sounds dumb but what I want now
is my mum, in the wings.
'Breathe in deeply…three times, in and out,
and give them what you've got.'

As I get into position in front of my
three dimensional wave,
I wait for the lights to dim
and the music to begin
and the UV effect
to mesmerise the judges
into that magical place
we all went on the night of the concert
but
I realise the reason
I can see everyone
is because of all the
sky-light windows
surrounding the whole auditorium.
My dance is lit by broad daylight.
My entire performance concept is
dependent on the effects of
UV light –
which only works
in the dark.

The horror. The horror.

The soundtrack begins,
I bend into shape
trying to blend into the backdrop wave
just dying with every aching sound of the pre-music ocean…
I shrink to hear my voice-over
whispering the poem
and then I have to begin
to dance.

Let me just say that I'm not a brilliant dancer.

This creation was an
Overall Concept –
not a ballet exam.
All lost now in the blandness of this
horribly bright auditorium light
with seven bewildered judges
sitting in the middle.

When the nightmare is finally over
I leave the stage
and change back into my sweaty A-sized bra
and T-shirt and uncomfortably hot jeans.
One of the judges collects me from the
stinky change room
and brings me back via the stage.

Mr Leather walks towards me
from way down the back of the auditorium.
He looks up at me, concerned and
makes some silly (nervous) joke about Lycra.
I feel dizzy. I try to banter back, jokingly, as I normally would
from up on the bare unmagical stage,
'Oh, shut up!' I say.
This turns his bothered face
into a teeth-gritting cringe because
though this was fine between us in private
this is not
how you speak (in public) to your teacher.

So I gesture both hands to the windows
(the heavens if you like)
with an accusatory shrug.
'Shhh,' he says, 'yes, a pity.'
A pity? My whole career just died in that blinding light.

The drive home is pretty quiet.
No ice cream.

I squint, trying to look for
fish and things
in the mirage that is mainly caused
by holding back the water in my eyes.

When he drops me off at school to catch the
afternoon bus home, he says,
'Don't worry. It'll be all right.'
What'll be all right?
What will be all right?

Part Four

1

After checking Dad and Bigstep are out of sight,
I climb with my bag up to the roof
and lay out my journal beside Empty Ness
who is stuck in a southerly direction. (Know the feeling.)

Late morning. Already hot. No rain for what feels like a century.
The yellow grass doesn't bend, it cracks. It's crunchy.
We can no longer keep our front lawn green.

Dear Journie,
  I've had breakfast & lunch for morning tea. Feel disgusting. She bought enough food for the 6 of us but the girls decided to go away with their Dad so I've eaten their share. It doesn't matter how much you eat, you can't swallow all of your feelings.
  Got out my box of B & H to find the packet empty. Must've smoked them all last night. Give up?

I see Hayzo and Pip double-dinked on the trail bike
heading down towards the waterless creek.
They carry their secret stash in backpacks now.
I told them, I don't care what you're up to
so long as you don't smoke in the dry grass.
How can a smoker tell another smoker not to smoke?
I give up. I don't care.
What's a fire when you're already in hell?

  Everyone in Australia's finished HSC but the pressure's not over for me. I rang to see if you could really get into drama school without passing. 'Occasionally, if the student is exceptional.'

This weekend it's my birthday.
'Hip hip hooray,' I say out loud, to nobody.
Then I speak like it's not even me.
'So, Lucindarella, where is your prince?'

Give up?

I shouldn't have ended it with Tony. It hasn't worked out with anyone else. He's the only one who loved me. Can there ever be anyone like him again? Will there ever be anyone else?

I close my journal. The binding is coming apart.
The red faux suede cover is marked and murky, more shiny than furry.
There's a quote on the front that's starting to rub off.
    'If we should fail?
    We fail.
    But screw your courage to the sticking place
    And we'll not fail.'
    (Mr & Mrs Macbeth)

And another one on the back:
    'Never give up. Never give up. Never give up.' (Winston Churchill)

I wish I could put a lid on the chimney
so I don't have to listen to Bigstep and Dad arguing.
I know he's frustrated because of his back
and not being able to do things
like work
but the fights are getting worse.

'That expense went towards looking after *your* children,
not *our* horses…'

I'm glad she's back though from visiting her parents and kids.
It was getting a bit exhausting being his helper.
Pity he couldn't bring his nurse home with him.

'Well, it was nice to have someone to
care for me for a change.'

I take out my book to practise my audition and
undo two buttons on my jeans. I wish I could stop eating.
My character, Sybylla, wouldn't fit into her corset.
Not that she wanted to wear one.
I practise out loud, to drown out their voices.

'Weariness! Weariness!'
I say it again without looking at the Miles Franklin book
and then read the rest out loud…

'This was life – my life – my career, my brilliant career! I was fifteen – fifteen! A few fleeting hours and I would be old as those around me. I looked at them as they stood there, weary, and turning down the other side of the hill of life. When young, no doubt they had hoped for, and dreamed of, better things – had even known them. But here they were. This had been their life; this was their career. It was, and in all probability would be, mine too. My life – my career – my brilliant career.'

I repeat as much as I can without looking at the book
and then I get back to my journal.

> *If I don't pass Art because of the dance, I won't get my HSC. If I don't get my HSC I can't be accepted into Drama School – unless my audition is exceptional. My audition needs to be exceptional. My audition will be exceptional. Only 1 more week. I'm too young for NIDA this year so I have to get into Vic College. If I can't be successful – what's THE POINT of me?*

2

The three of us are sitting at the huge dining table.
Bigstep's gone down to town again
for the weekend to be with the girls.
Nice to see Dad more regularly vertical
even though he has to wear
that huge white uncomfortable back brace
to hold him up.
Pipstar is tapping the table,
looking out at the daylight saving's sun
setting over his irritated face.
You can tell he's joined the dinner by obligation.
We're all trying to be nice because it's my birthday.

'Wow,' says Dad, 'seventeen…
What a lovely young woman you've turned into.'

I cringe. Not just because it's daggy
but because we all know that lately,
the only thing I've turned into
is a witch.

We're having Chinese takeaway,
specially delivered all the way from Kilmore to us, cold.
It's the only takeaway in the district
apart from fish and chips
and pies
and I'd be happy to never eat
sweet and sour pork again in my life.

I'm playing along because I feel sorry for Dad,
who's trying to do his best under the circumstances
and who lately seems a little pathetic.
His backbone is slowly mending
but the family backbone has slipped a disc.

'What's this?' says Dad,
composing with an unlit match in his hand.
'AC/DC,' says Pip.
'Who?'
'Schubert.'
'No!'
He's about to light the six candles on the pink-iced cake
(the novelty of the pink-iced buns wore off a year ago).
'It's Elgar's Cello Concerto', he says,
composing a little more to our deaf ears.
'Give it up, Dad,' says Pip, 'we're over the guessing game.'
Just as he strikes the match, the phone rings –
'I'll get it,' I say.

'Happy birthday, darling! Wow – seventeen.'
'Yeah.'
'Sweet seventeen. I remember my seventeenth birthday so well.'
'Mm,' I say, hoping not to remember this one.
I twirl the curly phone cord around my arm.

'I bet you've got a line-up of gentlemen callers to choose from?'
'What?'
'Anyone special?'
I'm thinking it might be best to get back to that old pink-iced cake
but I'd like to tell someone, anyone, what I'm feeling.
'I'm scared I might not pass HSC.'
'Oh, don't worry about that, darling.'
'I *am* worrying about that.'
'You can get through life all right without it. Look at your mother!
I'm just so proud of you for even trying.'
'But it's different these days. And if I don't pass HSC,' I say,
through the crackly line that may cut out any time…
'You've got your whole life ahead of you! You're still so young.'
(Did she forget I just turned seventeen?)
'You'll see when you get to my age that either way,
it won't mean a thing. Anyway, darling, guess what?'
I'm silent, picking forensic evidence out of the poo-brown carpet.
I'm not in the mood for guessing games or
pin the tail on the donkey.
'Remember I told you I had a surprise? This will cheer you up.
I was waiting until it was all confirmed.' She pauses…
'At last…we can come home.'

I can hear the emotion of it all in her breaking voice
as though she'd been walking on a tight rope since she left
and is almost safely at the other end of the rope.
And I've been imagining this moment for so very long
but maybe today is bad timing?
Some kind of protective numbness blankets me from
experiencing this reality.
'Darling?' she asks carefully.
'Really? Wow. Great,' I say,
with Jess's voice in the back of my head: 'Too late?'

'And darling? I've had tailored the most beautiful dress for you.
Will you do me the honour of being my bridesmaid?'
I throw my collection of forensics back onto the carpet.
'Bridesmaid?'

I pull the phone cord tighter around my wrist
until it makes a mark in my skin.
'Wow,' I say, 'that's a surprise,' with no surprise in my voice at all.
I dangle the phone from my wrist. It's heavy.
She seems concerned with the dullness of my voice
because the line goes very quiet except for the crackle.
'Darling? Is everything all right?'
'Yeah. Sorry, so tired after all the exam stress.'
'Of course, you must be exhausted. Can you go and see a movie?'
'There's no cinema in Kilmore, I told you.'
'I bet with all that study, you've been inside a lot.
It's not good to be inside too much. You can get a bit self-reflective.
Could you ask Christine to take you all out on a picnic?'
I slowly unwind the phone cord and tie up my reality.

'Mum, it's so great you're coming back,' I say, practising my acting.
'I just need to get back to the birthday dinner now and then
get ready for the audition. Gotta learn my lines!'
'Oh, of course darling, of course,' she says, vocally hurt.
I want to save her, hug her, start all over again
but I've run out of oxygen.
'Which piece did you end up choosing?'
I don't answer in case she thinks *My Brilliant Career*
doesn't suit me.
'I really wish I could be there for you,' she says.
Why does she always say that?
'Darling, we arrive back the week after your audition,
and I'm going to drive straight up to see you.
And I'll bring the dress for you to try on.
I *know* you're going to love it.'
'Great,' I say, like a robot on antidepressants.
'I can try on the dress and then we can all go on a picnic.'
'I love you, darling,' she starts to say, her voice breaking again.
She knows. She knows everything. We all do.
'Love you dar–'
I hang up the phone as though the connection accidentally cut out
except this time I got in first.

3

No breeze.
Everyone's doing their own thing with a quiet intensity
like they're reaching boiling point.
Which it is. Boiling. Around 37 degrees.

Bigstep's won the music war
and is playing a Clapton song about promises,
like yeah, '…till death us do part.'

A car comes up the drive
disturbing the hovering waves of volcanic energy in Doglolly House.
A long loud 'COOEEEeeee.'
It's Jess. I rush out.
'*Luce!*' She hugs me,
the same all-encompassing way as her mother does.
'Who brought you?'
She dangles the car keys. 'I'm *free*!'
Haven't done HSC but sure as hell got my *licence*!'
We scream.
'Come for a spin? I'm only up for the day.
Stacey lent me her car for a maximum one hour.'

It takes a few minutes to convince Dad
of the safety of the excursion
by promising to stick to the gravel road
behind our neighbours' property.

She's a bit clunky on the brakes of the old brown Datsun
and doesn't drive as fast as Dad
but she's not too bad –
with a cigarette in one hand and Jimmy Cliff's version of
'Wild World' on the cassette player.

Our hair is flapping around in the wind.
I yell over the chorus, 'You've got such an amazing voice.
It's so great you're going to do something with it.'

'I'm already doing something with it. I'm singing,'
she says and continues the song,
and when it ends,
she smiles like you could get by on one.

It's a stunning day,
blue sky forever
over beige fields full of
really relaxed cattle.

She doesn't drive where Dad suggested
but we do turn off onto an old dirt track.
The dust is so thick behind us that
you can't see where we came from.
She has one elbow out the window
like the way her dad drives his ute.
We start with the good news…
'I saw a great new movie,' she says. '*Puberty Blues*.'
'Oh, I wanted to see that when we were in town but I wasn't allowed.'
'Not allowed? Why? It's just us at the beach.'

I'm about to tell her that Mum's coming back when
suddenly
there's a loud smash. We can't see a thing.
I think we've been shot but it doesn't hurt.
She breaks hard. Nearly gives us whiplash.
'What the…?'
She stops the music and we take stock.
'Damn!' she says, banging the side door.
'Stone must've hit the windscreen. Stace will *kill* me.'

We sit there in shock.
The sun reflects through the millions of pieces of shattered glass
as the dust slowly settles behind us.

'Can't see, can't drive,' she says. 'Cigarette?'
I like her attitude.

We listen to the crackling sounds of the glass separating
and the car cooling down and the music of the insects
rising up from the bush as we drag on our cigarettes.

'Can you believe he was married?'
'Yeah, I thought he was.'
'Well, it's not like he mentioned it.'
'Maybe he didn't get the need.'
'Happily fucken' married.'

Outside my window a somewhat camouflaged palomino horse
curiously approaches the fence.
'I think I'm going to fail HSC. I totally needed a top art mark.'
'Who cares – just audition – actors don't need degrees.
You're still gonna boost the Australian film industry.'
'No,' I say, feeling dizzy. 'I'm not gonna bloody boost anything,'
'C'mon,' she says, 'if anyone's gonna boost anything, it's you.'
'No, you've got the wrong idea about me.
I'm no one. I'm nothing.'

It hurts talking about yourself like that. Especially if you believe it.
She leans over. 'Shut up, Luce,' she says.
'You're someone and something to me.
Stop turning everything in on yourself.'

It's good to cry with someone.

After a minute, she grabs her bag,
tips it upside-down on her lap,
rummages for tissues and then crazily offers me
Throaties, Tic Tacs, keys, diary, wallet, a silver bangle,
Redhead matches, a stray cigarette, Revlon lipstick, blue eyeliner,
musk oil perfume, Impulse deodorant Sensual Nights…
'Whatever you want. Take it,' she says. 'What's mine is yours.'
'Can I come and live with you next year?' I ask.
'Course.'

Through her side window I see a broken windmill,
which some cows are using for shade.

'Anyway,' she says, inhaling the smoke deeply,
'we're in the same boat.
After two weeks of not returning my calls I went over there
and found him with another girl.'
'In bed?'
'No, singing.'
'Oh,' I say.
'Might've handled it better if they were in bed.
He called later and said that she wasn't a better singer than me.
It's just that she didn't want a relationship,
so it was much less complicated.
But that wasn't much less complicated for me.'
She flicks the cigarette more times than she needs to.

'Fuck it. Who cares? Who needs 'em? Frankly.'
'Yeah, Dad always says, "Plenny of fish in the sea."'
(Dumb thing to say to a broken heart.)
'Pa says, "Plenny of time to milk all the cows,"' she says.
'Dad says, "All cats are black in the dark."'
'What?' she says, and we start to laugh
with tears running down our faces.
Strange how you can laugh right after a cry.
But then I realise it's Jess who is crying.
'He didn't deserve you,' I say.
'It's not that,' she says. 'It's Mum. She's got cancer.'

The news lands like a boulder on the already cracked-up car.
'Oh, God,' I say. 'That's terrible. So unfair.'
'I know,' she says. 'She never did anything wrong in her whole life.
All she wanted was to see us girls married and happy.'
I reach over and hug her a while until she pulls back
and looks at me seriously and says,
'Maybe you wanna get to know your mum.'

'Now,' she says, 'that we got all that stuff sorted out,'
which is funny, because we didn't,
'what the fuck are we gonna do about the car?'

The palomino snorts like it's Mr Ed offering us a lift
and so we laugh some more and she says,
'You gotta laugh,' and that is even more funny.

Eventually I say, 'Okay, you're going to stay with the car,
and I'm going to walk to the nearest farm house
and get them to call for help.'
I get out of the car, start walking, then come back to her window
just to check she's all right.
'Get outa my face, Bignose!' she says.
I tell her I love her too.

Cows look up as I walk past,
then go back to their munching.
It's weird the way the world just gets on with things
right after a drama.

Further down the road,
I hear the volume turned up on 'Wild World' again.
She sings along loudly,
Shit happens. But Jess makes it seem okay.

4

I'm finally on the Red Rattler
kerchunker-chunking down to Spencer Street.
All my lines are loud in my head
and sometimes fall out in a whisper.
'Weariness! Weariness!'
This is my big chance.
I don't know what I'll do if I don't get in.
I'll just die.
'I'm sure it's not any wish of mine that I'm born with inclinations for
better things.'

All the butterflies have left the fields
and dived into my stomach.

The heat sits in my carriage
like water
up to my neck.
Even with half the windows open, it's 'a stinker'.

'Summer is fiendish and life is a curse…'

We fly past Jess's farm.
I remember the first night I stayed there,
all cow-milkingly innocent
and so relieved to have found an oasis in the desert.
I think of her parents, a little stunned now
in their empty nest, watching *Young Talent Time*
with an abundance of home-baked biscuits.

'Day after day the drought continued…
wind…carried the dry grass off the paddocks and piled it against the fences…'

We fly through the farms of Wallan and Donnybrook,
then slow down through Craigieburn, and Coolaroo,
where women in their backyards hang washing on Hills hoists,
toddlers wander at their feet and dogs jump and bark at the passing train
then into Broadmeadows where houses get smaller and closer together
and then we're parallel to Fawner Cemetery.
'Ya gotta make the most o' life, don't ya think?'

This is it. Today's the day.

'This was life – my life – my career, my brilliant career!'

Angela's waiting at Spencer Street Station.
We get into her blue BMW and drive to the College of the Arts.
Nice of her to pick me up but I wished I'd been allowed a taxi.
I politely answer her small talk, though I'd rather eat glass.
I just want to focus.
You can tell she's got no idea what an audition involves.
It's hard to breathe because of the nerves
but also because of the strong scent of her perfume.

I wish Mum was 'in the wings'.
She'd say all the right pre-performance things
about breathing and stuff.

In the corridor where contenders wait anxiously
or warm up strangely
I view my competition:
a little older, taller, more beautiful,
and a lot more confident it seems to me.
Wearing some 'out there' outfits with original looks
like they fully decided who they were
by the time they were eleven.

Just before the audition begins
I'm shaking, sweating and heart-pumpingly nervous.
'Breathe,' I hear Mum say to me, 'breathe, one two three in…'
This is it. Give it your total absolute best. Come onnnnnn.

I start the monologue
and find I can really feel
the weariness
like a heaviness overwhelming me
and squashing me into the ground.
Just keep going, I'm thinking, it's good, it's good…
then I freak out that if I'm thinking about how it's going,
can it be going how it should?

'Hope, sweet, cruel, delusive Hope, whispered in my ear that life was
long with much by and by, and in that by and by my dream-life would
be real.'

I notice one of the judges leaning across to whisper to another.
Why?
I take a deep breath for the last lines,
and hold my head high looking beyond them
as though on the bow of a ship where I'm
heading towards my great expectations…

'So on I went with that gleaming lake in the distance beckoning me to come and sail on its silver waters, and Inexperience, conceited, blind Inexperience, failing to show the impassable pit between it and me.'

'Thank you, Lucinda,' says the same judge
who asked me to introduce myself at the start.
'All those accepted will be contacted by phone
between nine a.m. and noon on December 14.
Non-acceptance notices will be mailed by post soon after.
We wish you all the best.'

Are they that formal and distant with everyone?

Getting back into the BMW
with the perfume kind of staler,
I block out her please-like-me cheery-chit-chat,
as much as I can
and go over it all in my head.
I didn't forget any lines.
I did that section okay where I get down on my knees and pray.
Yes, it went well, I think, as well as can be expected.
I have to feel pleased.
Why don't I feel pleased?
Did they hate it?
Me?
I hated it.

5

Back at the ranch
on eggshells.
My nerves are smashed after the audition.
And I'm exhausted after the exams and the whole HSC year.
How am I going to be able to wait for that phone call?
Everyone else is on eggshells too,
for their own fragile reasons.

'How'd you go?' asked Dad.

'Okay. I don't know.'
'What do you mean?' said Bigstep.
'I mean I don't know,' I said firmly.
I'm so sick of people not getting what I mean.

Dad's getting more and more movement back
and therefore more impatience because he's got more energy
but less flexibility than he had before and he's still not working.
Bigstep's fuming about the nurse
and about having to do stuff for Dad when
I think they'd rather have nothing to do with each other any more.

Now that school is finished, Pip is stir crazy with boredom,
except when Hayzo comes over.
When he arrived this morning they ran down to the creek
shrieking with their backpacks of secrets
bouncing up and down behind them.

I'm up on the roof with my College of the Arts brochure,
reading it for the 200th time, highlighting bits that
I didn't highlight before.
Imagining what it's like there, where people respect you for
who you are
and want to help you shine.

I'm about to write in my journal
when I hear an almighty bang
like a gunshot
or something
way off in the distance.

I see Pip and Hayzo, running fast up the hill
over hungry crunchy grass.
Then I see it.
Smoke.
A trail of it, growing taller, wider.
I scramble down, almost jump off the roof,
nearly break my leg and go inside screaming,

'Call the fire brigade!' I'm gesturing outside. 'There's a fire!'

All hell breaks loose. Bigstep goes mad, calling the crazy neighbours to warn them and to get help with protecting the horses.

Dad gets Pip and Hayzo to hose the whole house
and the roof
where I left my brochure and journal.
I run down to open the gates for
Sails and Shimmering Fire and Pirate and the others.

The screaming sirens arrive
in convoy at the livestock entrance.
Three trucks, gleaming red,
out of place in the pale yellow paddocks.
The smoke is huge
and dark
and moving
up the hill.
Voices carry across the farm
as everyone tries to calm
the dragon eating the grass,
consuming it fast,
starving, like it's the last supper.
Trees fall down.
The hay shed explodes.
The fire is climbing towards us.
I feel a strange mixture of
horror
and peace
to witness a kind of hell
that has nothing to do
with the drama inside of me.
To be out of control
for once
is a weird relief.

6

We're standing on the patio
viewing the blackened paddocks
which smell as cooked as they look.
After yesterday's chaos
it all seems strangely quiet and still.
Eerie.

Everyone's upset. None of us slept,
all hyped up from the fire and worried about embers.
We were lucky the firemen stopped it reaching the house
but it feels like there's a fire inside
still burning.

Dad is scanning the paddocks. He seems more depressed
than the day before his operation. Shaking his head, he says,
'I told you to keep an eye on Phillip.'
'What?' I say. 'This is my fault now, is it?'
'I didn't say it was your fault but you're older than him.
You knew they were smoking.'
'But I tried to tell them,' I say,
defending myself, and them – but possibly not the truth.
If the firemen, the police and Dad knew
what I suspect – that it was not a cigarette
but some kind of 'Molotov cocktail' –
we'd probably all go to prison.

'It crossed the railway line and
came awfully close to the pine plantation.
Do you know how much that would cost to replace?'
I shake my head, feeling sick.
He continues, 'It's lucky no houses, no lives were lost.
Miles of fencing,' he says, forgetting we're metric now and
sitting down with some difficulty on the faded deckchair.
I stay quiet, all mixed up with a sense of injustice and guilt.
Could I have prevented this?

'Nothing left of the hay shed we filled last week.'

I don't need this information. I know we filled it.
I was there catching hay bales
with scratched arms and half a silo of dust up my nose.
'Half the saddle shed and contents up in smoke.
It's only lucky our neighbours were available, willing
and brilliant with helping to save the horses.
And that the fire brigade were able to protect the house.'
He shoos away a fly that wants to get to the source of the story.
'Bad reputation, that Hayes family.
The boy's already on six month's community service.
Imagine having a record at that age?
Bad influence, that kid. You should've told me.'
'Is this my fault?'
'No, but I wish you'd told me.'

He picks up the binoculars again,
takes his time scanning the paddocks.
'What a tragedy,' he says, shaking his head, like someone died.
Like something died inside him.
'All those beautiful trees.'

Bigstep comes out on the front lawn
with a crate full of Pip's plastic army soldiers and stuff
which she drops at my feet.
'That's for the tip.'
Dad starts to walk towards the house.
You can tell they can't even share the same fresh air lately.

'Where were you when you saw the smoke?' she asks.
'I was rehearsing lines.'
'Not *what* were you doing? I said *where* were you?'
'Why?'
She rolls her eyes. Dad pauses near the door, listening.
'Hey,' I say, 'I've been trying to keep an eye on him
since we got here. How come I have to keep an eye on him?
Why's that my job? In case you hadn't noticed,
I didn't bring him into this world.
I'm only four years older than Phillip, so that'd be impossible.

Yeah, breaking news. He isn't my child. I'm not his parent.
Where the fuck were you?'

'Don't you dare speak to me like that.
Maybe you speak to your mother like that but not to me,'
and she kicks the crate so the soldiers march across the grass.
'Hey,' says Dad. 'Enough swearing, Lucinda.
Tone it down immediately. Now come inside,' he says,
'and let's all calm down. It's been a hell of a night.'

Dad enters the house, calls out, 'Where's Phillip?'
Then tells me, 'Go and get him, Lucinda.'

He's on the floor in his bedroom,
surrounded by dirty clothes. Fuming.
'Dad wants you.'
'Dad and Bigstep confiscated half my stuff.'
'I know.'
'I'm on so-called good behaviour bond for six months,
which basically means I have to be their slave.
She's not my fucken' mother,' he says, copying my line.
I nod, torn between telling him I told you so
and taking his side
because I'm utterly over Bigstep and Dad.

'I'm not allowed to see Hayzo again – like that's it, never.'
'Well,' I say, 'maybe that's not such a terrible thing.
You have to admit he was trouble.
I mean this is totally bad enough
but it could have been a major fucken' disaster.'
'Yeah, well, ya know what?' he says,
desperately trying to defend himself and
fighting back the tears,
'It's been the most excitement
I've had around here in three years.'

I sit on the floor beside him
and his horrible feeling of being out of control.
Controlled. Isolated.

It's been a while since I saw us sitting
in the same sinking boat together.
I reach my arm around his shoulder but he pushes it away.

'Not fair,' I say, which surprises him, you can tell,
because he looks up at me like 'Hello…
is someone around here actually on my team?'
'It's fucked,' I say, kind of relieved to not be alone in the boat.
'It's totally fucked,' he says. 'I can't stand it any more.'
'I know,' I say.
'I'm gonna live with Mum,' he says. 'Fuck the courts.
I never wanted to come here in the first place.'
'I know,' I say, noticing a metal pipe sticking out from under his bed.
It looks familiar, like some kind of motorbike tool.
'As soon as she gets back…'

'What's that?' I say, pointing.
'What?' he says, moving swiftly, sounding shifty.
'That.'
I lean down to reach for it and he grabs at it,
tries to hold it under the bed.
We wrestle till I confirm what I thought.
'What the fuck are you doing with that?'
'Dad confiscated my stuff so I've confiscated his.'
'Jesus,' I say, a bit horrified. 'Does he know it's missing?'
'Not yet. But he'll know when he gets shot.'
'What? You're a fucken' idiot!'
'Shut up, I'm not gonna shoot him, ya idiot,
I just want 'im to see how it feels when they take ya stuff.'
He wipes his nose on his sleeve.

'Is it loaded?'
He shrugs.
'You don't even know if it's loaded?'
He shrugs, 'I thoughtcha understood?' he says, reaching for it.
'Right,' I say, 'okay, I get it, but I don't like it.'
'Well,' he says, pulling it out like a prize, 'I'm not giving it back.'
I move aside. I don't want to touch it.

I've always hated the hideous thing.
Poor ducks. Poor rabbits. Poor roos.
A confiscation is good but Pip shouldn't have it –
certainly not in this kind of mood.

I get a quick idea of how I can still be on his team
but get the weapon out of his room.
'Hey,' I say, 'how 'bout I hide it for you?'
'Whaddya mean?'
'Well, I know a place where he'll never find it.'
'Where?'
'Where it's impossible for him to find it.'
'Where?'
'Well, how about I don't even tell you and then
if he asks you where it is, you won't have to lie.'
He thinks about this a few seconds.
'Okay…maybe… You sure he won't find it?'
'No way. He can't. He physically can't.
I'll come and get it tonight when they're asleep.'
'Okay,' he says, nodding suspiciously. 'All right.'
'Okay, so leave it right under there. Don't touch it.'
'All right,' he says, putting it back under the bed
with a bit more caution. 'You're not giving it back?'
'No way.'
'Okay.'
'C'mon. Dad wants us.'
We get up, start to head out.
'Hey, Luce,' he says.
'Yeah?'
'Nothing. Thanks.'

7

A few days after the fire's out, there's a different kind of
simmering going on inside Doglolly House.
We've thoroughly inspected the damage.

It's bad
but it could've been worse.
We lost two cows that I could hardly look at.
I had nightmares about them.
Plus some rabbits, trees, the hay shed, the saddle shed,
lots of stuff
but thank the Rural Gods, no houses, no horses, no people.

My HSC results should be in the post box
but everyone's been preoccupied
with the tidy up after the fire.
Vic College are due to call with the audition results
tomorrow morning!

Bigstep comes past on her way to the laundry
with a huge pile of sooty washing.
'Was the letter in the post box this morning?'
'Obviously I didn't have time to get to the post box.'
'But it's my results.'
She drops the whole basket of laundry onto the floor.
Doesn't look accidental.
'Maybe you could help with this?' she says,
continuing towards the laundry without the basket.
'What's wrong?' I say, following her.
'What's wrong?' she calls from the laundry,
'What part of anything here is all right?'

I arrive at the laundry door to see her
pulling out a pile of clothes from the dryer onto the floor.
She stands up and flicks her wispy fair hair
which, like mine, hasn't been cut for months.
She looks tired. Her fingernails are short and dirty.
She used to splash on a bit of red lipstick or a bit of mascara
but these days she seems to have given up.
I remember Jess's mum said,
'The rich can look the way they want,
it's the poor that have to make an effort.'

'The fire was an accident,' I say,
taking a punt on the underlying issue and sticking up for Pip.
'Can you forgive him for getting mixed up with the wrong kid?'
She stares at me hard.
Was it us that put the gentle person she used to be
behind this shell of rigidity?
'Do you realise how much we lost?' she says, incredulously.
'Do you realise we nearly lost horses?'
'It wasn't my fault. I wasn't even there.
Why do you think everything's my fault?'
'If you really want to know what I think,'
she says, eager, it seems, for the opportunity to spill some ugly beans,
'I think you're pretty lost in your own little world of delusions…
In your own little egotistical fantasy world.'

'What?' I say, standing up, pushing the chair out
so it screeches on the floor.
'What's not real about wanting to make a mark?'
'The only mark you're gonna make
is a scratch on the floor,' she says, looking under the chair
then heading out to the lounge.
I follow her.
Dad's listening to his radio with earpieces
while trying to fix the broken record player.
'What the fuck would you know?' I throw back at her.
'All you know is horses! The dux of horses!
It's all because of the horses that we're here on this stupid farm.
In fact, this whole entire nightmare is actually your fault.'

'Oh,' she says, 'did you hear that, Richard?
At last you're here to witness her true behaviour.'
'What's going on?' says Dad, pulling out the earpieces
to hear Bigstep slam the glass door so hard
I'm surprised it doesn't shatter.
'What's up?' says Dad. 'Are you girls fighting again?'

I'm going to explode. I've got to get out. I can't stand it.
It was better when the fire was real and alive
than this burning hell inside.

'Is this what you call a *home*?' I say
and slam another door.

I walk
fast
down the char-grilled paddocks,
listening to the sound of its crunching,
tripping a bit on the uneven burnt grass.

I hear the eggshell-blue Volvo pulling out down the drive.

Occasionally I glance back to see
if anyone's following me (not)
and I notice my footprints in the blackened grass.
I'll make a mark. I'll make a mark.

Marching along
down past the dam and further
past the cattle yards then through the boundary fence
and onto the side of the road.
I keep on walking
fast,
all the way down to the underpass
under the Hume Highway and along the Broadford Epping Road
past the Wandong general store.
Wish I'd bought money for cigarettes.

Fuck it. Fuck everything. Guys, school, horses, family, love, results,
dodgy sex, stinky smokes, fat food, period pain, bus bitches,
married men, missing parents, broken homes, being alone,
pointlessness.
Everything's broken. Dad's spine. Jess's mum, Pip's friend,
marriages that don't last until the end…

It doesn't matter how fast I walk
nothing calms the turmoil –
the repetition of all the arguments, the chaos of the fire,
the visions and revisions of my audition,
the frightening non-possibilities if they don't choose me.

I walk and walk and
try and walk all the thoughts out of my head
but all I keep hearing are the scrambled lines of my audition –
'Weariness! Weariness! …the impassable pit between it and me.'
What if I don't get in? How will I get to matter?

I pass a sign: Mount Disappointment 14 km.
Maybe I'll get a better perspective
on top of a stupid mountain
with a tragic name like that.
Maybe they'll notice me more if I'm missing.

Putting myself in the hands of the Rural Gods,
I stick out my finger for hitching.
'Fuck it,' I say out loud. 'If I die, I'll be remembered.'
I'm not gonna be
no one and
nothing
forever.

Will I be remembered?
What if they don't choose me?
'…the impassable pit between it and me…'

A massive brown ute with tractor-sized tyres pulls over.
'Mount Disappointment?' I say
to the tattooed guy with the bulldoggy face.
He looks me up and down and says,
'Can only take you to the start of the state forest.'
'Whatever,' I say. 'That's plenty.'

He revs up the car to impress me, I guess.
Whatever.
I don't even put on my seat belt.
Fuck it. I'm over being careful.

'You all right?'
'Yeah,' I say. 'Got a smoke?'
He offers me a Winfield.

We pass an old fibro house with a panel van out the front.
'You sure you're all right?'
'Yeah,' I say, gritting my teeth.
I wanted a lift not a conversation.
'You meeting someone at the picnic spot?'
'Yeah,' I say.
He glimpses at me and grins.
I turn away, look out the side window.

We pass some clapped-out farmhouse
that's been abandoned.
We hurtle along, making dust and noise,
his radio is playing that idiotic song,
'Crazy Little Thing Called Love'.
Love's not a crazy little thing,
it's a big fucked-up monumental nightmare.

He's tapping along on the steering wheel
as if he was some kind of cool drummer
which he totally isn't.

They have to choose me. Don't I deserve it?
They have to see who I am.

He stops tapping, turns off the radio and says,
'Ya sure you're all right?'
Broken record.
I think of Bigstep's angry words,
'What part of anything here is all right?'
'Sure,' I say. 'Jus' running late for the picnic.'
He looks at me strangely.
'It's a bit late for a picnic, isn't it?' he says.
'Not where I come from,' I say idiotically.

Where do I come from? South Yarra? Wandong? Pluto?

'The only mark you're going to make…'

He turns into Main Mountain Road
at the start of the state forest.

'What's your friend bringing to the "picnic"?' he asks weirdly.
'Sandwiches,' I say.
'Right,' he says, nodding extra slowly, grinning
so I gather it's some kind of drug dealing place or something.
'What's ya name, anyway?'
Hell, I'm over the twenty questions.
Thankfully, I can see the sign up ahead
at the base of the mountain,
which isn't exactly a mountain in my books
but at least it's something to climb to get a look-out.
'Sybylla,' I say.
'Unusual,' he says. 'Where do you live?'
'Kilmore,' I say.
He turns the ute into Harry's Nose Road
and even though he said he wouldn't,
he drives further into the forest.
I get a wave of adrenalin
but it just mixes in with the fury.
'This'll do,' I say.
He looks at his watch, drives a bit more then pulls over.
'I'm late myself or I'd take you all the way up. All the way…'
he says grinning. 'Wanna give me ya number?'
I look at him, 'Sure,' I say, giving him a bullshit one.
What part of 'I'd rather fuck a bulldog,' doesn't he get?

I jump down from his fat rev-head truck, glad to get out,
and start speed-walking up the road,
reciting his number plate for about a minute
before I forget it.

Pretty soon I can't see anything but trees.
Massive tall gums blocking the light.
There's a sign that reads,
Blairs Hut Picnic Area 3.2 km.
I figure that must be the top.
Not that far.

Will they choose me?

Did they see my potential?
Was my audition exceptional?

I see two crows squabbling
over something dead by the road
then I get the fright of my life when a
wombat comes out of the dark bushes.
God there's some weird animals on this planet.

After a while
walking up and up,
I can't keep the same speedy pace
though I keep trying.

I'll make a mark. I'll make a mark.
I'll be someone and something.
Somebody who matters.
Someone who's missed.
Some horrible inner voice echoes back:
You're not going to pass.
You won't be accepted.
You're a hopeless loser.
You're nobody and nothing.

I send the judges the millionth telepathic message:
Choooooose Lucinda Smeeeeeaton.

I won't be no one and nothing forever.

The trees are full of screeching birds
arguing with the Gods
not to take away their daylight.
It's much cooler in here.
Lucky I'm warm from walking.

I should have bought something to smoke.
Or drink. Or eat.

I have a falling feeling;
what the hell are you doing
alone in a state forest?

Then something propels me to
keep on heading upwards.

I can feel my heart beating from walking
but also with rising anxiety.
I don't really want to be walking back in the dark.
I take a step down the hill
which feels right
but all wrong.
Fuck it. Let the Gods decide.
I deserve to get to the top.
I deserve to get the big picture, so to speak.
I walk defiantly upwards.

Behind me I hear
the low roar of a motorbike.
As it comes closer and louder,
it sounds like more than one.
Three Harley Davidson bikes zoom past,
ridden by spreadeagled men in black leather
with skull pictures and writing on their backs.
The way they sit makes them look
like they could circumnavigate the world in the air.

If they're riding up the mountain,
then they're probably going to have to
come back down.

Maybe this wasn't such a good idea.

I speed up my walk,
irrationally,
like I'm going to be late for the picnic.
What if it is a drug dealing hang-out?
Maybe I should just head back down?
Stuff the perspective.
Things are bad at home but
do I really need a picnic in hell with the Angels?

I pause a moment,
listening to the sound of the bikes fading
and the birds starting up
and the feeling of never reaching where I'm trying to get to.
I look up at the bits of sky between the treetops.
The passing clouds make me feel dizzy.
I'm exhausted.
Some part of me
wants to curl up
in the forest somewhere
and slowly turn into a fossil.
But how could you do it?
Just lie down and die?
It'd be like trying to drown yourself
by staying under water.
How could you not come up for a breath?

It can't be dusk already.
Maybe it's just the trees stealing the light.

I hear the bikes coming back.
Slower.
My heart starts thumping.
Should I walk faster? Run off into the bush?
Turn around and head down?
Before I've worked this out,
the bikes slow right down in front of me.
Oh God. Is this it?
Is this how I'm going to die?
Are they going to choose me?

They've slowed down enough to be
walking their feet alongside their bikes
to keep their gleaming machines vertical.

My heart is beating worse than in the audition.

They stop in front of me, blocking my way.
'Hey, love, what's ya name?'

'What?' I say.
They turn off their bikes,
which settle down with ticks and cracks like
monumentally exhausted creatures.
Know the feeling.
The lack of noise quickly makes the forest feel
vast and filled with a million invisible creatures.

Christ. What have I got myself into?

'What's ya name?' says the man wearing a black vest
with bare tattooed arms and a scar under his eye.
'Sybylla,' I say.
'Ya lost?' says the guy with the long beard on the biggest bike.
'Nuh,' I say.
I have nothing in my pockets. No defences.
'Did ya lose something?'
Yeah, I think, feels like everything almost. 'Nup.'
'You been up here before?'
'Nuh,' I say, roughly, trying to sound like a local.
'Never been to the top?'
I shake my head.
They wink and nod at each other.

I feel like saying, 'What do you want?'
but I totally don't want to know what they want.
'Whatya doing here, sweetheart?
It's getting late in the afternoon,'
says the third man. He has a ponytail
snaking out from under his black bandanna.
'Just walking. Exercise,' I say.
They look at each other.
'Where do you live?'
Never tell strangers where you live.
'Broadford,' I say, then remember that's where their base is.
I take a step forward, trying to indicate I'm over the chatting.
'Need an escort outa here?' says Scarface, smiling.
A shot of fear goes through me.

Escort? Nice word for the devil's ride into the next life.
What to do?

'C'mon,' says the Beardo. 'We'll give you a lift.'
'No thanks,' I say, finding it hard to speak.
'We're not gonna eatcha, darlin',' says Bandanna Man,
grinning like a cannibal.
Do their rituals involve eating things?
'I know,' I say, trying to smile, and start walking
around the obstacle of their bikes.
The upwards direction
feels insane now.
Where am I heading?

'Hey, sweetheart,' says Bandanna Man
as I walk around his bike,
'take the lift or you won't get outa here in daylight.'

What to do?
Scream for help? Who'd hear?
Run? How fast?
Hide? Where?
Pray? To whom?
How am I going to get home?
Do I want to get home?
Is home better than spending a night in the forest?

'C'mon, hop on,' says Beardo.
'She's all freaked out,' says Bandanna Man.
Scarface laughs, which proves to me
how sadistic he really must be.
'Hop on!' says Beardo.

Then I realise all the thinking is pointless.
Three against one.
If they want to do something unspeakable to me
there's no way I can stop them.

They're all staring.

I'll matter if I get murdered.
That's one way to be remembered.

'Come on, get on! Do we have ta lift ya?'
I get on the back of Beardo's bike.
There's a logo on his jacket that reads,
'Do right and no one remembers
Do wrong and no one forgets'.

I hold onto the sides of his leather jacket, wide.
He smells like a hamburger.
They start up their hungry bikes
then Scarface gestures with his thumb
up the mountain.
My stomach sinks.
They turn their bikes around too fast
for me to get off.

I shut my eyes and hang on.
There's so much power in the engines,
it feels like we've left the earth.

If I disappear now, so young,
such a nobody,
will it be like I never existed?

I'm more scared than I've ever been in my life
and at the same time
surrendered to the fact that I'm totally out of control.
It's a weird combination.

I want to be remembered
but does it have to hurt?
I console myself – once I'm dead
I won't remember anything.
Please, Gods, don't let it take too long.

We're flying along.

What if I passed?

What if I got accepted.
The phone could ring tomorrow morning
with the whole house calling LUCINDA!

She had so much potential, said the priest.

When they stop
I open my eyes to see the sign:
Blairs Hut Picnic Area.
They balance their bikes and Beardo walks ahead first.
'C'mon, love. Follow us,' says Scarface.
I pause a moment.
Couldn't they just do it out here in the open?
'I thought you were taking me home.'
'Trust me, this is a kind of home,' he says.
I feel sick. 'Where are we going?'
'Where's everybody going?' says Bandanna.
Scarface laughs, puts an arm around my shoulder,
guides me forward.
'C'mon, love.'

He leads me to a worn track
with Scarface walking behind me.
I could still run
but where?
My knees are weak.
The other two are in front.
Oh God, oh God.
Mum and Dad will be devastated.
Pipstar. Jess.
I should've left a note, like Mum always said.
Will they find my journal on the roof?
And Dad's gun? I wish I had brought Dad's gun.
Will they find me? In pieces?

Scarface and Bandanna arrive either side of me.
'Now for a surprise.'
They tie Bandanna's scarf over my eyes.

I'm shaking uncontrollably.
'One, two, three,' they say and
suddenly
lift me from under my arms.
I struggle,
they're strong,
they pull me along.
I squeeze shut my eyes,
feel them lifting me high...
Are they throwing me over the edge?

I land, feet first
on something high and
I feel them let go of my arms.
'Okay. Take the scarf off,' says Beardo.

I see that we've come out
into a small clearing.
See that I'm on top of a stone platform.
Am I a sacrifice?
They surround me below,
look up at me.
'Now turn around.'
I'm frozen.
'Turn around!' says Bandanna Man, pointing behind me.
The others laugh.
'That way.'

Is this some kind of
freaky routine
before they get on with
doing stuff
and then cutting me into pieces?

Slowly,
I turn around.
The three men are now behind me.
I look up.

I stand stunned
for a moment.
They stand still too,
all expectant.
And there it is. The entire city of Melbourne,
painted in rose-gold afternoon sunlight
in the fairy tale distance.

'Pretty fucken' spectacular, isn't it?'
'Hey,' says Bandanna Man,
'you've totally freaked her out.'
'Oh c'mon, love, siddown,' says Beardo.
I weakly sit down on the stone plinth,
with my legs dangling over the edge of it.

'What's ya name again, love?'
I can't speak.
'Cinderella,' says Scarface.
'Nah, Sybylla,' says Beardo.
'Well, there you go, Silly, whatcha think?'

All I can do is nod.

'See that?' says Bandanna Man,
pointing at the bronze plaque
stuck on the stone, under my knees.
'This is where the explorers came.'
He moves closer to read it.
'"Hume and Hovell" –
they thought they were gonna see Port Phillip Bay
but when they got to the top here,
there were so many trees,
they couldn't see nothin' at all
which is why they called it Mount fucken' Disappointment.'

The tears come
streaming down my face.

'Hell, it's not that disappointing?'
'No,' I say, half laughing, half crying.

Bandanna points to his scarf. 'Blow ya nose with that, love.'
Scarface says,
'It doesn't look disappointin' but it fucken' is
if youse are expectin' somethin' else.'

'You're all right aren't ya, darlin'? We was jus teasin'.'
'Yeah,' I say, 'I think so.'
'She's all right,' he says, 'it's all a bit overwhelmin'.'
I nod. Shaking. Blowing my nose on his scarf.

'You're from the city, aren't ya, love? Toorak?'
I nod. Near enough.
'You can tell,' says Scarface.
How can he tell? I just spent three years
changing myself into somebody from Broadford.
'You know what "Toorak" means in Aboriginal?' he says.
We all shrug. I shake my head.
'It means swamp. It was a fucken' mud pit.
So…mud-pit chicklet, you're a long way from home.'

Beardo starts singing a version of Dylan's song,
'One More Cup of Coffee'.
'Ah, shut up, Mack,' says Scarface. 'He can't sing to save himself.'
'Nor can Dylan,' I say in a haze.
Scarface laughs.
'What'd she say?' asks Beardo.
'Nor can Dylan.'
They laugh. I do too.
My terror and tears and fury and weariness
all merge into laughter.
Scarface exaggerates his laugh into a mad hyena.
Bandanna Man joins in
and then we're all inventing crazy laughs
and screaming and yelling and laughing and
scaring the birds and wombats and kookaburras
louder and louder
echoing across the mountain
like psychos freed from their 'cuckoo's nest'.

'Ahh,' says Beardo, 'haven't had a good laugh in ages.'
'Me neither,' says Bandanna.
'Me either,' says me, wiping my eyes with his scarf.

Bandanna Man pulls out a bottle of beer
from a bag strapped across his shoulder
and also a Violet Crumble
and he passes both around.

'So, you staying in Broadford?'
'No,' I say, 'I was just bullshitting
because I thought you were going to kill me.'
'Do we look like we're gonna kill ya?'
'Um, yep.'
They laugh.

Beardo lights up a smoke, and passes the pack
and we all sit, smoking in contemplation
as the light dissolves into the trees
and the sunsetting breeze wraps around
me and my Angels
on Mount Disappointment.

'Well,' says Beardo,
'can we give you a lift to where you're stayin'
or do you still think we're gonna eatcha?'
'Yeah,' I say to both questions.
'I live in the big shit-brown house on the hill
along the road from Wandong to Kilmore.'
'Oh, yeah,' says Scarface,
'that used to be owned by the mayor of Melbourne.
Remember? The house that got robbed and they questioned us?'
'Oh yeah. Isn't it haunted?'
'Yeah,' I say, 'maybe it is.'

As we walk back to the bikes,
we all join in singing Dylan's song, much worse than him.

Flying down the mountain,
my arms feel bare against the wind,
my hair flaps all over my face.
It's not like being on a horse,
it's meaner
but just as alive.
Scary alive.
Just the way you'd want to feel if you were about to die.
I want the ride to go on forever.

It's dark
when they slow down and pull over where I point to stop at
the livestock gates to our farm.
'Okay, Silly, if you don't want door to door service, this is it.'
'Thanks,' I yell over the bikes
still roaring.
I get off slowly,
savouring the last moments.

Bandanna holds his gloved hand up for a high five.
I go and smack it.
I offer the damp scarf but he shakes his head and winks.
Scarface holds two gloved hands up doing peace signs,
which he turns back and forth, twice.
I copy.
Beardo beckons me back to his bike.
You can hardly hear anything over the engines.
I yell out, 'Thanks – I won't ever forget this.'
He opens his arms out wide for a hug.
I move towards him,
he pulls me in fast,
slaps my back
like a great mate
and yells in my ear,
'You're all right, Silly. Don't you forget it.'
Then they hurl their mean machines off
into the future.

I climb the gate,
walk up the hill
with shaky knees,
amazed at my existence.

Maybe the Rural Gods don't hate me at all?

Back inside
I don't care if Bigstep hates me
or if Dad's furious I've been missing
or even if Pip's set fire to his bedroom
but what I find is
nobody knows I've been gone.
If I had been killed
it would've taken forever to find all my pieces.

I walk to the door of the TV room.
The house feels like a phoenix got burnt and buried.
All three are being quietly reassured watching
other people's disasters.
Without looking up, Bigstep says,
'There's leftovers in the oven.'
'Okay,' I say, 'great, thanks,'
and I give a double thumbs up to nobody.
'Nighty-night,' I say. 'Sweet dreams.'

8

The white hot sun is high in the midday sky.
I have no shadow.
The tiles are radiating so much heat
that I have to leave my shoes on.
Who cares if they hear me?

The acceptance results were going to be phoned in
between nine a.m. and twelve today.
I made sure no one used the phone
but now it's 12.25.

The phone has not rung.
At all.

It's a north wind that can't decide on
any particular direction.
Empty Ness is still stuck.
I try to turn her
like a chiropractor might turn a cricked neck
but her whole metal head comes off in my hands.
I lay her at my feet,
beside Dad's hidden shotgun.

When I stand up
the whole farm spins around
as though I was seeing it
from Empty Ness's perspective.
I haven't eaten all morning.
I've hardly eaten all week.
Usually I eat too much
but this close to the edge
I can't eat anything.

Mum's on her way here in a hire car
with the bridesmaid dress
and the picnic.
I chose today for her to come
so we could celebrate
the drama school offer
as well as her coming home.

I still haven't got my HSC results.
They'll be sitting in our post box at Kilmore
but Bigstep forgot when she went into town
and anyway,
maybe some part of me
didn't want to see them.

Pirate's been released on the front lawn
to escape the burnt paddocks and second-rate hay
and he's greedily munching the unmown grass,
though even this grass isn't green any more…
One, two, three bites then a step
then one, two bites then a step
then one, two, three bites again.
Munch, munch, munch, step, munch, munch, step…
The sound and weird rhythm is driving me crazy.
Combine that with Pip
who's hitting that god-awful ball against the wall again,
near where I climb to the roof and where I
have a feeling he saw me.
Whatever.

Munch, munch, step. Bounce, bounce, bounce.

12.45.

A fat black crow
writes a disgusted cry
across the sky
like the world had its chance to be great
but stupidly missed it.

I hear Dad and Bigstep's voices
rising up through the chimney.
'Of course she wasn't accepted.
Anyone could see she's been
barking up the wrong tree from the start.'
'She just needed us to believe in her.'
'Oh, give me a break.'

I stare across our property into the distance.
Something deep inside me
sinks
like cement falling
to the bottom of the ocean.

It occurs to me
that I've been climbing
Mount Disappointment
since we arrived.

I pick up the drama school brochure,
covered in coloured highlights, under-linings
and crinkly from getting wet.
I hold it over the chimney
and click my blue lighter under it
until I can't hold it any more
and it falls below to the empty fireplace.

'I'm not keeping it quiet Richard.
I'm sure your kids will be happy to hear
we're getting divorced.'

I wonder if they would notice me
if I fell down the chimney?
If I landed like good ol' fake Father Christmas?

I look up.
The sky is frighteningly empty and deep,
like nothing
could prevent the sun from falling out of it.

I watch a car drive along the road,
checking to see if it's hired.
It doesn't crunch up the drive.

'You'll have to sell the rest of the horses.
I'm putting the farm on the market.'

(For sale?)

'I'm not selling *all* the horses. This isn't the only place to keep horses.'
'Actually,' says Dad, 'they're not all yours to keep.'

I pick up my journal. It's pretty tattered now.
It got saturated during the fire-prevention hosing.

What's the point of a record of me anyway?
Who cares what I thought yesterday?
Even I don't.
I hold the lighter under the front corner,
near where it says, 'What if we fail?…'
It doesn't catch alight for long.
I try to hold it open a bit but then accidentally
drop it. 'Shit.'
Okay then, whatever. So what if they read it?
Maybe it's time for some truth.

'What was that?'
'What?'
'Shh, I heard something.'
'It's the kids.'

Kids. I've just turned seventeen.

'I know you were seeing Angela long before the operation.'
'Do you blame me? There was no affection in this house.
You gave more attention to the horses.'
'You were never here!'

I'm feeling dizzy and sick and mad.
The ball against the wall –
The munching –
The argument –
The heat –
The hunger –
The waiting, waiting, waiting…
Grovelling at the feet of an unreceived call.
Where's Mum?
I say it out loud, 'Where's my mother?'
Who cares if they hear me up here?
I've got nothing to hide any more.

Empty Ness's head blows onto its side
and slips further down the roof tiles.

I go to reach for it but it's too far then I
pick up the stupid gun instead.
Oh boy, the things I could do with this.
I wonder if it's loaded.
I unlock the safety catch.
He says he always cleans it unloaded
but there's been two stupid accidents already,
like our broken bedroom window.

'A better job of looking after the kids?' she says.
'Don't insult me. You can hardly look after yourself.'

I point the gun into the fathomless sky –
not a cloud or a star to aim at.
'They're going to live with their mother,' says Dad.

What? Hello? Did anyone ask me?
'DID ANYONE ASK ME?' I yell,
and aim all the way at
infinity
and shoot.

I'm jolted back.
My shoulder pulls, my ears ring and
the horse screams and bolts
as the shot pierces the district
and echoes across the ether.

Bigstep and Dad rush out onto the lawn
searching for the source.
My brother comes running out too.

'Did anybody ask *me*?'
They all turn around and look up, stunned.

'Hey!' says Dad. 'Give me that gun.
What the hell are you doing up there?'
I lift the gun back up to my shoulder.
'Shh!' I say. 'I've been listening to you two
long enough. It's my turn.'

A gust of hot wind unsettles us.
Pirate shies. We get dust in our eyes.
A car comes slowly crunching up the drive.

'Lucy, Lucy, put down the gun.'
'I'M talking.'
'Come on, you could hurt yourself.'
'I'M ALREADY HURTING.'

A car door slams. Footsteps.
'Yuuuhooo… Helloooo,' comes a voice
around the side of the house, followed by Mum,
with a pale blue chiffon dress
draped over one arm
and over the other is
a perfect wicker, red gingham picnic basket.

'What's going on? I heard yelling.'
Bigstep, Dad and Pip look up.
When Mum sees me with the gun she gets a fright
and drops the clinking basket.

'Come down, Lucy, come down now,' says Dad.
'Things aren't *that* bad, come on.'

'Stop telling me how things are,' I say,
'and where I'm going and who I'm going with
and what I'm feeling
and which idiotic wedding I'm going to next!
I'm not going to any weddings.
All that crap about "Till death us do part".
What a load of shit. Till *death*!
Well, guess what,' I say, lifting the gun,
'none of you are dead.'
Then I have to add, 'Yet.'

Mum drops the dress and moves closer to the others.

'Lucinda, I'm serious now, you need to put down the gun.'
'I'M SERIOUS NOW.

I went missing last night and nobody knew.
Whad'ya think of that?
Now I'll tell *you* who I'm gonna to live with.'

'Darling,' says Mum, carefully,
'aren't you being a little over-dramatic?'
'What?'
'Yes, calm down now, Lucy,' says Dad,
trying to sound all casual, which really fires me up.
'Dramatic? You know what? Yeah, actually,
I've been acting my fucking head off from the start.
Acting like everything's fine, everything's great.
Acting like everything's happy-family-terrific.
Well, you know what,' I say,
directing the focus and the gun at Bigstep,
'I'm a fucking *brilliant* actress.
But that's it. I don't care.
I don't care if I don't act another day in my whole entire life.'

Everyone seems small from up here.
It's weird to see Mum and Dad side by side.
I get a flash of them at the ballet concerts,
all smiles and applause in the audience.

'Come down now, Lucy,' says Dad.
'What for? What does it matter? OBVIOUSLY WE DON'T.'
I squeeze some tears back in.
'Don't be ridiculous, of course you matter.
How could you say that? We love you.
We give you everything. So many things.'
'THINGS!'

Pirate paces back and forth, agitated, snorting, looking for
escape – then stumbles on Pipstar's defeated plastic soldiers.

'You've turned everything upside-down
and you're about to do it *again*,' I cry.
'Made all your arrangements with your *lovers*.
Nobody asked *us*.

Your arrangements have NOTHING TO DO WITH US.'
I look for Pip for some moral support
but as with every argument
he's magically disappeared.

'Interesting *priorities*,' I say,
scanning the gun above their heads.
I take two steps forward.
The tiles feel loose under my feet and hot enough to crack.
It's getting heavy.
A wave of heat and dizziness spins up through me.
My eyes see white for a second.

'Of course you matter, darling,' says Mum gently,
daring to step a tiny bit closer.
'You have no idea how much you matter to us. To me.
I don't know how you could think that –'
'It's my turn to speak.
I thought people *hung around* for the things that matter?
Or did I not live up to expectations? Wasn't I *good enough*?'
'Oh, darling, please…no, no, you don't understand.
You've taken it all the wrong way.'
'I HAVEN'T FINISHED.'
I look at Mum and Dad, not Bigstep this time.
'Weren't we *good* enough to stick around for?'

'Lucinda, I'm getting angry now,' says Dad.
'Put the gun down. Enough's enough.'
'*You're* angry?' I point the gun at Dad. It feels drastic.
'Lucy, please, please, please put down the gun.'
'Maybe you're proud of how well I've been coping?
Well, guess what? What if I wasn't?
Sorry if it bothers you but what if I *wasn't* coping?'

Mum grabs Dad's arm.

'Let's see. If I wasn't around, would it be
a little more conveeeenient?'
'Lucy, stop it. Stop it, Lucy, please!'

'Luce!' – a voice from behind me.
I jump, all nerves. 'Shit!'
Pip's found his way up to the roof.
'Yeah, we're *sizzck* of it,' he says,
coming clumsily towards the chimney.
'Sick o' the farm, sick o' the horses,
sick o' the fights 'n' the crap.'
He kicks Empty Ness so she rolls noisily
down the rest of the tiles and all the way onto the ground.
Pirate shies with a whinnying cry.

'Phillip! Come – down – right – now,' demands Dad,
but Pip treads the tiles uneasily towards me.
'Here, give us it,' he says to me.
'What?'
'Was my idea,' he says, balancing his way closer.
I move further down. A tile cracks.
Bigstep, Dad and Mum step back.
'Put *down* the gun,' says Dad.
'*Stop* them,' says Mum.
'Give me the gun.'
'No, Pip. Get back.'
'Let's shoot the fucken' horse. I hate fucken' horses.'
I can't move further forward – I'm too close to the edge.
'Give it to me,' he whispers. 'My idea.'
'Pip, stop, be careful,' I say.
'C'mon,' he says, reaching for it.
'LUCINDA,' yells Dad.
'*Stop* it, Pip.'
I hold on tight,
but he lunges out
to grab the gun
and the way he grabs it
makes me
pull the trigger.

Our ears burst,
the world spins,
the horse screams, rears, bolts,
birds screech into the sky where I see
a blue chandelier
shatter in a million pieces.

The pull of the shot throws me off balance.
It's true what they say about accidents
happening in slow motion.

It even seems I've got enough time to stop the fall
as the ground looms up slowly beneath me.
But I can't at all.
And something in me welcomes the surrender of arrival.

I meet the earth with a numb thud,
see Pipstar above eclipsing the sun,
looking down at us all on the ground.
Then he seems to
spin around
and the echoing sounds
dissolve into the distance
until there is
whiteness,
shhhh…
and silence.

9

I had a dream.
It must have been set in winter
because my whole extended family
were sitting around a crackling fireplace
quietly crying
together.

In this dream
the crying wasn't sad.
It was nice and I wanted it to keep going
but a log cracked and fell out of the fire.
Then my journal went up in flames and
private words on ashes
went flying around the house.
I was trying to rescue them before they landed
when I woke up.

Now I can see a glimpse of dawn
through the curtains.
The sky is lilac, the colour of a bruise.
I reach under my bed to write the dream
in my journal
but my arm hurts like hell
and the book isn't there.
I remember where it is
and get up and limp-hop across the breezeway,
in through the TV room to the lounge,
shh, careful not to wake anyone up. Shhh.
When I get to the fireplace, I find it isn't there.

I sit on the couch.
Try to imagine the worst person to have found it.
Who's got it? Who's got my whole story?
Then I think maybe, now, in a sense,
everyone's got it.

The morning sun begins to filter through the glass doors
illuminating the paintings in the lounge.
It's going to be hot again but that horrible wind
has completely disappeared.
I watch the sun. It moves quite fast if you stare at it.
You can actually see Time passing.
Growing you up.

Lucky I didn't fall on the concrete porch.
The earth received me well.

My ankle is sprained, my wrist is strained
and my elbow is badly bruised
but hey, I could've broken my leg
like the back-seat bus-bitches wished for.
Proof that not all you wish for comes true.
Thank the Rural Gods I'm okay. I'm great.
I've had my say and though I'm limping,
I'm also kind of standing tall. I mean hell, this week,
I've survived a kidnapping, a shoot out and a fall.

After a while my brother comes in, all bleary.
'Hi, Pip.'
'You okay?'
I nod. 'You?'
'Yep.'
He sits beside me.
'Can I ask you a big favour?'
'Sure, of course.'
'From now on, could you call me Phillip?'
'Oh. Yeah. Okay. Sure.'
We both stare out the window.
Now the sky is really pretty.

Soon everyone's up.
Dad is sitting opposite us
also looking out the window.
It's strange without his radio.

The house smells divine.
Bigstep has cooked a miracle pile of pancakes
from an otherwise empty pantry. Some are even round.
She puts them down on a tray beside the tea
with heavenly options of lemon, honey, sugar and melted chocolate.
Phillip whispers to me, 'Everyone's being so nice.'
'Yeah,' I whisper, 'We must've done something right.'
He says, 'The shotgun worked a treat.'

We eat the pancakes slowly, savouring the sweetness.

Mum comes in looking mildly shell-shocked
carrying a plastic bag.
She's all showered but wearing the same nice outfit as yesterday.
And not sure where to sit, so Phillip gets up and gestures to his spot.
She asks how the pain is and how I slept.
'Really well.' Better than I've slept in months –
what with the Panadol, the overwhelm, the exhaustion.
She gives me the bag with the blue chiffon dress bundled up in it
and there's also a beautiful poetry book by Kahlil Gibran.
The dress is lovely enough for even me to get married in.
'I can't wait to try it on when nothing hurts!'

'Would you like a pancake?' says Dad to Mum. 'Delicious,'
though he and Bigstep haven't eaten any.
'No thanks, I should really head off,' she says,
sitting on the arm of the couch.
'Of course. You sure you wouldn't like a cup of tea?'
'Well, okay, just a tea'd be nice, thanks.'
Bigstep pours the tea.
Mum hugs the cup as though the weather was freezing.
I add extra chocolate to my last pancake.
Phillip uses his finger to clean his plate.
Nobody stops him.

'Well,' says Dad, after a prolonged silence,
'that was one horrible day,
but it could've been much, much worse.'
Everyone nods. For longer than they need to.

Eventually Mum says, 'Well, I'd better be off,
I'd better return the hire car.'
She stands, putting the half-full mug on the coffee table.
'Thank you for the bed last night.'
Dad says, 'Of course.'
'There was no way I could've driven back.'
Bigstep rises, 'Do you need any help with anything?'
Mum looks like she needs help with everything
but says very nicely, 'Oh no, I'm fine. Thanks again.'

Dad stands up carefully, holding his back
and goes to give her a brief kiss on the cheek.
It's nice, it's rare, it's sweet and
it's weird
to imagine them together, all those years ago,
passionately
making children.

'I hope you don't mind if I don't come out?'
says Dad, holding his back.
'No, of course.'
Bigstep stands and holds her hand up,
somewhere between a wave and a handshake.
Mum does the same and smiles and nods
like a comrade in a war they both fought.
I take a limping step.
'Don't come out,' says Mum. 'Darling, please.'
'Yes, you need to rest that, Lucy,' says Dad,
but 'No,' I say, 'I want to.'
Phillip lets me use his shoulder to get to the car.

Mum gets into the car and opens the window.
'I'm so proud of you both,' she says. 'Love you so much.'
'We love you too.'
'Better get this car back,' she says again,
and I'm reminded that since she left Doctor Dad
and the muumuu parties and South Yarra life,
she hasn't had any money.

We say our farewells, all teary but very temporary at last.
'See you soon, Mum,' says Phillip, peering into the window.

It's a pristine day. Perfect day for a picnic.
'Mum,' I say, 'we've got the rest of our lives for picnics.'
This makes her burst into tears.
The car is running, like some of her mascara.
'Wait!' I say, and get in the front passenger seat.
She turns off the engine and hugs me tightly.

'Oh, my darlings,' she says, crying again,
'there's just so much I couldn't tell you.
You have to believe me.
I tried hard. I tried so hard
to have you and Pip come and live with me. I really did.
Leaving you was the hardest thing I've ever done.
You *know* I wasn't in Paradise.'

Phillip comes closer to the open window.
His tired face is framed by the brilliant blue sky.
'You have to believe,' says Mum,
'you both have to believe you are very, very much loved.'
I look at Mum.
Though she hasn't had to sit HSC,
maybe she's had as hard a time as us
these past three years.

'We'll have a room for you, a lovely room, my darlings.
Please think it through, Lucy.
I know I can't make it all better right now,
but I promise – I'm going to spend the rest of my life
trying to make up for lost time.'
I hug her.
I love her.
I forgive her of course.
But everyone knows
there's no such thing as
making up for lost time.

Together, Phil and I watch the car go
all the way down the drive
and along the road towards the highway.
When it disappears,
he pulls a mad expression
like the ones we used to pull
in the dickie seat of the Volvo.
He mimes the playing of a violin and says,
'And they all lived happily ever after.'

I hop-limp on his shoulder around the front of the house
where it's a fright to see
the silver sections of Empty Ness
strewn across the lawn
and the red gingham picnic basket
shot to pieces.
But we start
to laugh
the way you can only laugh
when there's very nearly been a disaster.

10

Another brilliant day.
The sky, denim blue,
makes me remember the seaside.
I'm out on the front porch.
My voice is hoarse
from screaming because
miracle of miracles
I PASSED!

Only just.
But who cares if it's only by an ant's freckle?

11

There's a sign up at the start of our driveway
FOR SALE
with a sticker diagonally across it
SOLD.

Shimmering Fire's already been sold (well)
to the Aldrich Arabian Stud.
I thanked her for winning us ribbons
and teaching me
flying changes
and how to do ballet on a horse.

'You'll be really well looked after,' I said.
'Much better than you were with us.'
I told her that their horses are so shiny
you can see yourself in them.
She itched her chin on my shoulder
and pushed my ear with her nose
which tickled in such a way that I can
still sort of feel it. I hope I can always feel it.
It was hard when they drove her away.

The not-so-little Little Steps, are back to pack.
The heaviest stuff is the memories to file away.
My wrist is okay, my elbow's still bruised
and my ankle is much better.
This morning Dad asked for help with something that
he no longer needed help with. Bigstep and I
looked at each other like 'we are no longer your angels'.
She shook her head, I shook my head, we smiled and walked away.

Now we're down at (what's left of) the shed.
Had to loan some old saddles from the Crazies who aren't crazy.
Heading out for one 'last ride' before the floats arrive.
Bigstep has caught and saddled Sails for me.
I can walk but I probably shouldn't.
I'll be fine so long as I stay on the horse.

We head off, trotting across a paddock, still black,
but with patches of little green shoots coming through.
Bigstep asks Littlestep, 'You okay?'
'Sort of,' she says.
'Jackie?'
'Yeah, fine.'
'Lucy?'
'Great.'
Bigstep and I are side by side,
surrendered.

With everyone home
and the end of her dream
and the breaking up of the marriage,
there's nothing left to fight about.
After all, it's not her fault that she isn't my mother.
It's not our fault we got put in a
washing machine together
and the colours ran.

We're heading down towards Gallop Hill,
walking and trotting and looking around,
feeling all weird and sentimental.

At the base of Gallop Hill
the horses are bit-chompingly excited.
It amazes me that a horse would want to run up a hill
but they still get a thrill out of it.
We are trying to stall the take-off
while we check the girths and stirrups and hats.
I feel a well of emotion rise…
Where can you gallop across humanless fields in the city?

I look across at Bigstep,
who was already looking at me.
We both nod simultaneously. Ready.
Our horses take off from underneath us.
Midstep screams, 'Yeeehhaaaaaaaaaaaaaaaa.'
Littlestep screams, 'Slow down stop,'
and I just scream for everything that's happened,
'Aghhhhhhhhhhhhhhhhhhhhhhhhhh.'
And we fly
all the way up Gallop Hill
with pounding hoofs
and panting breaths
and tears streaming out of our eyes
from the wind and joy and sadness
and everything else about
living here
that we've hated and loved.

We arrive at the top
and stop beside the white dried out ghost gum,
stark and grand against the blue sky.
The horses are sweating,
their mouths are foaming,
their breathing and hearts beating fast
and I hold onto this feeling,
try to photograph it in my mind
to keep for any dull days ahead
waiting at tram stops in town.

Bigstep hops off to open the gate
and Littlestep goes through,
excited that she survived her first gallop without falling.
Midstep follows. 'That was exhilarating.'
She's practising extra syllable words for her school captain audition.
As I approach the gate I look to Bigstep and she looks to me,
'Thanks, Chris,' I say.
She gestures me through with the mimic of a royal bow.
I add, 'Thanks for everything.'
She smiles and nods like we got there in the end.

While she grooms her horse
we mix up a special last feed
with molasses, their favourite.
The girls let me put my arms around their shoulders
to take the full weight off my ankle.
We take the ponies to the closest paddock,
carrying three buckets, blue, red and green,
to the paddock nearest the road.
We sit on the grass, me in the middle,
watching the horses knock their noses around
in the buckets we hold between our knees.
They munch enthusiastically and
snort the dusty bits out.

The girls ask me about HSC,
boys and how it feels to have finished school.

Jackie asks if I can help her with her
school captain election speech.
'Superlative,' she says.

Sarah's fat bay pony, Anderson,
is so keen to get what's in the bucket
that with the strength of his nose
he knocks her over
which sends us into hysterics.
Then Jackie screams out, 'BULL ANT!'
and I fly up into the sky, but it's just a joke.
The whole morning is a nice relief
from the tensions up at the house,
with the packing, the uncertainty,
and the noisy silences between Dad and Chris.

With the girls either side of me
I get the feeling of them being
like sisters.
Ironic really, that just as we're getting on better together
the family is coming apart.
Or maybe we're getting on well now
because
it's coming apart?

Holding the empty buckets,
our horses follow us towards the gate where we hug them.
'I'll wait here, thanks. Pick me up?'

Sails starts munching on grass and I sit down beside him.
I'm sure he knows we're leaving him
but he's acting like he doesn't care.
Like I used to.
I pull out the apple I brought as a treat
and he eats it
bite by juicy bite
with his rubbery lips
and his tickly whiskers
and his feathery soft nose brushing my wrist.

I look into his lashy eyes,
thank him
for listening to all my secrets
and helping me get out of the house when things were bad.
For being the first horse to teach me to ride
and be out in a field with nothing but him
and the wind by my side.
I kiss the end of his velvety nose.
'I wish I could take you with me,' I say.
I stand up and he licks my hand
nuzzles my head and I hug his neck
for the last time.

With a heavy heart from the horsey farewell,
I hop over to the approaching ute
and wonder
after we leave the farm
if I'll ever see our horses again.
Then I wonder if I'll ever see the Steps?

12

Dad and I are on the patio deckchairs.
He's no longer wearing his brace. Yay!
Chris is down at the dressage arena
talking to people who answered the other horse sale ads.

'Bach Cello Concerto in C Minor,' he says,
not even bothering to quiz me.
It took a shotgun to kill that annoying game
but it sort of feels strange, him not asking.

'Do you really want to live with Jess?'
I shrug.
'You know I'll always have a room for you, as will your mother.'
'Thanks, Dad, I know. I'll think a bit more about it.'

Every now and then, in the light breeze,
bits of burnt grass drift onto us.
I brush mine off but Dad doesn't notice.

'Do you think this whole farm idea was all a big mistake?'
God, I think. How to answer?
'I didn't realise you were so unhappy.'
'I wasn't at first. I wasn't always.'
'No?'
'No.'
'I thought there were things you enjoyed?'
'Yes, definitely. The farm, the horses,
the small school with the inspiring teachers
where I wasn't just a statistic.
The Flowerdale trek. The chance to do the dance.
The friends I've met… Fantastic.'

I flick off some more burnt grass
and a million recollections.

'It's such a lot of hard work –
running a farm –
and it's really very expensive.
And then – the fire.
It just rips at your heart strings
watching the destruction of lovely things. You lose heart.
But it was good for a while, don't you think?
I mean we had some fun times, didn't we?'
'We did,' I say.
'It wasn't all bad, was it?'
'No, Dad. Of course not.'
'It wasn't all a big mistake?'
'No.'
I can't bear the sad look on his face.
'No, because if it was a mistake, I wouldn't be sad that we're leaving.'

He breathes in deeply, with a double intake, then sighs it out.
'I'll miss the farm,' he says. 'A number of things about it.'

'Me too.'
'But farming isn't something you can do as hobby.'
'No.'
'It's more a way of life.'
'Yeah,' I say, blowing a speck of ash off my arm.
'Anyway,' he says, '"Life wasn't meant to be easy".'
'That's true,' I say.
'Do you know who said that?'
'Yeah, Fraser,' I answer, glad to be back in the quiz.
'Well, yes and no. The person who said it originally?'
'I thought it was Fraser,' I say.
'No, Fraser was quoting George Bernard Shaw:
"Life is not meant to be easy, my child,
but take courage; it can be delightful."'
'Well,' I say, 'It's certainly not a picnic.'
And then we laugh,
like we both got away with robbery and murder.

13

I'm sorting stuff into boxes:
second-place horse-show ribbons,
what I wore the first night Tony came over,
a ticket to the Wandong Wingding,
a blue velvet hair ribbon from my first day at school,
a sample of White Sail's tail,
the ancient box of unused Trojans...
I even find the two parts of the wedding photo –
TILL DEATH (Mum)
US DO PART (Dad).
I hold the pieces together
back-to-front
so the writing reads
US DO PART TILL DEATH

I take another supermarket box out onto the lawn
and bang out the dust.

It's a calm day, seems quieter than last summer.
Not so many crickets this year, since the fire.

I scan the farm, thinking of the stories of our time here
scattered all over the paddocks like seeds,
then see a white panel van with familiar green curtains
coming up the road.
I quickly go inside and change out of my
old yellow 'rock 'n roll' T-shirt and bandanna scarf,
and put on a blue summer dress.

It's not just Stevie Maclain.
The whole gang pile out of the back;
Brett and Kate and Nick and Twin Two Timbo.
Stevie holds out a baby pine tree in a red pot towards me.
'Merry Christmas!' they all say.
'We thought you could do with a few more trees,' says Stevie
and puts it down at my feet.

Stevie and Timbo sit on the deckchairs.
Kate and Brett share an outdoor lounge.
Nick has one all to himself and
the lone pine is all bewildered in between us.

'Lucky your house wasn't barbecued,' says Stevie.
'I know.'
'Close call,' says Brett.
'Ken oath,' says Nick.
'Last fire, the pine forest burnt down for three whole days.'
'Very lucky,' says Timbo.
They all light up a smoke. I say no. I'm trying to quit.

'It's funny,' says Kate, 'how people pick out what's lucky –
when something really unlucky has happened.'
'Yeah,' I say. 'Pity I fell off the roof
but lucky I didn't break my leg.'
'Gotta look on the bright side,' says Brett.
'How else ya gonna get through this life?'

'Speaking of the dark side,' says Stevie, 'I heard
'that Hayes family's trouble. They've all got a record.'
'Yeah,' says Nick, 'it's a good thing you're leaving.'
'No, it's not,' says Kate. 'We're really upset you'll be gone.'
'Yeah, we are,' says Stevie. 'Will you visit us sometimes?'
'Of course,' I say. 'Yes.' And then wonder.

I look at them all
in a moment of silence
while the light fades another shade
and a lone kookaburra
starts a laugh
but for some reason doesn't finish it.

'Luce, we're heading off to Tina's,' says Stevie.
'Her parents are away again. Wanna come?'
'I'd love to,' I hear myself say,
'but I've got to help with the packing.'

They banter on.
The conversation surrounds me and after a while
something pulls focus
like a camera,
away from the sorrow of leaving
and I'm outside the group –
observing them all,
watching, like a scene in a play.
Watching,
like an outsider.
And there's something about
being outside
that feels different this time
and this kind of different actually feels okay.

'You're very quiet,' says Stevie,
scratching his knee through faded jeans.
Such a gentle soul. He's sure to make someone happy.
It could've been me.

'Sorry, so much on my mind,' I say,
'and I'm sorry I haven't been around much lately.
The shit kinda hit the fan.'
'No worries.'
'Yeah, we know about shit hittin' fans,' says Nick.

'Hey,' says Kate, 'I heard you passed! *Congratulations!*'
They all give me high fives.
'I reckon you should just get a medal for finishing it,' she says,
generously, given that she dropped out along the way.
'Promise you'll come up and visit us,' says Stevie.
'And send us your new address,' says Kate.
'Sure,' I say.
They hug me.
Brett pretends to hug the little tree.
'I really love it.'
'Yeah, well, everyone's gotta love something,' says Nick
and they head off in a bundle of banterings.

I watch the white van disappear down the road and
the light continue to dissolve from the sky.
'Farewell,' I whisper, 'to my local princes.'
We had our own kind of ball.

14

It's been raining all morning.
Stormy, steamy.
A rare occasion.
Thunder cracked open the sky
and you can feel the fields drinking.

Jackie writes down the last of the speech that
we worked on together.
The girls are missing their athletics day, by choice.
She said, 'If you're good at swimming –
no point trying out for the hurdles.'
Even though neither of us are any good at either.

Her speech is focused around the Shakespearean quote,
'... To thine own self be true...'
She'll get brownie points for this old Will quote I gave her.
'There,' she says. 'Finished.'
'Okay then, let's try it?'
She stands, all earnest, at the far end of the vast lounge,
reciting the speech out loud.
'... So, elect me to be the ambassador of our reputable school
and I will ensure all your natural gifts
are celebrated with great significance.'

'Hm. It kind of doesn't sound natural,' I say.
'Maybe try it again – just be yourself
and say it like you mean it.'
She starts again. The same.
'Okay, not bad,' I say, even though it was terrible.
'How about you put down the notes
and say the speech a couple of times without reading it?'
'But I won't remember it.'
'I know, but just ad-lib, to get the gist of it across.'
'But we wrote exactly what I want to say.'
'I know, and you can use it again but just as an exercise –
so you get the meaning and the feeling
and the freshness back into it…
Just try it as an exercise without the script and we'll see.'

It comes out a bit muddled but with a hell of a lot more
truth and strength and at the end I applaud and she says,
'Okay, I see.'
Then she picks up the paper
and reads it – this time, quite differently –
occasionally ad-libbing a bit but keeping mostly on track.
I nod here and there to encourage her.
She's connected with the point of it now and the meaning.

'Great. Much better.'
'You're really good at this,' she says.
'You'd be a good teacher…or a movie director or something.'

She has one more go at her speech.
'Excellent! You got it.'
'Thanks,' she says, 'That was great.'
'Pleasure.'
She walks towards me. 'You're nicer than you were before.'
'Oh,' I say.
'Yeah. Definitely. It was hard to talk to you before.'
'Sorry.'
She shrugs. 'It was like you were sort of above us or something.'
'I was,' I say. 'I was on the roof.'
She laughs.
'Sorry,' I say once again. 'Maybe I've only just landed.'

15

Phillip calls me into his room.
'Sit down,' he says,
patting his faded superhero doona cover
turned inside-out to hide the outgrown heroes.
'Hey,' I say, 'if I give up smoking, will you?'
'Maybe,' he shrugs. 'I don't inhale.
Now,' he says, all business-like. 'You really gonna live with Jess?'
'I don't know,' I say. 'I'm not sure.'
He nods. You can tell he's glad I'm not sure.
I think of what Jess said:
'Maybe you might want to get to know your mum.'
I could share with him my decision process but won't.
He likes me to answer questions but not in detail.
He's developed a kind of
'Anything can happen – wouldn't surprise me' attitude,
which is useful, I dare say, to survive a life
but is also a little bit sad in a way –
like, 'Let's not feel too much. It could be dangerous.'

'At least I've got a choice now,' I say.
But maybe it was good that we had no choice before.
If you love both parents equally, how could you possibly decide?

'Got a surprise,' he says in a monotone.
'Um,' I say, 'I'm not sure I could handle any surprises.'
He hands me a plastic bag with something wrapped in it.
'What is it? A book?'
'Mm, sort of.'
'Huh?' I say, unwrapping the bag.
And there it is, worn from use,
crinkly from water, burnt in the corner –
my battered red journal.

'Oh, my God,' I say, 'thank you! I thought Chris had it or Mum!'
'Nuh, found it in the fireplace,' he says.
'Thank you! Oh, my God…' I hug the journal. I hug him!
'I like it when you call me God.'
'I can't tell you what a relief this is,' I say, letting him go.
'Well, I thought I should use it for blackmail but a reward is just fine.'
'Yes. Yes! Definitely a reward!'
I go to hug him again
but once was more than usual already and obviously plenty.
'Interesting reading,' he says. 'Bit too interesting in places.'
I cover my mouth, scanning my memory for the worst of it.
'Could've done with a few less sixty-niners. Ugh,' he says.
'Oh, my God,' I cringe and cover my whole face.
'And all that palaver about your teacher. Oh, and the poems.'
I peek through my fingers.
'But overall,' he says, 'quite a good record of the time –
at least from your point o' view.'
Then he adds, 'Which is nothing like mine.'

16

Dear Jerkoff,
      This is Phillip. Lucys brother. Thanks 4 the read. Freaky. Just 4 the record… Lucy can be pretty anoying too…and Chris (Bigstep) can be really nice. My sister's version of reality is warped. That's why I niknamed her 'Rose'. She's a dreamer. But at leest she smells better than a cabage. (Sometimes.)
      Phillip the Pipster.

Dear Journie,

Sorry you got read by my brother! Aghhh. I always thought I secretly wanted you to be read but in the end I didn't! Thank the Rural Gods it was Pip (sorry) Phillip!

MIRACLE OF MIRACLES – I PASSED!

I thank the Gods for this and everything in the world that's good. I've realised I only thank them when things go well and wonder if they'll forgive me for being biased!

Too much else to tell. So much told already. Out loud.

PS. Chris's dream is over. Like mine. Maybe it's a relief…for her as well.

PPS. Maybe I should be a teacher or a director? Yeah, maybe I'll get offered my backup choice, teaching Drama & English.

PPPS. Coming to the end of your blank pages. Thank youuuuuuuuuuuuu………………………

PPPPS. Found interesting quotes in Mum's Gibran book about how it's sad to leave a place, even if not all your days there were happy.

17

Late morning. A clear day –
the kind of day you could decide you wanted to
to live on a farm.
Can't believe we're leaving tomorrow.

Phillip is digging a hole
for my pine tree
in the top paddock behind the house.
The hole is nearly deep enough.

I think of him going back to finish at the private boys' school.
I wonder how he'll cope? Lucky I've finished.
I know I'm not that Grammar girl any more.
But maybe he'll resume the life we lost
and start again where we all began.

Maybe he'll marry a private school girl
raise a big beautiful family
in a nice part of Melbourne
and grow old together
all cosy and secure
until death do they part.

He stops a minute, all sweaty,
puts his foot on the spade like a farmer,
scratches his nose on his sleeve. Pauses.
'Could've been digging a grave,' he says dryly.
These days, you never quite know if he's serious or not,
except for the glint in his eyes that maybe he caught from Hayzo.
The kid's getting awfully witty in an old killer-tone kind of way.
Let's face it. The kid is no longer a kid.
He goes back to digging.

'Would've been digging for a week,' he says. 'She's enormous.'
'Our mother or our stepmother?' I ask.
'The horse,' he says.

We half laugh
but below the joke,
shake our heads and
shiver at the thought.

He digs three more shovels full.
'I think that'll do it. After you,' he says,
gesturing for me to step in.
'No, no,' I say, 'please, after you.'
He throws the shovel to the side
and picks up the pine tree pot.
'Okay,' he says, 'you hold the pot – I'll pull.'
It comes out in one piece and we place it in the pit
and fill the gap with dirt.
He gets up saying, 'I think it'll be happy here,'
and I view, with a little jealousy, the little pine's stability.
It's the only thing around here with its feet firmly planted.

'We'll come and visit it when we're old,' he says,
putting his arm around my shoulder.
'Okay,' I say, pretending his beautiful gesture is normal,
and noticing that he's almost as tall as me.

The sound of a motorbike arriving takes our attention.
I think of my Hell's Angels.
My brother works out who it is before me.
'I knew he'd come back some time.'
I forget to exhale when the rider takes off his helmet.

He sees us and comes straight towards the embankment.
'Might leave you guys alone,' Phillip says
and winks and salutes Tony.
'Thanks,' I say, transfixed by the approaching apparition.

'Nice tree,' he says, staring at it,
nodding slightly ironically in dark glasses.
There's an uncomfortable silence where
the little tree seems to shudder in the breeze.
'Don't leave me…'

'Let's watch it grow for a minute,' he says.
And we do.

He's still upsettingly desirable in a gritty magnetic way.

'Can't believe you're here today.'
'Just riding past. Saw the sign.'

I push down some dirt
around the base of my tree with my foot.

'We're leaving tomorrow.'
'Yeah?'

He seems stronger.
Not just in his body
but in himself.

'So, ya goin' back to the city?'

'Yeah.'
'Thought you might in the end.'
I nod.

A semitrailer hurtles past in the distance.
They don't usually use this back road.

He takes off his leather jacket.
I wish he'd take off his glasses.
His legs look strong, in faded jeans
and motorbike boots –
legs I used to
sit on
lie on.
Legs that used to be mine to touch –
legs that belonged to me.

He sits on the grass.
'Must be hot riding around in all that leather?'
'Better hot than dead,' he says.
Laying the jacket on his right side he
pats the grass on the left, gesturing to me.
I sit down beside him.
'So how've you been?'
(What can I say? I've been everything.)
'Okay. You?'
'Yeah, yeah, good… Did ya pass?'
'Yes.'
'Toldja.'

I don't want to talk.
I just want him to put his arm around me.
To hold me as still and firm on the earth as my tree.
The breeze picks up, throws my hair over my face.
I keep brushing it away, grateful for something to do.

'Got a good job,' he says.
'Great. What?'
'Interstate refrigeration.

As far away as possible from me ol' man.'
'Fantastic.'
'Drivin' the trucks for now, but they're training me up to be manager.'
'Great,' I say again, nodding, nodding.
He's nodding, nodding.
I wish we could just forget all the small talk
and the history of everything and the future of nothing and
hang on tight
and dissolve into each other.

'Got a new girlfriend.'
'Really?' I say, way too enthusiastically.
I hang onto my knees, rein myself in,
hold myself together.
'She's nice,' he says. 'You'd like her.'
I bite the inside of my cheek. 'That's great.'
'She's nice, but she's not you,' he says,
taking his sunglasses off and smiling.

I fall a bit
inside
when I look in his eyes –
still dark
still deep.

I help myself by thinking about
interstate trucking refrigeration…
and wonder exactly what part of that lifestyle I might have enjoyed.
Maybe things work out for the best.
Maybe we get led to where we're really meant to be?

'Good timing. Were you really just passing?'
'Nuh,' he says. 'I heard you were leavin'. Come ta say goodbye.'

He looks beyond the tree, slowly, from left to right,
across the farm, taking it all in
like Empty Ness did.
'I could say I'm gonna miss you
but you know I already have.'

He nods like he understands everything.

I wonder if I can ever choose someone
who I can really be with
and who can really be with me?
A relationship without an inbuilt mechanism for
departure.

I don't know what's next. It's scary.
I think I need to be planted.
I'm holding back a flood that could water my tree
for a year.

He must sense this because he leans over, reaches out, holds me.
'Sorry,' I say, 'bit emotional – everything, the move.'
'You'll be all right,' he says quietly. 'You'll always land on your feet.'
He hugs me.
'Now, just sit with ya tree and make a wish,' he says.
Then he kisses me
on the lips,
firmly,
but briefly.

'Won't ever forget you,' I say.
'Fucken' better not,' he says
and puts on his dark glasses,
picks up his jacket and leaves.

I continue to hug my knees,
watch his bike spin some gravel,
then I make three wishes.

18

It's a hot night. So still.
Can't sleep. My mind's racing.
Everything's packed for the trucks tomorrow.

I've got my Walkman on, the same song over and over,
'Romeo and Juliet',
but it isn't calming me down…

How's it going to be, moving back to Melbourne
and living with Mum after all this time
and not living with Dad
and going to teacher's college
and missing the horses and the
fresh air and the roof and
everyone and everything?

Through the glass doors
I can see a boat-shaped moon
floating in the sea of the universe.
How big is this sea?

I go out onto the front lawn.
The grass is cool. I breathe in the air.
The sky is filled with so many stars.
It makes the universe seem enormous.

I hear music.

I walk towards the patio as the volume increases
and I see a tiny glow moving on the outdoor lounge
and smell the smoke of a cigar.
'Hello?'
I walk closer, slowly, just in case it's not Dad.
'Hah!' he says, which terrifies the life out of me.
'You gave me such a fright,' he says.
'Me too!'
'What are you doing up so late?' he says, curious, not cross.
'Couldn't sleep.'
'What about you?'
'Just a little contemplation…'
'Total fire ban,' I remind him. 'No smoking.'
'Shh,' he says. 'I'm being very careful.
It's one of life's little pleasures, a fine cigar – and I don't inhale.'

'Nice night.'
'Stupendous,' he says. 'Feel like I'm in heaven…
Balmy. Clear. Full of stars, *full* of stars.
Look at them, everywhere, and listen, listen…'
'Ah,' I say, then surprise him as much as myself with,
'Schubert's String Quartet in C Major, second movement.'
'Oh, you heard the announcer.'
'No.'
'You guessed it? You recognised it?'
'Mm,' I say proudly.
'Bravo! Bravo! Ahhhhh,' he says, and I join in too,
'the most beautiful piece of music ever written.
Have I said that before?'
I smile.

'A balmy night, a fine cigar, a Schubert quintet
and a visit from my lovely daughter…
What more could you possibly want in life?'
That's one thing about Dad –
he knows how to appreciate the small things.
Or are they the big things really?

'Have a seat,' he says. 'Join me?'
I lie on the deckchair next to his.
'You can see the entire Milky Way,' he gestures like a maestro.
'You could almost reach out and touch it.'
'Yeah. Millions and trillions of stars,' I say.
He takes a couple of puffs. The familiar scent wafts my way.

'You know I'm very proud of you, Lucy.'
I'm not sure what he's proud of exactly
but I like the sound of it.

He says, 'I've been watching the little lights
of the cars on the freeway. Can you see them?'
'Yeah.'
'Over there.'
'Yeah.'

'If you blur your eyes, they look like little comets.'
'Oh, yeah.'

'Dad?' I say.
'Yes?'
I feel a sudden urge to tell him I love him
but it's really hard to say.
'What is it? Eh?'
'I was just going to say – you're all right.'
'You think so? Even with all of my faults and foibles?'
'Even with all of your millions and trillions of faults and foibles.'
'Well, that's it then,' he says. 'I must be in heaven.'

19

The trucks will arrive any minute now
and everyone rushing around packing last minute things
and checking the labels on boxes.

I feel like smoking a cigarette
but I'm trying hard not to have one.
Maybe ever.

The maggies are gurgling away in the trees as if to say,
'Ah, they come and they go – these townsfolk.'

Over here by my pine, looking up at the roof,
I wonder if one of the new owners' kids
will find Empty Ness,
put her head back on right
and share with her all their secrets.

I sit on the grass,
pick a dandelion flower and blow it,
watching the furry feathers
all come off
in one go.
Some land on my tree.

I send a little prayer
to Tony
and another one
to the girl that I was
when I arrived
and the girl I became
to survive here
and one more
for whoever I'm becoming.

20

Heading south
on the Hume Highway,
following Dad's Scary Canary
in the old blue Volvo.
Poor Dad, at last he's able to drive but
none of us were in the mood
for Stravinsky and cigars.

The two big Wilson trucks are a little way behind us.
Phillip's keeping an eye on them
though he's too big for the dickie seat.
I'm up the front beside Chris.
Jackie and Sarah are in the back seat
and Phillip is leaning over their seat
to join the game I invented.
It's to try and take our minds off
the crazy-uncertain-what-the-hell's-next kind of feelings
and to distract us from the fact that
something big is ending and that
this family
of sorts
which has only really just come together
is about to come apart.

The Steps will stay with their grandparents
until they find a new house.

Phillip and I are going to try
what it's like to live with Mum.

The game goes like this:
we each take turns to tell a true story
that happened on the farm.
You have to tell it
like you're someone else in the family,
and as though it's happening to you.

So far it's quite amusing. Especially Phil
who mimics me practising Shakespeare:
'Out damned spot!'
And Jackie's just finished being Dad,
serving up Ayers Rock duck for dinner.

When it's Chris's turn she gets stuck a few times
trying to be Arnie, our riding instructor,
so I have to jump in to help her.
'Stop!' she says.
'You're making me laugh too much. I can't see the road.'

She's playing her favourite tape, Van the Man's *Wavelength*.
I like how he sings about
spirits and stuff
helping us along the road of our
tricky existence.
Her great music collection
has pulled us through some lonesome times.

I turn to face forwards and see the skyline of Melbourne,
a mirage ahead in the distance.
What stories await us there?

A charge of Hell's Angels bikies go speeding past us,
one at a time. I touch the bandanna in my hair to check it's there
and scan each rider for recognition.
'Don't pull a face,' says Jackie, 'they might attack like Mad Max.'

But Phillip's not focused on the bikies.
'I can't see the trucks!' he says. 'Oh, wait, yes I can, yes,'
and he turns around and rests his head
over the seat between the girls again.
I give him the thumbs up and he gives me one back
which feels less to do with spotting the trucks
than our overall survival.

I don't know if we'll ever revisit my pine tree
on Doglolly Hill,
at Wandong –
with the 'second largest truck 'n' country festival
in the southern hemisphere'.
I've seen inside the trunks of trees,
the way they have rings
that mark every year of their existence.
Maybe there's something similar in humans,
something that marks the Wandong time inside us?

Wandong –
sounds more like a Chinese rice paddy,
than a one-shop pit stop,
along the train tracks to Sydney.

I've got a faint feeling
I've left something behind
but maybe we all do.

References

References are made to the following works, quotes and organisations:

Astro Boy, Tezuka Productions, dir. Ishiguro N., 1980 [television programme].
Aznavour, C. and Kretzmer, H., 'She' (Barclay, 1974) [CD].
Bach, J.C., Cello Concerto in C minor, W.C77 (ca1755).
Beethoven, L., Piano Sonata No. 31 in A-flat major, Op. 110 (1822).
The Blue Lagoon, dir./prod. Kleiser, R., USA, 1980 [video].
Brahms, J., Piano Concerto No. 2 in B-flat major, Budapest: Various (1881).
Bryant, F., 'Bye Bye Love' (Cadence, 1957) [CD].
Calvin Klein, Levi's Jeans advertisement, Brooke Shields (model), 1980.
Churchill, W., *The Complete Speeches of Winston S. Churchill*, ed. Robert Rhodes James (NY: Bowker and London: Chelsea House 1974).
Clapton, E., 'Promises', from album *Backless* (Polydor, 1978).
Close Encounters of the Third Kind, dir. Spielberg, S., USA, EMI Films, 1977 [DVD].
Costello, E., 'Accidents Will Happen', from album *Armed Forces* (Radar, 1979).
Cross, C., 'Ride Like the Wind', from album *Christopher Cross*, (Warner Bros. Records, 1979).
Dawes, C. and Sigman, C., 'It's all in a Game', sung by V. Morrison, from album *Into the Music* (Warner Bros., Mercury, 1979).
Dire Straits, 'Down to the Waterline' and 'Six Blade Knife', from album *Dire Straits* (Vertigo (UK), Warner Bros. (USA), 1978).
—, 'Tunnel of Love' and 'Romeo and Juliet', from album *Making Movies* (Vertigo, Warner Bros., Mercury, 1980).
—, 'Where do you think you're going?' and 'Follow Me Home', from album *Communiqué* (Vertigo, Warner Bros 1979).
Dylan, B., 'One More Cup of Coffee', from album *Desire* (Columbia, 1976).
The Eagles, 'Desperado', sung by L. Ronstadt on album *Don't Cry Now* (Asylum, 1973).
Edwards, B. and Rogers, N., 'Le Freak', from album *C'est Chic* (Atlantic, 1978).
Elgar, E., Cello Concerto, Op. 85 (1919).
Eliot, T.S., *Murder in the Cathedral* (Harcourt, Brace and Co. 1935).
Foreigner, 'Cold as Ice', from album *Foreigner* (Atlantic, 1977).
Franklin, M., *My Brilliant Career*, (Sydney: A&R Classics, 1979) (pp. 17, 21, 22, 27).
Fraser, J.M., 'Life wasn't meant to be easy', Alfred Deakin Lecture 20 July 1971. Based on a quote from the G.B. Shaw play *Back to Methusela*.
Gallipoli, dir. Weir, P., Australia, Associated R&R Films, 1981 [DVD].
Gilligan's Island, Sherwood Schwartz, USA, (CBS, 1964) [television programme].
Gone with the Wind, dir. Fleming, V., USA, MGM, 1939 [video].

Harry, D. and Stein, C., 'Heart of Glass', from album *Parallel Lines* (Chrysalis, 1979).

Hokusai, K, *The Great Wave off Kanagawa*, c. 1830, from the Thirty-six views of Mt Fuji series 1826–33 (colour woodblock print), National Gallery of Victoria, Melbourne.

Jarre, J-M., 'Oxygène Part VI', from album *Oxygène* (Dreyfus/Polydor, 1976).

John, E. and Osborne, G., 'Ball and Chain', sung by Janis Joplin with Big Brother & The Holding Company (Universal Music Publishing Group, 1968).

Kristofferson, K. and Foster, F., 'Me and Bobby McGee', sung by Janis Joplin on album *Pearl*, (Columbia, 1969).

Looney Tunes, Warner Bros, 1930 [television programme].

Mad Max, dir. Miller, G, Australia, B. Kennedy, 1979 [DVD].

Mahler, G., *Song of the Earth* (Universal, 1909).

The Man From Snowy River, dir. Miller, G., Australia, 20th Century Fox, 1982 [DVD].

Melbourne Symphony Orchestra, Australia's oldest orchestra, http://www.mso.com.au/

Mental as Anything, 'The Nips Are Getting Bigger', on album *Get Wet* (Virgin, 1979).

Mitchell, J., 'Clouds', from album *Clouds* (Reprise, 1969).

Morrison, V., 'Venice USA' and 'Checking it Out', on album *Wavelength* (Mercury 1978).

Musica Viva, Australian chamber music organisation, https://musicaviva.com.au/

My Brilliant Career, dir. Armstrong, G., Australia, Peace Arch, 1979 [DVD].

Oliver, dir. Reed, C., UK, Romulus Films, 1968 [DVD].

One Flew Over the Cuckoo's Nest, dir. Forman, M., USA, Douglas, M. and Zaentz, S., 2016 [DVD].

Paterson, A.B. ('Banjo'), 'The Man from Snowy River', 1st ed. First published in *The Bulletin*, Australia (1890).

—, 'Waltzing Matilda', song based on ballad by B. Paterson, melody by C. Macpherson, based on 'The Craigielee March' by J. Barr, 1818, Australia, 1895.

Picnic at Hanging Rock, dir. Weir, P., (1975), Australia, H & J McElroy, 1975, [Based on the novel by J. Lindsay (F.W. Cheshire, Penguin, 1967)].

Plath, S., 'Daddy', in *Ariel* (London: Faber and Faber, 1965).

Puberty Blues, dir. Beresford, B., Australia, Limelight, 1981. [DVD]

Queen, 'Crazy Little Thing Called Love', on album *The Game* (EMI Elektra, 1980).

Reddy, H. and Burton, R., 'I Am Woman', on album *I Don't Know How To Love Him*, (Capitol, 1971).

Rodgers, R. and Hammerstein II, O., 'Climb Ev'ry Mountain' and 'Edelweiss', from *The Sound of Music*, USA, 1959.

Schubert, F., String Quintet in C major, D.956, Op. posth. 163 (1828).

Shakespeare, W., *The Tragedy of Hamlet, Prince of Denmark*, c. 1599–1602.

—, *The Tragedy of Macbeth*, c. 1606.

—, *The Tragedy of Romeo and Juliet*, c. 1597.

Shaw, G.B., *Pygmalion*, premiered Hofburg Theatre, Vienna, Austria, 1913.

Shazam! USA, Warner Bros. TV Distribution, 1974 [television programme].

Sherbet, 'Howzat', on album *Howzat* (Festival, 1976).

The Sound of Music, dir. Wise, R., USA, 20th Century Fox,1965.

Stevens, C., 'Wild World', sung by Cliff, J., on album *In Concert – The Best of Jimmy Cliff* (Reprise, 1976).

Thatcher, M., 'The lady's not for turning', speech to Conservative Party Conference, 10 October, 1980, http://www.margaretthatcher.org/document/104431, accessed 4 July 2015.

TV Week, Bauer Media Group, Australia, first published 1957.

Vogue magazine, Condé Nast, USA, first published 1892.

The Wailers, 'Get Up, Stand Up', on album *Burnin*, (Island, 1973).

Wouk, H., *Don't Stop the Carnival* (USA: Doubleday, 1965).

Young Talent Time, (1971–1988, 2012.), Network 10 Australia, producers, K. Lewis & J. Young [television programme].

3XY, popular Melbourne radio station in the 70s and 80s now broadcasting as Magic 1278.

www.ingramcontent.com/pod-product-compliance
Lightning Source LLC
Chambersburg PA
CBHW030902080526
44589CB00010B/113